Policy and Politics in
Japan

Policy and Politics in Industrial States

A series edited by Douglas E. Ashford, Peter Katzenstein, and T. J. Pempel

T. J. Pempel

Policy and Politics in
Japan

Creative Conservatism

Temple University Press

Philadelphia

Temple University Press, Philadelphia 19122
© 1982 by Temple University. All rights reserved
Published 1982
Printed in the United States of America

Library of Congress Cataloging in Publication Data

Pempel, T. J., 1942–
  Policy and politics in Japan.

  (Policy and politics in industrial states)
  Bibliography: p.
  Includes index.
  1. Japan—Economic policy—1945– . 2. Japan—Social policy. 3. Japan—
Politics and government—1945– . 4. Public administration—Decision
making. I. Title. II. Series.
  HC462.9.P4   338.952   81-14464
  ISBN 0-87722-249-5   AACR2
  ISBN 0-87722-250-9 (pbk.)

To
Alice McDowell Pempel

Contents

Editors' Preface

All industrial states face a tension between bureaucracy and democracy. Modern governments have found it increasingly difficult to formulate policies adequate to the complex tasks they undertake. At the same time the growing specialization and widening scope of government have led many to question whether it can still be controlled democratically. Policy and Politics in Industrial States explores how some of the major democracies have dealt with this dilemma.

Policy is a pattern of purposive action by which political institutions shape society. It typically involves a wide variety of efforts to address certain social problems. Politics is also a much broader concept, involving the conflict and choices linking individuals and social forces to the political institutions that make policy. Comparative analysis of the interaction between policy and politics is an essential beginning in understanding how and why industrial states differ or converge in their responses to common problems.

The fact that the advanced industrial states are pursuing many similar aims such as increasing social well-being, reducing social conflict, and achieving higher levels of employment and economic productivity means neither that they will all do so in the same way nor that the relevance of politics to such behavior will always be the same. In looking at an array of problems common to all industrial states, the books in this series argue that politics are shaped primarily by the manner in which power is organized within each country. Thus, Britain, Japan, the United States, West Germany, Sweden, and France set distinctive priorities and follow distinctive policies designed to achieve them. In this respect, the series dissents from the view that the nature of the problem faced is the most important feature in determining the politics surrounding efforts at its resolution. Taken to its logical extreme, this view supports the expectation that all states will pursue broadly similar goals in politically similar ways. Though this series will illustrate some important similarities among the policies of different countries, one of the key conclusions to which it points is the distinctive approach that each state takes in managing the problems it confronts.

A second important feature of the series is its sensitivity to the difficulties involved in evaluating policy success or failure. Goals are ambiguous and often contradictory from one area of policy to another; past precedents often shape present options. Conversely, adhering to choices made at an earlier time is often impossible or undesirable at a later period. Hence evaluation must transcend the application of simple economic or managerial criteria of rationality, efficiency, or effectiveness. What appears from such perspectives as irrational, inefficient, or ineffective is often, from a political standpoint, quite intelligible.

To facilitate comparison, all the books in the series follow a common format. In each book, the first chapter introduces the reader to the country's political institutions and social forces, spells out how these are linked to form that country's distinctive configuration of power, and explores how that configuration can be expected to influence policy. A concluding chapter seeks to integrate the country argument developed in the first chapter with the subsequent policy analysis and provides more general observations about the ways in which the specific country findings fit into current debates about policy and politics. Each of the six cases also follows a common format. The first section analyzes the *context* of the policy problem: its historical roots, competing perceptions on the problem by major social groups, and its interdependence with other problems facing the country. The second section deals with the *agenda* set out for the problem: the pressures generating action and the explicit and implicit motives of important political actors, including the government's objectives. The third section deals with *process*: the formulation of the issue, its attempted resolution, and the instruments involved in policy implementation. The fourth and final section of analysis traces the *consequences* of policy for official objectives, for the power distribution in the issue area, for other policies, and for the country's capacity to make policy choices in the future. The element of arbitrariness such a schema introduces into the discussion of policy and politics is a price the series gladly pays in the interest of facilitating comparative analysis of policy and politics.

An important feature of these cases is the inclusion, for each policy problem, of selected readings drawn primarily from official policy documents, interpretations or critiques of policy by different actors, and politically informed analysis. We have become persuaded that the actual language used in policy debates within each country provides an important clue to the relationship between that country's policy and politics. Since appropriate readings are more widely available for Britain and the United States than for the non–English–speaking countries in the series, we have included somewhat more policy materials for these countries. In all instances, the readings are selected as illustration, rather than confirmation, of each book's argument.

Also distinctive of the series, and essential to its comparative approach, is the selection of similar policy cases. Each volume analyzes at least one case involving intergovernmental problems: reform of the national bureaucracy or the interaction among national, regional, and local governments. Each also includes two cases dealing with economic problems: economic policy and labor–management relations. Lastly, each book includes at least two cases focusing on the relationship of individual citizens to the state, among them social welfare. Our choice is designed to provide a basis for cross-national and cross-issue comparison while being sufficiently flexible to make allowance for the idiosyncracies of the countries (and the authors). By using such a framework, we hope that these books will convey the richness and diversity of each country's efforts to solve major problems, as well as the similarities of the interaction between policy and politics in industrial states.

D. E. A.
P. J. K.
T. J. P.

Preface

The subtitle of this book, Creative Conservatism, attempts to convey what I believe are the two most important dynamics in modern Japanese politics. On the one hand, Japan is undeniably conservative in the bias of its politics. Traditional values such as the family, the Emperor, hard work, collectivism, duty and self-sacrifice permeate the official and unofficial vocabulary of Japan's citizens and its rulers. These rulers gain their major support from conservative segments of society and respond in kind, by providing these segments with disproportionate shares of the benefits of public actions. At the same time, unlike many manifestations of conservatism, which have been mired in the past and resistent to change, Japan's brand of conservatism has been creatively adaptive to new circumstances.

The creativity of Japan's approaches to many of the problems common to all industrial democracies has made that country an increasing source of curiosity to many in the West. Japan's impressive economic success, accomplished without the surrender of social cohesion, has been at the core of this curiosity. While much of North America and Western Europe confronts combinations of high inflation, low productivity, loss of foreign exchange and international competitiveness, Japan's economy is among the healthiest in the world. And while other nations can boast of some comparabilities in the field of economics, few have matched Japan's social achievements.

Many explanations have been offered for Japan's successes, but two of the more popular strike me as unnecessarily one-sided. Japan is by no means just an example of the success that can emerge when private enterprise is allowed to compete and flourish without "excessive government interference." On the contrary, government actions have been very much at the core of the bulk of Japan's public policies, in economics as well as elsewhere. At the same time, it makes no sense to ignore the importance of competitive private enterprise, as is too often done in attempts to demonstrate that Japan's successes are the result of little more than government manipulation of private industry in a collusive effort to build an economically successful Japan at the expense of the rest of the industrial world. Government actions have been critical to much of Japan's success; but so too has private initiative.

In focusing on Japan's successes it will not do to ignore their many darker sides. Clear social costs have accompanied most of Japan's accomplishments; undeniable social tradeoffs have been made.

I try in this book to explore these successes and failures, as well as their causes and consequences. But I begin with an explicit conviction that such assessments can best be made in a comparative context. Japan has its unique features, as does any country. But what is truly unusual about Japan is not always best perceived by simple binational comparisons with the United States. When the context of comparison is broadened to include other industrialized countries, Japan's uniqueness fades. The broader context may simply reveal that the United States is the unusual case. What emerges to me as most comparatively significant about Japan is its historic combination of creativity and conservatism. This interweaving forms the predominant theme of the book.

The Series Preface outlines the origins of this project. A special word of thanks, however, is due to my colleagues, Douglas Ashford and Peter Katzenstein. The unflagging persistence of their curiosity about Japan, combined with the tough–mindedness of the questions they asked, forced me continually to reassess much of what I had long considered undeniable folk lore about Japan. That they approached the problems of policy and politics from two strikingly different vantage points helped me to realize the merits of trilateral cooperation. In addition to their intellectual support, I would also like to acknowledge their unremitting patience. Both have been of great value to me.

I have incurred innumerable other debts of gratitude during the course of this project. John Creighton Campbell, Horie Masahiro,

Ishida Takeshi, Kitamura Kazuyuki, Ellis Krauss, Margaret McKean, Mizuno Kunitoshi and Shioji Koji, as well as one anonymous reader provided invaluable and charitably phrased comments on specific chapters or the entire manuscript. Frank Baldwin, Kano Tsutomu, Patricia Murray, Ayako Timmons, and Tsunekawa Keiichi helped in the location, selection and translation of many of the documents used. Andrew Feldman, Richard Friman, and Mark Moquin gave stalwart research assistance with a combination of skill and good cheer unwarranted by the ambiguity and immediacy of most of the requests made of them.

The Ford Foundation provided important financial help to our project. Cornell's Government Department and its China-Japan Program supported much of the work involved in this volume.

I should say a word about the conventions used in this book. Japanese personal names are presented in Japanese form, namely family name followed by surname. Spellings follow the modified Hepburn system. Most figures have been given in yen. From the late 1940s until August, 1971, the exchange rate was ¥360 to one United States dollar. It then appreciated to about ¥300 to a dollar and later went as high as ¥189 to a dollar in 1973. For most of the period since then it has hovered in the neighborhood of ¥220–250 to a dollar. Throughout the book, references have been kept to a minimum. Usually, references are given in one of three instances: where a point of fact or interpretation is sufficiently controversial to warrant additional support; where a significant but unusual point has been made as a result of someone else's work; and where references are so important in their own right that the reader should be alerted as to their existence. I have made or supervised most of the translations. In several instances, I have relied on official translations done elsewhere. Where gross misspellings or grammatical errors existed in the original they have been corrected without additional notation; in most other instances the original has been retained untouched.

T. J. Pempel

Ithaca
June 1981

Policy and Politics in
Japan

1 Introduction

Contemporary Japanese politics contains two fundamental anomalies: conflictual outbursts in the midst of consensus, egregious failures submerged in conspicuous success. The first involves the processes of Japanese politics; the second, the public policies that emerge from these processes. The processes of politics in Japan are widely treated as highly consensual. The most respected students of Japanese society and Japanese psychology stress the importance placed on group solidarity. The individual family member is expected to suppress personal desires in the interests of family unity, the family is expected to do the same for community harmony, and so on up the hierarchical ladder. Success in Japan is measured in terms of achieving group, rather than individual, goals. "Egoism" is regarded as a social evil; conformity is the anticipated norm. This widespread expectation is reflected in the predominance given to the proverb, "The nail that sticks up will be hammered down" (e.g., Nakane, 1970; Fukutake, 1967; Doi, 1973). Typically, most Westerners who have observed Japanese behavior stress their belief that greater conformity, more group consciousness, and more consensual behavior are found in Japan than in their own societies (e.g., Rohlen, 1974; Bayley, 1976; Dore, 1958; Vogel, 1963).

This general social orientation is mirrored politically by studies suggesting that the most successful Japanese leaders are low-key consensus builders, and that collective, rather than individual, decisions are preferred. It is also seen in the importance attached to avoiding or minimizing open conflict in decision making, in the frequency of blurred compromises rather than forceful decisions, and in the relative ease with which decisions, once made, are

3

accepted. "Japan, Incorporated," namely, Japan as a unified political whole when it confronts "outsiders," is a predominant image that vividly captures this concept (Kaplan, 1972).

Although many would agree that the inclinations toward political consensus are strong in Japan, they must confront numerous empirical examples of nonconsensual behavior. Months of massive street protests marked the politics surrounding the United States-Japan Security Treaty, both in 1951–52 and in 1960. During the late 1960s, scores of Japanese universities were closed by students, outfitted in helmets and wielding long wooden poles, who battled unceasingly with police and one another. Consensus was hardly the prevailing norm in the massive citizen protests on environmental matters during the later 1960s and early 1970s. Furthermore, the Japanese parliament, while often so tranquil as to cure insomnia, is periodically the site of vitriolic verbal and occasionally physical attacks. And even within the confines of such allegedly consensual bodies as the Liberal Democratic Party or the Japanese bureaucracy, there are frequent and well-documented battles among competing factions, sections, and agencies (e.g., Thayer, 1969; Donnelly, 1976; Johnson, 1977). Although Japan typically presents a highly consensual image, this consensus is offset by numerous explosions of conflict.

Much of the same duality exists when one examines, not the processes of decision making, but the content of the decisions that are actually made. Contemporary Japan appears to many as a Panglossian political success story. Historically, the country modernized earlier and faster than any other non-Western nation-state. And despite its experiences with authoritarianism and expansionism in the middle of the twentieth century, it presently exhibits laudably high levels of internal democracy, social freedom, and external restraint. Today, Japan also reveals numerous policy accomplishments when compared to other industrialized countries. The unparalleled growth of the nation's economy from the early 1950s through the early 1970s was later matched by an exceptional capacity to continue expanding world market shares while holding down inflation and unemployment at home. Japan seems a paragon of comparative success in other areas ranging from control of crime, disease, and population to the quality of its education, transportation, and communication systems. The country's successes have become so pervasive that many individuals have been wont to describe Japan with such laudatory labels as "Number One" (Vogel, 1979), a "Superwelfare State" (Nakagawa, 1979), or "Asia's New Giant" (Patrick and Rosovsky, 1976).

Yet such successes, shining as they may appear, have their darker sides. In areas such as pollution, old-age benefits, housing, labor rights, civil liberties, and land use policy, for example, Japan has lagged considerably behind most other advanced states. In these areas, the country's performance must be labelled more failure than success. Even within Japan's successes, certain failures are conspicuous. Economic growth was marked by long periods of inflation and by high rates of bankruptcy. A modern international airport is isolated by a failure to create local transportation links with the central city. Unlike the generally high-quality primary and secondary education system, many schools in the higher educational system have been noticeably deficient. Thus in performance as well as in procedure, Japan presents an anomaly. In this case, the curiosity is that of conspicuous failures sandwiched between far more noteworthy successes.

Is there anything unusual in this? Surely, every political system strives for consensus and success but occasionally lapses into conflicts and failure? In what way is Japan unusual? Certainly, any claim that these terms help one to understand Japan better can only be made in light of the relative balance among these elements. Any sensitive assessment of Japan's successes and failures and its concensus and conflicts must consider a relatively broad range of behavior and must view both in comparative perspective. What appears to be a success or a failure in a country's own context may appear quite differently in other countries. Successes in one area are often balanced by failures in another. Thus, Japan's rapid economic growth over a period of twenty years was unparalleled among industrialized countries, but it was carried out at the expense of developing the social infrastructures that are taken for granted in most of Western Europe and North America. Unemployment "soared" to over 2 percent in Japan during the recession of the mid-1970s, but such rates were the envy of political leaders and workers in most other countries. Many castigate the high cost of poor-quality housing in Japan, but Manhattan's young singles typically pay far higher rents for even smaller apartments than most people in Japan pay for their "rabbit hutches." Regional concentration policies may have appeared to be blessed with foresight in the 1950s, but environmental, population, and transportation factors in the 1980s suggest otherwise.

From such a perspective it is impossible to label Japan either an unqualified success or an unqualified failure. Japan certainly faces many of the problems that confront other industrialized countries. In some instances, it has opted for solutions similar to most others; in a few cases it has taken a relatively unique path. Some of its successes are compromised by the failures they have caused in other areas. Elsewhere, the successes and failures of one time–period seem reversed a decade or two later. Yet, when one compares Japan's overall policy performance over the period since World War II to that of other industrialized countries, the image of success remains predominant.

Much the same can be said for the balance between consensus and conflict in Japan. Britain, the United States, and West Germany have often been characterized as demonstrating broad social and political consensus on questions of foreign policy, economic policy, and social distribution. And British "Butskellism," "Tweedledum-Tweedledee" electoral choices in the United States, and the West German Grand Coalition of 1967–69 have no real parallels in Japan. As a result, in such areas Japan appears to be far more conflictual than many of its industrial counterparts. But Japan loses far fewer man hours to strikes than either Britain or the United States; political terrorism is neither as feasible nor as widespread as in West Germany; and crime rates in Japan are vastly below those in these other countries. Again Japanese consensus seems predominant.

Pervasive as the two separate images of success and consensus may be for Japan, they remain somewhat ephemeral. What is success or consensus on one issue, or in one country appears a failure or conflictual in another context. Random parallels to or differences with other societies prove little, inviting as they may be. Far more intriguing and far more analytically interesting than the presence or absence of consensus or success on any single issue are the patterns of both consensus and success. How do successes and failures combine into a cohesive whole? How and when is consensus upset by conflict? How do consensual or conflictual processes interact to generate successful or unsuccessful policy consequences?

In the Japanese case, as I will argue throughout the book, this mix or blend is not random. Rather, the areas of consensus and conflict and the areas of success and failure are relatively predictable as explicit consequences of the character of Japanese politics. Moreover, there are identifiable and systematic links between the areas of consensus and those of conflict while the areas in which Japan is accounted a success or a failure are also systematically interwoven. Before elaborating on this point, however, it is wise to make a few observations on the relationship between politics and public policy in industrialized democracies.

Policy and Politics in Industrialized Democracies

It is a central premise of this book and of the series of which it is a part that one of the most fruitful ways to understand the politics of any single country is through a comparative assessment of its public policies. What choices were made? What political factors lay behind such choices? Why does one country choose path X rather than paths Y or Z that seemed so logically adopted in countries with relatively similar situations? More importantly, how do the various individual policy choices blend or conflict with one another? In short, the bundle of a country's public policies viewed collectively provides a strong lever with which to gain entry into a country's politics.

A comparison of contemporary public policy in a number of problem areas reveals that most highly industrialized capitalist countries face a host of common problems. At the same time, despite the many similarities in problems faced, the national definitions of these problems, the political mechanisms used to handle them, and the ultimate policies adopted often differ widely from one nation-state to another. To different degrees, for example, all modern governments are involved in national-level economic policy. But for Britain this long meant relying on the banks in the City of London to protect the international value of sterling. In more recent years, economic policy has focused on government efforts to gain the consent of labor to a national incomes policy and price stability. In France, by way of contrast, economic policy meant government efforts to create internationally competitive "national champions" in key industrial sectors and to draw private attention to periodic national economic plans. In the United States, economic policy typically revolved around Keynesian-inspired fiscal and monetary efforts by the President, the Congress, and the Federal Reserve Board aimed at smoothing out the peaks and troughs of the business cycle and, more recently, at securing the nation's reindustrialization.

Most industrialized countries have also been faced with the need to reorganize their central administrative apparatuses. Yet, in Britain the key aims have been recruiting top-level bureaucrats more representative of Britain's diversified class structure and introducing more functional expertise and scientific management into top levels of the civil service. West German policymakers, in contrast, have seen the problem of "administrative reform" partly in terms of securing top bureaucratic positions for their partisan supporters and partly in terms of using administrative centralization to overcome federal fragmentation. In most of the Nordic countries, reform has involved concerted efforts to reduce abstract bureaucratization and make agencies more responsive to public needs, largely through the introduction of institutions such as the ombudsman. Under presidents Nixon and Carter, the problem in the United States was seen to involve top-level administrative coordination and political responsiveness. The result was a trend toward superagencies designed to oversee the work of many decentralized government agencies. Most United States presidents have also interpreted administrative reform to imply purging top layers of those in the civil service whose policy predispositions were antithetic to their own.

Japan has been no exception to this pattern. The country faces multiple problems common to all industrial societies, yet efforts to deal with them are typically distinct. Yet they are not so unique or exotic as to preclude insightful comparison. For a long time, economic policy in Japan meant protecting the value of the yen; but, unlike the British pound, the yen was internationally undervalued, not overvalued. For many years, it also meant using the national bureaucracy and the Bank of Japan in an industrial policy similar to that of France; but Japan's economic policy aimed at maximizing Gross National Product (GNP) growth in a manner that caused inflation rates that would have made most French, German, or Swiss policymakers blanch with disbelief. By the mid- to late-1970s, economic policy shifted to stricter control of inflation and to an internationalism and liberalism in many sectors that seemed a revival of the laissez-faire philosophies predominant in nineteenth-century Britain and mid-twentieth-century United States.

In administrative reform, Japan has shown little national concern with changing the socioeconomic composition of its civil servants, and political responsiveness has not been perceived as a major problem. Instead, attention has concentrated primarily on reducing the size and cost of the national bureaucracy. As a result, Japan was the only major nation in the industrialized world to curtail national bureaucratic growth for over a decade (Nutter, 1978).

Such a wide variety of responses to relatively common problems suggests that there is a prima facie basis for questioning the logic of most policy studies. Contrary to the predominant functionalist assumption, economic management, housing, or sanitation are more than technical problems common to all industrial societies, problems which can be dealt with in common fashion. It is a central argument of this book, and of those in the series of which it is a part, that the technical character of a problem is not paramount in determining that problem's solution. The political perception of such problems differs in different countries, and politics plays an essential role in the manner in which they are resolved.

Nor are such variations in public policies the simple result of what are often called "political inputs." Pluralist models stress these "political inputs"—interest groups, political parties, elections, and public opinion, and tend to ignore differences in "political outputs"—legislation, policy initiatives, etc. Such outputs, when they are treated at all, are typically treated as the direct consequences of some interaction among inputs. As a result, the role of the state as an actor in the shaping of political choices is played down. Again, this book and the series attempt to develop a counterargument, suggesting that many policy choices are heavily shaped by state actions.

Finally, Marxist studies provide little help in understanding variations in public policies such as those noted above. There, the focus is on the modes and the relationships of production. Just as pluralist studies minimize the role of the state as little more than the reflection of political inputs, Marxist studies tend to see state actions as the undifferentiated reflection of the economic relationships in a society. Moreover, in Marxist studies the primary distinctions are those drawn between capitalist, socialist, and other modes of production. As a consequence, the Marxist framework provides little help in differentiating *among* the specific behaviors of different capitalist states. Variations in the way individual capitalist states deal with specific policy problems are of little interest to Marxist or neo-Marxist scholars in the attempt to show how such actions reflect, reinforce, or reduce the common economic power-relationships within society.

All of the countries explored in this series are both capitalist and pluralist. As such, they share many commonalities which differentiate them from noncapitalist and nonpluralistc countries. But we are less concerned with this differentiation than with exploring how these capitalist and pluralist nation-states differ from one another. In what specific ways, and with what degrees of success, have they attempted to deal with the various political problems they have faced. In this respect, we are first interested in differentiating *among* the industrialized democracies rather than in understanding what unites them. In what ways are the combined politics and policies of a single industrialized country relatively distinct from those of other industrialized countries? How does such political uniqueness characterize public policies across a range of different problem areas?

With such broad country-to-country distinctions established, it is then possible to explore, in some detail, second-order questions regarding the specific politics surrounding the many discrete issues any single country faces. Thus, even though some broad logic may shape all politics within an entire country in a general way, this logic is usually played out differently in regard to different problems at different points in time. And, finally, we are concerned in at least exploring a third set of problems, namely, the ways in which politics of a single issue in country A may be similar to the politics of that same issue or a different issue in countries B and C. Thus, throughout the series the authors are concerned with country-to-country comparisons, with issue-to-issue comparisons within each country, and with whatever cross-country comparisons seem to emerge logically from these first two.

To understand how the politics of any single country differs from that of any other, it is essential to understand the particular character of each country's political regime. More concretely, it means understanding the character of the social forces within a country, the character of that country's political institutions, and the ways in which these are related. Each book attempts to isolate the combination of social forces and political institutions that in the mind of the author best differentiates each of the six countries from one another and to examine how these shape the outcome of particular political quarrels in systematic ways. Simultaneously, we are interested in how the resolution of particular political issues, in turn, either reinforces or alters the character of the regime.

This book's primary argument seeks to explain the particular mix of consensus and conflict in Japanese policymaking processes, and the blend of success and failure in policy outcomes. Specifically, I argue that what sets off the politics of public policy in Japan is a twofold combination: first, the conservative nature of the social support–base of government in Japan; and second, the relative strength and cohesiveness of the Japanese state apparatus. Both of these factors are rooted deeply in the lateness of Japan's industrialization, but they continue to be influential today. Both combine to produce Japan's peculiar blend of conflict within consensus, failure within success.

In brief, Japan has consistently been governed by conservative political regimes in which organized labor has been completely missing as a social support–base and in which state institutions have been cohesive and strong. This combination has had a consistent influence on the character of Japanese politics and Japanese public policy. Part of this influence has been manifested in the peculiar characteristics of both consensus and success in Japanese public policy.

At the same time, the Japanese regime is by no means fully homogeneous, cohesive, or comprehensive. Divisions are pervasive within the social groups that support the regime and within the various institutions that collectively constitute the state. And nonconservative groups and nonstate actors can, on specific occasions, restrict the boundaries within which the conservatives are free to move. Unlike authoritarian or totalitarian regimes, Japan is pluralistic and democratic with all the complexity of bargaining and influence these terms imply.

Further, to say that the Japanese state is strong is not to say that it is continuously and actively involved in the shaping of policies affecting all areas of society. Japanese governments have, in fact, been highly selective in the scope and direction of their actions, intervening forcefully in some areas but remaining only on the periphery of many others. Alongside varying spurts of activism since the nineteenth-century, successive Japanese governments have shown a parallel proclivity toward nonintervention in many areas. As a consequence, different areas of public policy manifest different levels of state involvement. And even within the same problem areas, the extent of government involvement typically ebbs and flows (Pempel, 1978a).

Many, though not all, of the conflictual and unsuccessful dimensions of Japanese public policy lie embedded in these latter features more than in the conservative and centralized character of the regime. As a consequence, internal divisions, external opposition, and privatization are all aspects of Japanese public policy that must be examined along with the centralized state institutions and the conservative social forces that control these institutions, these being the most fundamental features of the Japanese regime.

The Japanese State: Toward Cohesion and Strength

When Japan was forced to open to Western commerce in 1854, it had to overcome a 250-year history of centralized feudalism. Some 250 individual fiefs were only loosely governed *de facto* by the military shogunate in what is now Tokyo, while the emperor and his court exercised *de jure* sovereignty from Kyoto. The bickering and dissension that marked the country's internal politics in the decade after the coming of the West was only the most blatant manifestation of the relative weakness of the country's decentralization. The Meiji reformers realized that a strong state apparatus, parallel to that of Prussia, was essential if Japan was to develop the "rich country and strong army" designed to preserve national autonomy from the threats of Western imperialism (Akita, 1967).

The Meiji political system rested, therefore, on the principles of political centralization and the citizen's duties to the state rather than on popular sovereignty, local autonomy, checks and balances, or the rights of man. Under the Meiji Constitution, sovereignty rested exclusively in the emperor, whose decisions, though typically the ratifications of decisions made behind the scenes, were absolute and unchallengeable. Day–to–day administration was carried out by a talented and powerful national bureaucracy whose members were "servants of the emperor." Their powers to rule by administrative decree and to appoint local officials were indispensible tools for the centralized state apparatus. The cabinet, the prime minister, and the privy council were all appointed at the direction of the emperor, as was the upper house of the Diet or Parliament (the House of Peers). Parliament was created late and only the relatively weak lower house (the House of Representatives) was directly elected. And as suffrage was sharply curtailed, so was parliament's social responsibility. Strict legislation aimed at "peace preservation" limited political dissent. A strong police force and a national military added to the capacity of the nation's governors to enforce their will.

Strong as the Japanese state was during the prewar period, the tendency toward the centralization of state powers was by no means unique to Japan. Many present-day democracies emerged from comparable traditions, and at the end of the nineteenth century most of Western Europe leaned more toward centralization of authority than toward administrative decentralization and citizen autonomy. But Japan was much closer to the etatist traditions of Germany and France than to the traditions of circumscribed authority of the later English or Swedish monarchs or of American presidents (Gerschenkron, 1962; Moore, 1967).

Furthermore, the state by no means exercised comprehensive control. Although unlike the liberal regimes of Britain, Canada, or the United States, Japan was almost equally distant from the totalitarian and authoritarian model of modernization represented by the Soviet Union. Unification was not complete and control was far from absolute. The numerous institutions in the national government controlled various resources of power, and there were wide fluctuations in their relative influence. Political infighting was rampant on most central issues. Though hemmed in by both law and custom, citizens were rarely in personal terror and enjoyed many of the individual freedoms associated with political democracy. Under the Meiji regime, the lower house of parliament slowly gained the ability to exercise important influence over some issues (Akita, 1967). Yet, even compared to strong states the Japanese orientation was clear: the country developed no analogue to the French

Rights of Man, for example, nor was there an attenuation of state power in the 1920s comparable to that of the Weimar Republic.

Where the prewar Japanese state was most different from totalitarian states was in its toleration, even actual encouragement, of the private sphere. State institutions, while powerful, were not comprehensive in their activities, leaving many critical functions to private or civil society (e.g. Kajinishi, et al. 1973; Marshall, 1967; Nagai, 1971). In this regard it strongly resembled another late industrializer, Sweden.

Unlike Sweden, however, Japan did not develop a widespread public system of social services. Although the government supported a public system of primary, secondary, and university education, private systems developed parallel to and in competition with the public system. Labor markets were left essentially unregulated by the state. Private newspapers and, later, radio stations were allowed to function largely without censorship. Freedom of private association was permitted. Perhaps the most noteworthy example of the tendency toward privatism involved the economy where, in contrast to direct intervention and control, the Japanese government supported the rights of private ownership and economic competition. Following a brief flirtation during the immediate postrestoration period with state establishment and control of vital industries such as munitions, shipbuilding, coal mining, and communications, the government withdrew from direct ownership and management, leaving these aspects largely to the private sector. As a result of the government's decision to abdicate ownership to the private sector, the more highly capitalized and technologically sophisticated industries critical to Japan's economic strength came to be controlled by a limited number of highly concentrated, oligopolistic combines (*zaibatsu*), about which more will be said later. But the significant point here is that the economy remained in private hands and operated largely around competitive principles.

The government, in turn, encouraged and utilized this competitive situation to steer the economy in the "national interest." Positive stimuli, such as tax rebates, attractive conditions for investment, contracts, market privileges, and the like, gave successive governments the leverage to stimulate private industry to follow their official wishes. Thus, while the state did not retain direct managerial control over the economy and actively encouraged the private sector, it also did not leave key economic questions to the marketplace. Government intervention in the economy was frequent, systematic and, for the most part, publicly accepted. Japan's rapid economic growth, its success in loosening the constraints of the unequal treaties imposed by the West in the 1850s, and its ability to gain control over Asian territories all testified to the basic effectiveness of this government policy.

These two prewar legacies—a strong state and the tradition of privatization—left their marks on postwar Japan. But at the same time, the authoritarian state of the 1930s was an early target of the Americans during the Occupation. State institutions were drastically revised. Under a totally new constitution, reflecting a combination of the United States and British systems, popular sovereignty was introduced, and the emperor was reduced from the rank of absolute sovereign to that of "the symbol of the state and the unity of the people." Both houses of parliament were made elective, and parliament became "the highest organ of state power." Along British lines, the cabinet was made responsible to parliament, while an independent judiciary was vested with American-style powers of review. The legal rights of citizens and the powers of local governments were substantially expanded.

Such changes sharply altered the nature of Japanese politics, particularly insofar as popular support became a vastly more important political factor than it had been under the Meiji Constitution; the ability to command a parliamentary majority became essential to continued and effective governance.

The transformation under the Occupation is undeniable, and the Japanese political system was undoubtedly at a major historical crossroads during the years immediately following the war. Various factors, including United States Occupation policies, international conditions, and socioeconomic developments in Japan, could well have nudged the country in any one of several drastically different directions. The combination that evolved, however, worked to revitalize, albeit in somewhat different form, strong and cohesive state institutions.

In particular, little was done to drastically alter the power of the national bureaucracy. In fact, the military nature of the Occupation and its use of domestic government organs to enforce Occupation policies actually reinforced the power of Japanese government ministries. So did the prevailing sense of crisis and the need for strong central direction, particularly in areas related to economic reconstruction. The postwar Japanese bureaucracy, therefore, emerged from the Occupation with few of its inherent powers altered. Despite subsequent fluctuations in its powers, it has remained to date at the center of the state's wide-ranging authority (Johnson, 1975), much as its counterparts in France and Sweden.

Under the present Japanese political system, there are numerous sources of division among state institutions. This is particularly true of Japan's parliament. The freedom of debate, the increased role of political parties, the tightness of the parliamentary calendar, the relative autonomy of parliamentary committees, the media coverage given to parliamentary activities, and a host of other factors combine to make the parliament the major institutional locus of conflict between the government and opposition parties. Executives and legislators in perfectural, city and town governments are freely elected and are much less under the thumb of Tokyo than they were under the prewar constitution. This newfound autonomy has also proved to be a source of political controversy (MacDougall, 1976). The judicial system gained institutional autonomy which, in turn, decreased the comprehensive control of the prewar political system. Beyond these elements, Japan has at least a normal component of divisions based on personality clashes, factionalism, cliques organized around school ties, marriage connections, regional links, personal ambition, and ideology. These divisions serve as undeniable sources of cleavage, tension, and controversy throughout state institutions, forcing continual modifications, delays, and compromise in state actions pressed by any single group or organization. Democracy presumes conflict; no democratic government is close to either omnipotence or freedom from conflict.

At the same time, the collective effect of government in Japan is toward a national cohesion and centralization rather than toward the dispersion of power and the institutionalization of conflict. The Japanese state is capable of making decisions and of enforcing them once made. There are two different sources for this centralization of power: institutional and personal. Institutionally, numerous centripetal forces pull Japanese political actors toward one another. Within the parliament, party solidarity is the watchword, as it is in almost all parliamentary systems. It is extremely rare for an individual to vote against his party. And although there are clear lines among parties in the parliament, these divisions are minimized by the House Management Committee, the development of a neutral speaker, and the trend toward concurrent majorities (Krauss, 1980). Thus, from July 1975 to June 1980 there was not a single no-confidence motion introduced against the cabinet, and in 1977 over two-thirds of all cabinet legislation was passed without opposition. When Communist party opposition is excluded, this figure rises to about 80 percent.

Even more significantly, the cabinet has been a force for unity and effective implementation through its ability to oversee the bulk of parliamentary activity. The cabinet calls the parliament into session and controls the bulk of the legislative calendar. Through the Cabinet Legislative Bureau (Naikaku Hōseikyoku), the cabinet oversees legislative technicalities, and draws up and presents the bulk of the legislation on which the parliament acts. As in nearly all democracies with cabinet governments, most of the actual legislation presented in Japan is initially drafted within the various ministries. In fact, 85 percent of the bills introduced in the Diet between 1945 and 1975 were drawn up and sponsored by government ministries, and over 90 percent of all the legislation passed in Japan was government sponsored. It is extremely rare for a nongovernment bill to pass; it is also rare for important government bills to fail (Pempel, 1975).

Another occasional impetus toward consensus in the Japanese government involves the nearly 250 advisory councils and numerous other study groups and research committees attached to government agencies. The members of these bodies are appointed by the ministry from various public and private organizations ranging from interest groups to academic institutions to media. Membership may range from less than a dozen to over 100 when specialists and others are included in the count. These councils may be charged with examining a problem as narrow as how to regulate masseurs and acupuncture specialists, how to ensure safety with high pressure gas, or how to develop the Amami Island group, or it may range over broad topics, like the entire social welfare system, the industrial structure, or energy. In all cases, however, the council is expected to provide a forum for discussion and investigation of a problem, to work toward resolution of different positions and opinions, and to present a unified proposal for action to the government. Such unanimity is not always readily forthcoming, and two advisory bodies often propose different courses of action. Still these bodies serve as important lightning rods for dissent, and normally they help to conciliate the differences among their members. Not only is a more unified set of proposals presented to the government, where it tends to have a consensus-forming influence, but the procedure itself serves to create a core of respected advocates for whatever positions emerge from the councils. Perhaps only Sweden outdoes Japan in the prevalence given to such bodies.

Naturally, there are differences of interest and opinion within the government. When these differences are among the ministries, they are typically referred to the Conference of Vice-Ministers. Although this conference has no legal standing, it includes the most senior civil servant from each ministry, and it meets just before each cabinet session under the direction of the chief cabinet secretary in an effort to iron out interministerial differences.

Cabinet cooperation is also facilitated by a number of *ad hoc* cross-ministerial councils and permanent bodies such as the National Defense Council or the Science Council, which are composed of the prime minister and usually five to eight additional ministers whose agencies are directly involved in the problems under consideration. The permanent bodies meet regularly to define broad policy guidelines, cutting across ministerial specialization. These guidelines then become the major principles directing specific ministerial actions, and the minister and the senior civil servants bear a heavy collective responsibility to see that such broad cross-ministerial agreements in fact guide policies within their individual ministries, both in policy formation and in policy implementation.

Local governments and the judiciary are also potential sources of institutional conflict within Japan. Under the postwar constitutional system, most local officials are elected. Consequently, partisan conflict has become more salient both within local governments and in local-central relations than was the case under the Meiji system. Particularly during the 1970s, local level partisan conflict took on important significance for the system as a whole (MacDougall, 1975). Yet, the bulk of local government financing comes through the central government, giving the latter an important lever over local activities. As in France, the central government has used

financial dependence to limit local autonomy and to ensure conformity with central governmental policies. A large percentage of
local governmental legislation involves the passage of model bills
drafted by and passed at the suggestion of the national government.
Police and educational functions, frequently the most important
activities carried out by local governments in other countries, are
under central direction in Japan. The prewar Home Ministry, which
had exercised control over local government, was dissolved during
the United States Occupation, but was reconstituted as the Local
Autonomy Ministry in 1960 and provides a dimension of centralization to local government. (Interestingly, while the ministry's name
in Japanese has remained the same since then, in the mid-1970s the
English-language translation of the agency's name was switched to
Ministry of Home Affairs.) Finally, since the Occupation there has
been a reconsolidation of local administrative units into larger
bodies, and there is continual discussion of even further consolidation. In short, there is an important impetus toward centralization
that weighs heavily against the centrifugal forces of Japan's numerous local governments.

Turning to the judiciary, the pull toward the center is also very
much in evidence. The courts do have the power of judicial review
over the constitutionality of legislative and administrative actions
(Itoh and Beer, 1978). And as will be seen, particularly in the case
of environmental pollution, many have been happy to take an
activist stance (McKean, 1977). The Supreme Court, however, has
largely supported government policies. Its members are appointed
by the cabinet and it oversees the administration of the entire court
system, including the appointment of lower-court judges. Throughout its history, the Supreme Court has been far more active in
reversing antigovernmental decisions made by lower courts than in
challenging any important government actions. Decisions by the
Supreme Court holding that governmental actions were unconstitutional are few in number and none has been of serious political
significance. Meanwhile, among other things, it has reversed lower
court decisions that held that the existing military forces were
unconstitutional; that limited the rights of the police to regulate
political demonstrations; that held that public sector employees had
the right to strike; that undercut the nation's stringent antipor-
nography laws; and that limited the Ministry of Education's right to

grant military–base rights to United States forces. In short, the Supreme Court has been an important, if frequently unrecognized, vehicle for preserving the status quo in Japan and for reducing the capacity of the courts to reverse executive actions.

All of these structural features of Japanese government provide bridges among competing institutions and press toward cohesion rather than diversity, toward obedience rather than dissent. But perhaps the most important structural feature fueling the cohesion and effectiveness of the Japanese state is its small size. As noted earlier, when Japan began its industrialization in the late nineteenth century, the government initially created and managed a number of critical industries. But by the turn of the century, industrial ownership was almost exclusively in private hands. In most areas of social welfare, the government also avoided direct involvement, explicitly rejecting the Bismarckian approach to German industrialization, namely, combining growth with extensive social programs. Even in the 1980s, the Japanese government continues to be among the smallest in the industrialized world. Japanese government employees represent 9 percent of the labor force, compared to 14–20 percent in most North American and European countries. The Japanese government spends about 22 percent of the nation's GNP; in Europe and North America, the figures range from 31 percent in Switzerland to nearly 60 percent in most of the Scandinavian countries (Nutter, 1978). The reasons why the Japanese government is so small and the mechanisms whereby it has remained so, are complicated and will be explored in more detail in the subsequent policy chapters. At this point, it is sufficient to note that the government has not taken on many of the functions handled by its counterparts in other industrialized societies, leaving large numbers to the private sector. This is particularly true in matters of social welfare, regulation of labor and internal commerce, health care, higher education, research and development, and a host of other areas. The government has also kept its military expenditures proportionately lower than those of most other countries. As a consequence, both the size and the cost of government in Japan are markedly below those of most other countries.

The relatively small size of the Japanese government is particularly conducive to internal government cohesion. Forced, in effect, to choose its targets of action from among a wide range of potential problems, the Japanese government must strive for greater coherence on goals than governments which have a wider scope of action and more numerous agencies to take on new problems. While the bureaucracy has remained very powerful, its power has not been used to direct and control society in minute detail, unlike its French or Swedish counterparts. Japanese government has not sought to be all things to all of its citizens. Immediately after the war, the bureaucracy was heavily involved in many essential aspects of the economy and society. As economic growth increased, and as the need for such direct controls as rationing diminished, the bureaucracy, like its prewar predecessor, moved more into the background (Honda, 1975; Patrick and Rosovsky, 1976). Private initiative rather than government direction; selective government intervention or direction rather than a constant presence; and a small and efficient government rather than a lumbering bureaucratic monstrosity tended to characterize Japanese politics. Instead of government by autonomous agency, Japan has had government by central design.

In addition to the many structural factors which contribute to coordination and cohesion in Japanese governmental institutions, one must also take account of the personal factors that do the same. Grossly oversimplified, everyone who is anyone in Japanese government knows everyone else, or at least someone who does. This common knowledge contributes to the consensual nature of much of Japanese politics and also aids tremendously in increasing governmental effectiveness (Nakane, 1970; Thayer, 1969).

Like France, Sweden, or England, but unlike West Germany or the United States, Japan has one geographical center, its capital city, Tokyo. The country's political, commercial, financial, media, and cultural centers are all concentrated within a radius of less than five kilometers. A short limousine ride can put the head of a major corporation in touch with the prime minister, the editors of the nation's largest magazines or newspapers, his major financial supporters, or his major sales outlets. A politician, banker, or reporter has similar ease in achieving direct communication. Meanwhile, old school ties, family linkages through marriage, and a host of informal study groups, research associations, and social groupings also make it easy for many of the most important members of the government and the private sector to remain in fairly constant communication with one another. Equipped with a common language and style, these members of the Japanese elite can transcend many formal institutional roles and deal with one another in a fluid and flexible manner.

Ease of communication is also facilitated by the common socialization that most of the important members of government (and many leaders in private spheres) have achieved. Tokyo University remains an important vehicle by which to enter the national elite. Education in administrative law also provides a commonality of background among top officials. In the early 1970s, over 60 percent of those holding the rank of section chief or above in Japan's national ministries were graduates of Tokyo University. In 1972–73, 77 percent of the bureau chiefs and 91 percent of the administrative vice-ministers were graduates of law faculties. Despite claims that this dominance is becoming less significant, in 1976, 49 percent of the successful applicants in the senior civil service examination were graduates of either Tokyo or Kyoto universities. Whereas these two universities had 654 successful applicants, the next most successful institution had only 51. Only fifteen universities out of the more than four hundred in the country placed 10 or more of their alumni on the passing list. When one looks at the top positions in the cabinet and the judiciary as well as in the private sector, the commonality of educational background is similarly distinctive. The common socialization-experiences of Japan's top leadership makes for ease of communication and for common perspectives and points of reference. Finally, Japan's newspapers, magazines, and television all have national circulation, giving breadth and simultaneity to most of the important events viewed by these leaders. These features are essential to the centripetal pull in Japanese politics.

If Japanese state institutions are powerful and cohesive, are they also autonomous? To what extent are they capable of initiating policies and forging social conformity as opposed to merely reflecting socioeconomic divisions of power? This is perhaps one of the most vexing questions that arises in the discussion of any state: To what extent does it function autonomously of the society it allegedly governs? Is the state, as Marx and Engels suggested in *The Communist Manifesto* "but a committee for managing the common affairs of the whole bourgeoisie?" Is the state, as the liberal pluralists have for so long implied, little more than an ultimate ratifier of socially arrived at bargains? Or is it more? Do state actors have interests separate from and in conflict with powerful social groups? Can they forge and enforce policies that reflect such separate interests, even in the face of opposition from the socially and economically powerful?

The best test of such questions requires an assessment of situations in which state and society have sought goals directly antithetic to one another. When state actors, for example, want an alliance with country A and major social groups prefer country B, what happens? If an alliance is struck with country A, there is a reasonable basis for concluding that the state is autonomous, whereas if the alliance is struck with B, one would be forced to conclude the opposite.

Easy to imagine in the abstract, such situations are comparatively rare in real life. Actual political struggles rarely pit a unified state so starkly against an equally unified society. More often political alliances cut across state-society lines while most political solutions involve adjustments and compromise that make it difficult to isolate one total winner and an equally total loser.

An important real life surrogate for such a test situation often takes place when one government is replaced by another with drastically different priorities. Do entrenched state officials have the capacity to effectively resist the altered priorities of new social coalitions or is the new government capable of taking control of state institutions and enacting its policy proposals? Unfortunately, for purpose of analysis, Japan, as will be seen below, with a cohesive conservative coalition controlling the reins of government since the end of the 1940s, has not experienced any such clear test of state autonomy. Thus one has no real sense of what would happen within the state bureaucracy if, say, a socialist government came to Japan. Would new socialist policies be introduced and implemented with comparative ease, or would the bureaucracy effectively resist changing past practices? One can only speculate; two points are clear, however. First, the state institutions are currently closely interwoven with, rather than hostile to, the predominant social forces in the country. And second, while these social groups provide a broad ideological framework within which most government action must take place, the state bureaucracy has a good deal of leeway so long as it does not challenge the boundaries of this framework. But within this framework, Japanese bureaucrats are quite free to take policy initiatives, and to press hard to carry them out. In each of the policy cases explored in subsequent chapters, there are several clear instances in which bureaucratic power prevailed when matched against that of important social or economic groups. At the same time, what is most consistently predominant is the *combination* of conservative social power and strong state institutions rather than the consistent predominance of one or the other. The Japanese state shows flashes of autonomy, but it hardly exists in a social vacuum.

This discussion provides a logical lead into what may well be the most significant reason for the cohesion, consensus, and cooperation in Japanese politics, namely, the homogeneity that links the members of Japanese society to one another, and, more importantly, the consistent political dominance of Japan's central political institutions by a single social coalition.

Japanese Society: The Conservative Coalition

Compared to most societies, Japan is strikingly uniform. Since the country began its industrialization, it has been racially, ethnically, and linguistically homogeneous. Virtually no significant numbers of people outside the country's reasonably well-defined geographic boundaries speak the language or count themselves as Japanese. Although two major religions, Buddhism and Shinto, prevail throughout the country, religious ties have been weak and most Japanese have been comfortable with both. Regional loyalties, while strong in the mid-nineteenth century, were not reinforced by drastic differences in language, culture, ethnicity, or religion. They thus blurred rather rapidly. Geographically isolated, Japan has seen little migration in or out of the country as has Europe and North America.

This natural homogeneity was reinforced throughout the prewar period by ideologies of the "family state," "Japanism," the "national essence," and the "emperor system," all of which developed and reinforced notions of Japanese uniqueness and their separateness from all other peoples. Whatever class, regional, occupational, or other differences separated one group of Japanese from another were blurred in the emphasis on national unity, the collectivity, and the importance of social harmony (Nakane, 1970). A rapidly introduced, comprehensive, and governmentally over-seen public school system reinforced these perceptions for many young citizens. Military conscription, press censorship, and public indoctrination drove them home for many more. The built-in pres-sures toward social conformity in a society that until World War II was over 50 percent agricultural also undoubtedly contributed to the sense of national homogeneity.

Censorship, conscription, massive indoctrination, and most ves-tiges of agricultural isolation have been eliminated in contemporary Japan. But ethnic, linguistic, religious, and regional divisiveness are, if anything, far less salient in the 1980s than they were in the 1860s. Moreover, the national school system remains highly confor-mist, with textbooks and curriculum strictly controlled by the Ministry of Education. For most citizens, additional homogeneity is generated by the uniformity and national pervasiveness of the mass media. Three rather standardized national dailies blanket the is-lands of Japan twice a day, and the country's readership per capita far exceeds that of any other industrialized society (548 papers published per 1,000 inhabitants compared to 312 per 1,000 in West Germany, 388 per 1,000 in Britain, 287 per 1,000 in the U.S., and 215 per 1,000 in France). In a similar fashion, radio and television provide comparably standardized and widespread programming.

Thus, even today the Japanese frequently refer to themselves without the slightest trace of self-consciousness as *wareware Nihon-jin* (we Japanese) while a commonly used word for "Japan" remains *wagakuni* ("our country"). Such terms suggest to the foreigner a presumed uniformity and homogeneity not typically found in most other countries. The word gaijin (literally "outside person") com-monly used to refer to foreigners also conveys the sense of national exclusiveness.

This general homogeneity of Japanese society contributes natur-ally to the consensual nature of decision making in the country, and to the ease of implementing decisions once they are reached. The broad-based social homogeneity of the country contributes to grea-ter ease in communication among competing individuals and orga-nizations. Having relatively broad bases of commonality in such things as speech, upbringing, and information, if not in specific values and objectives, minimizes or at least clarifies the areas of potential disagreement, confusion, and misunderstanding that can often arise in more diversified societies. These, in turn, make it easier to reach agreements, or at least to know why agreement is impossible. They also make it easier for decisions, wherever made, to be accepted throughout important segments of society.

Yet the relatively undifferentiated homogeneity of the Japanese populace is complicated by many lines of organizational and social cleavage. Like any complex society, Japan is laced with a great variety of economic, regional, cultural, generational, and other organizations. It is hard to find many Japanese who are not members of one or more groups or organizations. Such organizational pervasiveness tends to minimize the extent to which individual citizens float autonomously outside the boundaries of society and outside the effective jurisdiction of the state. In this way, social communication is facilitated and citizen involvement increased.

The most politically salient of Japan's social groupings have usually been those purporting to reflect the economic or occupational interests of several broad social sectors, agriculture, business, the military, and so forth. Because the interests of these sectors have by no means been fully congruent, cleavage lines have consistently marred the facade of Japanese harmony, national unity, and consensus. Yet throughout its contemporary history, Japan has managed to fuse essentially disjointed social sectors into relatively cohesive ruling coalitions.

One of the earliest divisions of significance in modern Japan was that between business and agriculture. Because the major goal of the Meiji government was the rapid industrialization of the country, business and commerce rapidly acquired political influence with the modernizing elite. Since this industrialization was being carried out largely with capital raised by the land tax of 1873, however, the rural sector had a vested economic interest in opposing the government and its business allies. This opposition took the form of the People's Rights Movement, an embryonic political party movement, and eventually a well-organized demand for a constitution and a parliament. When these were achieved in 1890, they allowed agricultural interests to check government expenditures and the rapid advancement of industrialization and military expenditures. Representation was sharply limited, however, and it was really only a small segment of large landowners who enjoyed parliamentary representation. Not unlike most countries in comparable stages of industrialization, the bulk of the peasantry was disenfranchised. Despite initially incompatible interests, by the turn of the century a working conservative coalition, which papered over many of the early divisions, was formed among governing bureaucrats, the landlords, and the largest business organizations. Industrialization proceeded, with the peasants and the urban underclass, not the landlords, footing most of the tax bill. In turn, pork-barrel benefits to specific localities reinforced the regional influence of the landlords. Political parties, even when their influence was at its peak in the 1920s, served largely as vehicles for fusing business and landlord interests, rather than as challenges to them or as channels for their separate articulation.

Continued military expenditures and overseas expansion catapulted the military into ever-increasing influence over government following World War I, and particularly from the 1930s until the end of the Second World War.

The major social forces driving Japanese politics during the prewar period, therefore, were essentially four: the state bureaucracy, the rural landowning elite, big business, and the military. Despite the battles that took place among these diverse elements of Japan's ruling coalition, and within the sectors themselves, there was broad agreement on such basic goals as rapid industrialization, a strong international military and security position, and a stable political system able to achieve these goals. This social coalition was also consistently more conservative in its approach to fundamental questions of economic management, political organization, and social redistribution than its West European counterparts. The coalition's predominant position was bolstered at the mass level by the ideological cement by such quasi-mystical notions as "protecting the national essence" or "preserving the Japanese spirit," as well as by the widespread perception of Japan's international vulnerability.

The most important exception to Japan's prewar social unity was provided by labor. As industrialization proceeded, factories dotted the land, and workers came to bear a disproportionate share of the public burdens, the heretofore alien ideologies of unionization, liberalism, socialism, and communism gained credibility. In the two decades following World War I, consistent efforts were made to organize unions and to develop political parties with a predominantly working–class base and a leftist ideological orientation. The alien nature of these ideologies and their presumptions of inevitable social conflict reduced their mass appeal. Virtually all unions took the form of enterprise unions, where loyalty to the firm and employer paternalism reduced any horizontal class appeals the union movement might otherwise have had. Large pools of female and seasonal agrarian workers reduced the unions' potential for economic clout. Government, business, the major parties, landlords, and the military were almost uniformly opposed to the threat posed by the left to their hold on power and the directions they were following (Marshall, 1967). As a result of all these factors, the left achieved only limited success. At the height of union development in 1936, only 6 percent of the labor force was unionized. Its greatest electoral success came in the 1936 and 1937 elections when parties of the left combined to win about 10 percent of the vote (Scalapino, 1968). Both figures are markedly lower than those for any European counterparts at the time. Thus, at no time during the prewar period did organized labor begin to penetrate the ruling coalition or to influence public policy as it did in Western Europe and North America. With the establishment of the Imperial Rule Assistance Association in 1940, all autonomous political parties and interest-associations were dissolved, and the consolidation of power by the state and the conservatives reached its apex.

Following the war, the Americans sought, particularly in the earliest stages of the Occupation, to introduce a number of changes into Japanese society and politics. As a result of the War Crimes Trials, a purge, and the constitutional prohibition against the maintenance of an armed force, the military was eviscerated. Simultaneously, an extensive land-reform program virtually wiped out the landlords as a cohesive and nationally relevant social grouping. Thus, two vital elements of the prewar power structure lost virtually all political significance. Moreover, the oligopolistic character of industry and commerce was slated for massive deconcentration. Meanwhile, organized labor received a major injection of vitality from Occupation policies designed to organize unions and legalize a variety of union activities prohibited under the prewar regime.

From the late 1940s onward, the Cold War, the polarization of international politics, and the consolidation of communist control in China generated a drastic reassessment of United States foreign policy and Japan's role as enemy or ally. Within the United States, strong pressures developed from business and a Republican-dominated Congress to hasten Japanese economic recovery, to check the radicalism of the new labor movement, and to stifle anything vaguely resembling socialism in Japan.

By the latter years of the American Occupation, a new conservative coalition had begun to emerge and the social forces of big business and organized agriculture were its most prominent constituent elements. Meanwhile, organized labor remained its most conspicuously excluded sector.

Although several of the major prewar business combines (*zaibatsu*) were dissolved or reorganized under the Occupation, the bulk of them regained national economic predominance. Starting in the middle of the Occupation, business as a whole began to take on an impressively well-organized character. Elaborate subcontracting arrangements linked numerous smaller firms to a limited number of larger firms. The major banks began to aid business reorganization on the "one set" principle whereby each bank sought to develop extensive ties to one major steel company, one major chemical company, one major trading company, and the like. Government and the banks aided the formation of cartels in such areas as electronics, fertilizers, steel, and machine tools (Kaplan, 1972). Mergers and industrial reorganizations provided further integration. Meanwhile, individual firms and sectors were hierarchically organized into approximately six hundred trade and industrial associations with elaborate powers to shape the domestic and international behavior of their member firms (Patrick and Rosovsky, 1976: 753–811).

At the national political level, three peak associations became spokesmen for the interests of big business. The Federation of Economic Organizations (Keidanren) with its membership of 100 major trade or industrial associations and some 750 major firms is considered the political capstone of Japanese business. Its president is frequently referred to as the prime minister of the financial world. The Japan Committee for Economic Development (Keizai Dōyūkai), with fifteen hundred individual members, is also a major voice in the coordination and articulation of business interests. Some 30,000 employers are organized into the Japan Federation of Employers' Associations (Nikkeiren) through which they attempt to speak with a unified voice on matters involving labor-management conflicts.

As a result, Japanese business, especially big business, is pervasively and hierarchically organized. As with any social sector anywhere in the world, Japanese business is not without its internal disagreements and divisions. But the organizational mechanics exist to allow business to sing out in a rather loud and harmonious chorus on important matters. And in this chorus it is the *basso profundo* of the largest corporations and banks which is most prominent. In turn, when decisions are reached at the upper echelons of these organizations, individual members can be expected to carry them out with relative rapidity and effectiveness.

Much the same is true of the conservative coalition's second major partner, organized agriculture. Individual farmers were tightly organized into a single agricultural organization, the Imperial Agricultural Association (Nōgyōkai) during the 1940s. When the war ended, autonomous agricultural cooperatives were formed at the behest of the Americans and with the willing collaboration of most Japanese farmers. The new groups inherited the properties, tasks, and employees of the wartime association, and soon provided comprehensive organization for most of Japan's farmers. Although membership was technically noncompulsory, the cooperatives soon counted 99 percent of Japan's farmers among their membership. At the village level, the cooperatives provide purchasing, marketing, and credit facilities, common crop spraying, and often commonly owned equipment. At the regional and national levels, they press for legislative and bureaucratic decisions favorable to agriculture and particularly to rice farming. From the local villages up to the national level, the cooperatives are organized into The National Association of Agricultural Cooperatives (Nōkyō) and, even more than for its business counterparts, Nōkyō is a comprehensive organization of a politically essential sector of Japanese society.

Holding these elements together has been a vague consensus on the merits of the capitalist economic system (despite different interpretations of what that specifically entails), Japanese nationalism (both economic and political), support for traditional values and institutions (ranging from the Imperial system, the family, and the peasant class through the work ethic, respect for superiors, and the introduction of more moral teachings into the school system), hostility toward communism and socialism, and a foreign policy based on cooperation with the United States and Western Europe.

Japanese labor presents a striking organizational contrast to Japanese business and agriculture. Only about one-third of the labor force are union members. This figure is more than that of the United States, Canada, or France, approximately equal to that of West Germany, but lower than that of the Scandinavian countries and Britain. Moreover, it has not grown at all since the end of the Occupation. Furthermore, as will be examined at greater length in Chapter 3, most unions are of the enterprise variety and, therefore, they rarely transcend the boundaries of the individual firm (Cole, 1971; Dore, 1973; Hanami, 1979). As a result, the organizational links between the local and the national levels are extremely weak. Finally, labor's voice is organizationally diluted at the national level by the fact that two major and several minor federations have attempted to provide the national organizational locus for labor. *Sōhyō*, the largest, represents only slightly more than one-third of the nation's unionized workers and has only limited representation in major manufacturing firms. *Dōmei*, the next largest, contains less than one–fifth of the total unionized work force and rarely works closely with *Sōhyō*, whom it sees as a rival. The rest of the unionized work force is organizationally even more dissipated at the national level. Such fragmentation in the ranks of organized labor has long mitigated its overall political influence.

Thus, as was noted earlier, organized labor has never provided the support base for government in Japan. With only a peripheral exception for a six–month period immediately following World War II, Japan has, since the beginnings of its industrialization in the mid-nineteenth century, been governed by conservative political regimes for which organized business and organized agriculture have been the primary social supporters. Japanese labor has played a preponderantly opposing role, in contrast to its counterparts in all other industrialized countries. In these other nation-states, despite variations in the character of its penetration, organized labor has been at least partly involved in government. In some countries, labor has been the prime source of a hegemonic left-of-center regime, such as that in Sweden or Israel, from the 1940s into the 1970s. In other countries, such as Britain, West Germany, or the United States, organized labor has been an essential supporter of one of the major political parties in control of government for sustained periods of time. Finally, in countries like Italy and France, labor is internally divided, and large and generally radical segments are excluded from power; still, important and more conservative portions of organized labor have supported the governments in power and have been suitably rewarded. Japan represents an extreme case because organized labor has been uniformly outside government institutions. Unessential to the dominant social coalitions that have formed the base of government within the country, organized labor's influence on politics and public policy in Japan has continuously been that of the outsider looking in, demanding, cajoling, criticizing, and carping, but rarely making or shaping decisions.

Of course, the picture of Japan's political society as composed of big business, agricultural, and labor groups is oversimplified. At various times, groups such as veterans, former landlords, senior citizens, students, environmentalists, doctors, small businessmen, bathhouse owners, war widows, teachers, and numerous others have influenced important political decisions. (Campbell, 1977, 1979; Kitamura and Cummings, 1972; Pempel, 1976; Thurston, 1973). Yet the size, importance, and scope of activities of these groups have been far less significant than those of the three main groups explored above. Most of these other groups have smaller memberships, are less well organized and/or less comprehensive in the range of their interests. Often important when a single issue is involved no one of them exerts the same continuous, long-term, and systematic influence over the conservative coalition and its progressive opposition as is exerted by big business, organized agriculture, and organized labor. As such, they are less essential to an understanding of the character of the political regime.

Linking the Social Coalition to the State: Parties and Elections

Although the character of state institutions and the nature of the dominant social coalition have been analyzed separately, in fact the Japanese regime, with its peculiar blend of consensus and conflict, success and failure, is really the outgrowth of their interrelationship and mutual reinforcement. The cohesive and comprehensive character of the Japanese state has depended for its continuance on the predominance of the conservative coalition. In turn, there is little likelihood that the coalition could have retained its internal cohesion without the reinforcement provided by continual control over the major organs of state power. The most important institutional glue holding the two together has been the party system and the electoral system. In the postwar period, it has been the Liberal Democratic Party and its electoral success that have linked the more powerful Japanese social organizations to the institutions of the state.

Elections and political parties became the essential vehicles to political power in Japan only recently. The central political problem Japan faced in the late nineteenth century was industrialization and protection of its sovereignty from external threat. Internally, the country was, as noted above, blessed with a high degree of social homogeneity. Thus, at this critical stage of its early creation, unlike most of its European and North American counterparts, the Japanese state was less pressured to create political institutions designed to guarantee the rights of powerful social minorities. The legitimacy provided by elections was not needed while the strong state was a logical concomitant of a defensive and defenseless Japanese society.

Political parties did not enter electoral competition in Japan until the 1890s, and when they did, the franchise was limited to about 1 percent of the population. In only four of twenty-two elections between 1890 and 1946 did a single party win a majority in the lower house of parliament. Universal suffrage for most males over twenty-five years of age was not introduced until 1925. For most of the period, parties were more a mechanism whereby state officials ensured parliamentary support, and less a device to guarantee societal checks over state actions. Not until the 1920s did the parties establish their power to form governments on the basis of strength in the lower house of parliament. And this power lasted only a decade.

Thus, of the forty-four cabinets formed between 1890 and the end of World War II, at most seventeen were headed by party leaders. Since this figure includes eight cabinets formed by individuals who left high positions in government or the military to head parties, it is more reasonable to speak of eight of forty-four, or about one in five cabinets, as being headed by individuals who had made their careers largely through electoral and party politics (Pempel, 1978b). With the increased role of the military during the 1930s, this short-lived ability of the parties disappeared once again. Elections, parties, and the parliament thus played only a limited role in linking state and society and in determining government actions. Electoral strength was but one element in the struggle for political influence. At least equally significant were economic power, military strength, administrative autonomy, and proximity to the emperor. Although segments of the conservative coalition occasionally relied on elections, parties, and parliament to exert influence, there was no constitutional or practical requirement to do so.

With the new constitution in 1946 electoral strength and party organization became a far more important currency of political exchange. Practically speaking, it has been virtually impossible to become a cabinet member without being a parliamentary party member; all cabinets formed under the new constitution have been headed by party leaders. Parliamentary support is essential to cabinet longevity.

After several multiparty coalitions in the first decade following the end of the war, Japanese parties in 1955 took on the organizational form that remains primary even today. In that year, the hitherto-divided socialist parties came together to form the Japan Socialist Party (JSP), while the conservative parties united to form the Liberal Democratic Party (LDP). Between them, the two parties accounted for over 98 percent of the parliamentary seats. From 1955 until the mid-1960s, these two rival parties dominated the elections and parliamentary activity. But since the union-based JSP was consistently unable to gain more than one-third of the seats in parliament it never gained a foothold in the cabinet, while the LDP, with consistent ties to organized business and organized agriculture, held comfortable majorities in both houses of parliament and dominated all cabinet posts.

From the 1960s through the beginning of the 1980s, smaller rival parties sprang up and gained electoral significance. The most noteworthy were the Democratic Socialist Party (DSP), a conservative spin-off of the JSP; the Japan Communist Party (JCP), which had been in existence since 1922 but which only regained its electoral appeal during the late 1960s; the Clean Government Party (CGP or Komeitō), a political affiliate of a fundamentalist Buddhist sect (Sōka Gakkai); and the New Liberal Club (NLC), a group that broke away from the LDP in 1976.

The LDP is a vague and amorphous amalgam of conservative economic and cultural values supported electorally and financially by the key elements of the dominant coalition. While business provides the funding for the party, agriculture long provided a hefty chunk of the votes. In turn, a succession of LDP governments has protected the capitalist economy and pursued specific policies designed to improve the domestic and international competitiveness of big business. For agriculture, these governments have provided broad support for traditional moral and political values plus a system of lucrative agrarian price supports.

In these basic orientations, the conservatives have been quite consistently opposed by the labor-based parties (JSP, JCP, and DSP) and occasionally by the other minor parties. At various times, these parties have called for a foreign policy less closely linked to the United States and Western Europe, for economic policies aimed at greater redistribution, for a more extensive social welfare system, for decreased centralization of education and the police, and for an overall increase in the privileges accorded to organized labor, consumers, and the common man. But strident ideological positions have been more frequent than opportunistic adjustments to meet public sentiments. The JSP, for example, continues to advocate a "dictatorship of the proletariat," a slogan long since abandoned even by most communist parties, including Japan's.

Yet JSP strength declined from nearly one-third of the vote in the mid-1950s to about one-fourth in the late 1970s and early 1980s. And as of the 1980 elections no other party has ever succeeded in gaining more than 11 percent of the popular vote. As a consequence, throughout the period since its formation in 1955 the LDP has managed to garner enough seats to dominate the parliament and to form the country's cabinets unilaterally, while the party opposition has been severely fragmented. This combination of electoral, party, and parliamentary strength has allowed the conservative coalition to retain preponderant control over the nation's political institutions and its public policies.

The political consensus of the right and the seemingly unshake-able majority of the LDP in turn increased the power of the state apparatus. Unlike most bureaucracies in industrial democracies, which must accommodate periodic alterations in the political direction of the government, the Japanese bureaucracy for most of the postwar period knew that there would be few fundamental changes in basic governmental policies. Thus, by working closely with the dominant party it could increase its own ability to shape society. So long as bureaucrats were willing to work in conjunction with the broad policy orientations of the dominant coalition and the LDP, there was little likelihood that bureaucratic powers would be severely circumscribed. More of a fusion than an antinomy took place between party and government, much along the lines of other regimes in which a single political party enjoyed a long period of rule, such as Italy, Sweden, and France. Political stability made it possible for the bureaucracy to engage in long-term planning without fear of unfamiliar political pressures.

Retaining conservative control over the mechanism of the state has been much more a function of elections than in the prewar period. Oddities in the Japanese electoral system help to preserve the conservative coalition, while at the same time the system has also buffered the Diet from rapid shifts in national opinion. It is relatively easy for any candidate to run in Japan; it is extremely difficult to win. To run, all that is required is a relatively small cash deposit which is returned after the election if the candidate polls approximately 5 percent of the votes cast. To win, on the other hand, a candidate almost always requires the endorsement of one of the country's major political parties, a strong local support-base cultivated for at least several years, and a good deal of cash. None is easy to secure, particularly in a short time; acquisition of all three by no means ensures success.

Japanese election laws are among the strictest in the world. The official campaign period is limited to three weeks. House-to-house canvassing is prohibited. So too are signature campaigns, buttons, leaflets, food, drink, or other presents to voters; speeches, spending, campaign materials, newspaper ads, and media use are strictly circumscribed. Indeed, the law also prohibits anything designed to "raise the ardor" of the voters, such as bands, sirens, parades, marches or any other clamor. The model of virtually any successful

Western-style campaign would have to be totally revamped under Japanese law.

Campaign realities differ greatly from what the law prescribes. Campaigning is almost a year-round process. Food, drink, and presents, including cash, flow freely. Defacing an opponent's posters and putting up one's own are regular nocturnal activities for any hardworking campaign staff. Winners often spend as much as ten times the amounts legally allowed. And anyone listening to hour after hour of polite but high-volume voter solicitation from a candidate's touring campaign car would have to wonder whether a band and a parade might not be more soothing to the ears than what is legal. At the end of a typical election period, charges of election law violations are filed against upwards of 25,000 individuals, and most pundits suggest that the job of a campaign manager is essentially to pay the fines and serve the allocated jail terms, leaving the successful candidate free to serve in the Diet.

Under such a system, there is premium placed on a candidate's having long-standing familiarity within the district. Gaining such recognition in a short time, through media exposure, for example, or as a result of a single issue, is extremely difficult, even though the campaign laws are modified by realities. Even more constraining is the electoral system itself (Nishihira, 1972).

The House of Representatives may be dissolved at any time by the prime minister, so long as this occurs at least once every four years. Except for one minor deviation, members of the lower house are all chosen from "middle-sized" districts in which each voter casts only one ballot with the top three, four, or five vote-getters being seated.

The House of Councillors (formerly the House of Peers) has a twofold electoral system. One-half of its 252 members are elected every three years, the other half stand three years later. In any one election, one–half of the seats are allocated to the top fifty-one vote-getters in a national constituency. The remaining fifty-one are chosen from districts similar to those of the House of Representatives. In upper house elections, each voter may cast one vote for the national constituency election and one for the district. Among its other features, the House of Councillors, with its six–year terms of office, serves as a force for conservatism.

There is a drastic imbalance in the number of voters in individual districts. Since 1964 there have been several expansions in the number of lower house seats, aimed at reducing some of the extreme inequities. Still, the basis for the original allocation remains a census taken immediately after the war, when the rural population was massively higher than it is today.

There are several significant implications of such a system. Most obviously, there are severe inequalities in the number of votes needed to win in an urban in contrast to a rural area. Thus, even after the 1975 redistricting it was possible for a JCP candidate in the metropolitan third district of Osaka to be defeated although he received 115,000 votes, while in rural Ehime an LDP candidate who received only 37,000 votes could be elected. In 1980, one JCP candidate in Hokkaido's first district received 126,000 votes and lost, while in the second district of Kagawa barely over one-quarter this number was sufficient to elect an LDP candidate. In the 1977 upper house election, 187,000 votes secured a victory in Tochigi, while 549,000 votes in Osaka was not enough.

The system also means that to win a majority within the House of Representatives a political party must elect more than one candidate from each district. (As of 1980, there were 511 seats in the lower house, with 124 electoral districts. To attain a working majority of 256, a party would have to elect an average of slightly more than two of its candidates from each district.) But with each elector casting only one vote, there is a good deal of intraparty competition to attract the potential party supporter to one's own candidacy. Most frequently, with voter sentiment relatively fixed regarding party or camp, the real electoral battles are among members of the same party.

A final and perhaps the most significant consequence for the argument of this book is that the system makes it extremely difficult for the nation's voters to "throw the rascals out" if and when a high degree of national dissatisfaction develops with the government in power. Except in a very indirect way in the national constituency election for the upper house, most voters have little leeway to act or react to national issues. And though all small- to medium-sized-electoral-district systems are biased toward local, rather than national, influence, in a single-member-district system such as prevails in the United States or Britain, a vote *against* an incumbent and his party automatically beomes a vote *for* the challenger and his. Hence, a shift of a few percentage points within a district can easily alter the electoral results and the party of the representative. In Japan, however, since most candidates receive somewhere between 12 percent and 25 percent of the district's vote, even a 10 percent shift in a major party's support usually means only a 3–4 percent shift in the support level of each individual candidate from that party. In some cases, this is sufficient to ensure defeat for one of them, but the potential for the individual elector to vote effectively against the party as a whole is almost nil. Protest votes are frequently cast against an incumbent but for a different member of the same party or for an independent candidate associated with that party. At other times, such protest may be directed in favor of one of the several opposition parties, but rarely with such consistency as to cause a rapid shift in the balance of forces. Far more frequently, the number one vote–getter in a district may fall to a still–successful number three or four. In other cases, a "new face" candidate from the same party will win instead. But drastic shifts in the balance of party forces is extremely rare.

Thus, in the election following massive protests against the United States–Japan Security Treaty in 1960 and a plummeting of public support for the government, as indicated by all opinion polls, the LDP actually increased the number of seats it held. Following the Lockheed scandal, when public disgust with the government was again consistently reflected in national opinion polls, ex-Prime Minister Tanaka and four of the five LDP representatives implicated in the scandal were returned to office due to local support. As in most countries, incumbency has been the most important element in electoral success. From 1955 to 1976, over 75 percent of the incumbents who ran were returned to office. "New faces" in the Diet, in contrast, shrank from 41 percent in 1949 to 24 percent in 1976.

The Japanese election and party systems, therefore, have come to play a vital role in linking social forces with state institutions. In particular, they have been the vehicles whereby the conservative coalition has retained hegemonic control over the state apparatus since its formation. The electoral system, in particular, has built-in biases favoring the conservatives and reducing the potential for electoral politics to result in sudden alterations in government or in public policies. Elections and party politics are vital components of the Japanese polity, and the outcome of their interplay provides broad boundaries within which policies must be set. But if governments rise or fall as a result of their policy platforms and performance in countries such as Britain or the United States, such factors are far less salient and immediate in Japan.

From the end of the Occupation until the late 1960s, parties and elections were the main political link between state and society in Japan. In particular, opposition to the state and efforts to redirect state actions revolved around party and electoral competition. Until 1960, the Japan Socialist Party more or less monopolized such efforts. With the splintering of the JSP and the rise of several small parties, political opposition in Japan broadened somewhat; but for most of the 1960s, opposition was still largely confined within the party system.

During the decade of the 1970s, political opposition could no longer be so conveniently categorized (Hashimoto, 1975). The established parties were not always quick to respond to new issues and the election system provided numerous barriers to rapid change. Student groups, consumer groups, local residents' movements, and various single issue pressure groups sprang up toward the end of the 1960s. Most of these chose to act independently of the established political parties and to pursue their objectives outside the electoral arena.

These groups have added increased complexity to Japanese politics and to the meaning of political opposition within the country. Their impact on several policy issues will be clear in subsequent chapters. Collectively, their influence has provided an indictment of political weakness against the established parties at the same time it poses a challenge to them. Could the parties again recapture their roles as the most important links between social groups and state institutions? Could political competition and conflict again be reconfined to the electoral arena? Or would Japan witness the increased influence of such groups and their single issue politics, much as has happened during the same period in the rest of the industrialized world?

The Policy Implications

Japan thus emerges as a democratic regime in which a cohesive conservative social coalition has remained relatively unchecked in its control of strong state institutions. It is also a regime from which organized labor has been consistently excluded. The effect of these elements on different public policies provide the bulk of the material in the remaining chapters. Overall they combine to give the Japanese political system its peculiar blend of policymaking based largely on consensus occasionally brusquely interrupted by conflict plus public policies that generally prove highly successful, though occasionally marred by failure.

The consensus in Japanese politics lies in the consensus of the conservative coalition. On key questions of economics, social welfare, labor relations, higher education, the environment, and the character of the national bureaucracy, as well as on a wide range of other issues, the major components of the conservative coalition have been in general agreement. Their internal divisions are of the sort that lead to bureaucratic and interest–group infighting—vigorously fought out, yes—but not leading to massive and rapid shifts in governmental priorities let alone to conservative schism or civil war. In reaching and maintaining agreements, the major social organizations have been aided by the electoral predominance of the LDP and by the numerous structural and personalistic elements of state institutions pushing toward policymaking cohesion.

This consensus is, of course, a limited one. The cohesiveness between the conservative coalition and the strong state makes for ease of adjustment particularly because the major challengers of that cohesiveness can be systematically excluded from formal policymaking roles. But on those occasions when policymaking moves outside the ring of consensus to include nonconservative actors, conflict, usually of a particularly nettlesome variety, results. At least two different types of nonconservative actors have, with some regularity, jarred the tranquility of conservative policymaking. The first is the domestic Japanese opposition, led largely by the JSP and the national labor federations and later by the single–issue groups. The second, about which little has been said thus far, involves foreign actors. In neither of these cases is the Japanese political system particularly well–adapted to anticipate, incorporate, or adjust. The systematic exclusion of the left and organized labor makes it unnecessary for the conservatives to go through, on any regular basis, the series of multiple minor adjustments of position that might bring the two sides closer together. Occasionally they do so, and serious conflict is thereby avoided. But so is any public credit to the opposition. Their systematic formal exclusion, therefore, provides the opposition with the opportunity, temptation, and occasional need to pull out the stops, violently jarring the policymaking process through street demonstrations, parliamentary boycotts, and the like. Only in this way, in effect, can it force the public and the government to take it seriously on what it deems to be critical issues, attempt a redefinition of the conservatives' rendering of the political agenda, and generate a publicly visible rationale for its own existence (Pempel, 1975).

The situation is somewhat different with regard to jars from abroad. But the roots of the problem are the same, namely, the exclusiveness and closed nature of the conservative coalition. No government systematically includes foreigners, but most are more continually involved with them than is the Japanese government. Culturally, linguistically, racially, and geographically isolated, with a narrow definition of its foreign policy interests, Japan has little of the regularized foreign stimulation that the European Economic Community provides to its members nor of that provided to the United States by its role in the creation and maintenance of the Pax Americana. Consequently, Japan is often much less well-poised to anticipate and to deal with overseas events. And as with the domestic opposition, foreign governments, in particular the United States, frequently find it in their own interests to wrench the attention of the Japanese government away from its narrow and cohesive focus, forcing it to consider a broader set of problems or alternatives.

The nature of the Japanese political regime does not allow one to predict just when and in what form such violent shatterings of the prevailing consensus will arise. But it does suggest that they will occur with regularity, and it helps to identify their predominant sources. So long as policymaking involves members of the conservative coalition, the process will be largely consensual and bureaucratic; when the conservative circle can no longer encapsulate the preponderant forces relevant to a policy decision, there is a strong likelihood that jarring conflict will result.

The closed nature of the regime is also important in understanding the pattern of success and failure that characterizes Japanese public policies. The regime has been extremely adept at solving problems central to its own existence and in ensuring that these solutions will be consistent with its own long–run ideological preferences. Relatively free from the need to continually reexamine basic premises, the government has been able to overcome most competition among agencies and to move consistently and coherently on most problems. Rarely has it been in the position of having one set of policies directed toward ends that conflict sharply with other policies, as happened, say, in Britain with regional policies versus manpower policies or in the United States with alliance policies versus human rights policies.

Thus, Japan's economic policies have been highly successful, initially in achieving structural transformation, high rates of growth, and export markets and later in controlling inflation and in expanding overseas investment. The government has also been successful in doing all of this with remarkably low rates of unemployment. By most international standards, transportation, education, and agricultural policies have also been successful. Even more striking is the fact that the government has largely been able to do what it has set out to do, and such achievements must be regarded as at least instrumental, if not necessarily normative, successes. In contrast to many governments that continually lament their inability to effect their policy goals, the Japanese government has been able to achieve a large portion of what it has sought to do.

The instrumental successes of many policies have, in fact, been associated with what many would see as normative failures. The government has thus avoided massive social welfare expenditures, built an extensive but largely privatized higher educational system, and held down the size of its administrative apparatus. It has measured all of these as successes, and in these judgments it has been supported by many at home and abroad. But conservative successes have often been obtained at such high social costs that the liberal would regard them as failures (Yokoyama, 1979).

The government has also been quite successful in coping with problems once they have reached crisis proportions. This was true of policies designed to end the student radicalism of the 1968–69 period, policies introduced to deal with the suddenly–discovered problem of the elderly in the late 1970s and policies designed to reduce the massive environmental catastrophe that threatened the nation in the late 1960s and early 1970s. While its structure may not have been equipped to anticipate such problems, it has been comparatively well-suited to facing and dealing with crises from a creatively conservative perspective once they do appear.

But there have been failures to anticipate these very problems, especially the failure to consider ideologically unappealing alternatives until they are forced on the government, largely through policymaking crises. For example, the government did little to change the higher educational system that was a major contributor to the student protests before these reached mammoth proportions (Kitamura and Cummings, 1972). The same was true of environmental problems. Only after epic ecological blight, hundreds of deaths, and thousands of injuries did the government begin to act. The same pattern existed in the government's long-standing efforts to preserve the low international value of the yen. Only when faced with the "Nixon shocks" of 1971 was the government forced to revalue. Finally, the government's limited role in developing social welfare programs, if dubbed a normative failure, was the consequence of a clear and long–standing decision that to establish such welfare programs was neither politically necessary nor congruent with the predominant conservative ideology.

The actual working–out of these interactions is examined in the subsequent six chapters, dealing respectively with economic policy, labor-management relations, social welfare, higher education, the environment, and administrative reform. All the cases show the impact of the overall conservative orientations of the regime and particularly the impact of the systematic and long exclusion of labor. In addition, the issues highlight in much greater detail the previously defined mix of success and failure, consensus and conflict, that predominates in Japanese politics.

But lest the picture remain too cybernetic, rigid, or closed, it is well to note that certain issues show broad policy shifts. As was noted above, the election system in Japan works to reduce the likelihood that rapid shifts in opinion will force equally rapid shifts in government and public policy. Still, political democracy in its fullest sense has proven to be a meaningful, although often very slow–moving mechanism whereby discontent with government policies has been injected into politics and policy. This was most clearly revealed during the decade of the 1970s, when locally and nationally the unqualified control of the LDP began to ebb. Progressive coalitions gained control of executive and legislative branches in many large cities and prefectures. Various smaller parties collectively began to drain seats away from the LDP and the JSP at the national level. Citizens' and single-issue movements began to combat a variety of ills growing out of past policies. Local and judicial influence also increased. Thus, while the politics of the 1950s and early 1960s primarily reflected a business-labor division on many issues and produced bipolar electoral and party politics, the politics of the 1970s reflected more complexity and more issue-specificity.

LDP dominance grudgingly gave way to broader appeals and occasionally to policy and programatic compromises in parliament, especially on social welfare, higher educational, and environmental problems. The long–standing prevalence of the dominant conservative coalition and the strong state was at a critical juncture. Would the coalition be forced to expand, split, or reorganize? Would it fall apart completely or would it regain its earlier predominance? Would state power prevail or be hemmed in by more plural political forces? These were the key political questions facing Japan in the 1980s. But despite the changes of the 1970s, the Japanese regime remains one of conservative social dominance and strong governmental institutions. Moreover, it is still a regime in which social democratic or labor–based penetration of government has been totally absent. Given the drastic changes taking place in Japan's industrial structure and the seeming stagnation of organized labor and the political parties it supports, it remains unlikely that Japan will ever undergo the major shifts in policy-orientation on economic and social questions that took place when labor entered governments in North America and Western Europe. Certainly, the phenomenal local electoral successes of the LDP in the late 1970s and the party's overwhelming triumph in the national elections of June, 1980 suggest that the long–standing characteristics of the Japanese regime may well continue for many years into the future.

2 Economic Policy: State-Led Capitalism

More than any other single policy area, economic policy is at the core of Japanese politics. It has been the domestic political issue given highest priority by Japan's conservative regime. It has almost certainly been the issue to which most public and private energy has been allocated. As in most countries, it is also the area where the interaction of the two can best be seen. Similarly, economic decisions most clearly reveal the priorities of the conservative coalition and its ability to achieve them.

Economic policy emerges as an area in which there has been tremendous success in achieving conservative goals, a success marked by side effects that many would surely rate negatively. It is also an area in which the processes of politics have been largely consensual but in which serious challenges to this consensus have periodically emerged.

From the end of the war until 1971, economic policy was the umbrella under which policies in other areas had to squeeze; failing to do so meant being left out in the rain. During the 1950s and 1960s, the general coherence, coordination, and success of economic policies made the umbrella appear watertight. But during the political and economic torrents of the early– to mid–1970s, the umbrella began to leak. Component policies suddenly seemed failures by many standards, and more vigorous conflicts emerged over both means and ends. By the early 1980s, these again seemed less striking than the fact that Japan's economic policies were proving to be considerably more effective and consistent than those of almost every other major industrial nation. Productivity and growth increased while inflation remained low. Whether this success marks the raising of a new Japanese umbrella or simply luck in finding temporary shelter is the key political question that Japan will face in the 1980s.

Context

The most persistent influence on economic policy in Japan has been the relatively hostile international environment perceived by the country's political leaders. Throughout Japan's modern history, external circumstances have been seen as threatening to its economic development and, more fundamentally, to its political sovereignty.

Japan's political elite has been continuously sensitive to the country's international vulnerability, but this perception was acute at two critical junctures: from the mid-nineteenth century until the beginning of World War I and from the end of World War II until approximately the beginning of the 1960s. This perception of international vulnerability laid the basis for the agenda and instruments of Japanese economic policy until the 1970s. It remains an open question whether it will recur in a different guise in the 1980s.

The country's lack of most natural resources made it imperative for Japan throughout its modern history to be heavily involved in international commerce. To fuel a modern economy, Japan has always had to import large quantities of raw materials. To pay for these raw materials, it has been similarly compelled to export large quantities of manufactured goods. Recognition of this basic fact has continually helped to generate consensus domestically on key aspects of Japanese economic policy. Carrying out this combination of vigorous exporting of finished products and aggressive pursuit of raw materials, however, has frequently made Japan appear an international pariah, and its economic interests have frequently come into conflict with those of other major powers.

The foundations of Japan's 250 years of feudal solitude were forcibly undermined by the demands of the nineteenth-century industrial powers that Japan open her borders to international commerce. Military, technological, and economic weakness, combined with internal political divisions, made the country vulnerable to the imposition of a series of commercial treaties, under which monetary and tariff control were surrendered and special commercial and legal privileges were offered to Westerners. With the Meiji

Restoration (1868), Japan came to be governed by a political elite convinced that rapid, state-directed industrialization was the key to national survival, and that ultimately this would provide the basis on which to build an internationally powerful Japan. Such a course was seen as one which would allow Japan to fend off the threats of the West, and eventually to compete with the Western nations on more equal grounds for the fruits of international economic strength.

This Japanese choice was in keeping with the comparative lateness and defensiveness of its industrialization. Whereas Britain, the United States, and other early industrializers generally found it economically, legally, and socially advantageous to follow patterns of private ownership, limited state intervention, and international economic liberalism, latecomers such as Japan, Germany, and Sweden almost inevitably found it necessary to rely on greater government direction and economic nationalism. Capital assets in private hands at the beginning of the Meiji period, for example, were limited. Furthermore, these assets had traditionally been utilized for little more than usury, commodity purchases, and extractive monopolies. The riskier ventures associated with the creation of a national industrial infrastructure appealed to few holders of private wealth. Nor were most private owners of capital in a good position to overcome the technical difficulties of initiating the large-scale industrial development that would make them internationally competitive. Thus it fell to the state to develop and initially to maintain modern industries in areas such as shipbuilding, railroads, communications, textiles, and armaments. As will be noted in Chapters 3 and 5, the government also took on a major role in providing the infrastructure to develop sufficient trained manpower to manage and work in these industries. By 1880, the government owned three shipyards, fifty-one merchant ships, five munitions works, ten mines, fifty-two factories, a national telegraph system, and about seventy-five miles of railroad. It also had taken the lead in developing model factories in less-critical areas such as cotton spinning, tile works, and cement.

Rather than following a permanent strategy of direct state management of key industries, however, starting in 1880 the government began to sell off the bulk of its holdings to the private sector, usually on terms highly favorable to private owners. Several characteristics of this policy deserve to be underscored, particularly because of their historical legacy. First of all, the sale of these industries on such favorable terms won the government many important allies in private industry and provided a basis for subsequently close cooperation between the public and private sectors. Unlike government in some other industrial countries, government in Japan has not been perceived as the historical adversary of business; it has been more typically seen by business and industrial leaders as a catalyst to growth. Second, the released holdings became the basis for the formation of a limited number of huge business conglomerates which came to dominate the most dynamic sectors of the prewar Japanese economy. These conglomerates, with government assistance, were the major force in carrying out the successful transformation of the nation's economic structures during the late-nineteenth and early- to mid-twentieth centuries. Meanwhile, numerous smaller, less capital-intensive, and less technologically advanced firms were dependently linked to these large, more sophisticated conglomerates through subcontracting arrangements. Finally, it is worth noting that although a limited number of conglomerates acquired oligopolistic control over key areas of commerce, industry, and finance, government also preserved elements of the private market and industrial competition. Throughout the prewar period, typically, two, three or four conglomerates would receive government largess in some particular area, such as shipping or banking. Rarely would any single conglomerate or firm gain monopolistic power. Consequently, even though Japanese industry and commerce were rarely characterized by vast numbers of entrepreneurial and highly competitive firms, such as was initially the case in much of Britain, the United States, or Belgium, for example, the country was not insensitive to private sector competition and market stimuli. Furthermore, the government retained a good deal of autonomy and influence in choosing when and how to distribute its patronage in the private sector. Rarely was it the pliant victim of private monopolies.

Important as private finance and banking were during this period, the government never conceived of its economic role as that of the night watchman, the conception behind the major economic doctrines of British and American government at that time. Through both the successes of the period following World War I and the failures following the Great Depression of 1929, the government sought to monitor business activities so as to ensure conformity with governmentally determined objectives. The government was also active in maintaining a stable currency, creating a strong central banking system, promoting Japanese exports, and protecting domestic industry. The generally close ties forged between government, business, and finance were further strengthened during the wartime mobilization, starting with the formation of the Planning Board in 1937 and continuing with the passage of the National Mobilization Law in 1941. Meanwhile, as will be discussed in more detail in the next chapter, organized labor and the socialist left were internally divided and subjected to government repression. Thus, unlike the case in most other industrial countries, they could be largely discounted in the formulation of national economic policies. Prewar economic policies were thus the joint and rather exclusive affairs of government and big business. Together they tried to make Japan economically competitive with the European and North American powers.

The defeat in World War II and the subsequent occupation by the American military altered this situation far less than is frequently imagined. Although initial American goals focused largely on economic deconcentration and on breaking up the links between government and business, by 1947 the United States, for a variety of domestic and international reasons, decided that an economically healthy Japan was essential to its interests. Government-business cooperation and economic concentration were seen as more essential than deconcentration, competition, or redistribution. The strong bureaucratic institutions of the central government emerged virtually unscathed, and the country's economic ministries and central banking system were at least as strong by 1950 as they had been in 1930. The United States Occupation did witness the development of a vigorous labor movement that, along with the political parties labor supported, entered government for six months during this period. But this government was the only one of its kind and it never implemented any of its major programs. Thus, labor emerged from the Occupation as a force which could not be as fully excluded from economic policymaking as had its prewar predecessors, but its role remained far less important than that in virtually any other industrialized state.

With the end of the Occupation in 1952 and with the consolidation of conservative political dominance, Japan soon had a domestic political context highly advantageous to economic policies favoring big business. However, national economic productivity lagged far behind that of the victors of World War II. Hence, the government was again in a position of trying to formulate policies that would allow it to catch up, just as it had done during the Meiji period. But with a hostile political left challenging the regime at home and with the world's strongest economy as a vigorously supportive international ally, the context within which specific goals were identified and the instruments by which they were pursued were somewhat different than they had been eighty-odd years earlier.

Despite certain fluctuations, this context remained relatively fixed from the 1950s until the early 1970s—a cohesive government-business partnership and a radical but limp political opposition at home, the United States as a friendly political and economic ally abroad.

By the early 1970s, this context had changed, both internationally and domestically. Internationally, there was a jump in world inflation rates starting in the late 1960s, followed by a drastic decline in world growth rates. In 1971, the world monetary system collapsed. The United States and Europe pressed feverishly for import and capital liberalization in Japan while increasing protectionism at home. Finally, there was the oil crisis of 1973, which threatened the basis of Japan's energy-dependent economy. The seeming permanence of the long-standing agenda and policies of the 1950s and 1960s meant that most Japanese leaders were truly shocked by these dramatic twists in international events. Few, if any, had been anticipated, and for a period of time there was tremendous uncertainty as to how Japan could best deal with them.

At the same time, within the country the comfortable electoral margins that the LDP had enjoyed for the first fifteen years of its existence began eroding, and new opposition strength developed. The nation's opposition parties, single issue groups, and parliamentary politics all became more important. Both opposition parties and individual pressure groups were able to bargain for greater government financial assistance, which led to increased deficit spending. Many internationally successful Japanese businesses clamored for looser government oversight and more investment abroad, while at the popular level the economic successes of the past were broadly challenged as their environmental and social costs became more vivid. Public readiness to sacrifice present for future economic rewards turned to insistence upon a reexamination of priorities. Individual and collective demands for improved living conditions, even at the expense of lower growth rates, recurred constantly. The opposition parties were outspoken in their challenges to the policies of high growth (see Reading 2-4). As a result of all these changes in the context of economic policy, a substantial shift took place in both the agenda and the process of Japanese economic policy. But it is worth noting that the consequent reassessment of both the agenda and the instruments of past economic policies came not so much because they had failed but precisely because they had been successful.

Agenda

There were several competing agendas for Japanese economic policy during the early years of the United States Occupation. One strand of American thinking was punitive, pressing for the total dismantling of basic industries and at least a temporary fixation of the economy at 1934–36 levels. A different strand among the Americans, and one shared by most conservatives in Japanese business and governmental circles, involved the economic revitalization of Japan, partially with American help but largely through the reconstruction of basic private industries. Finally, on the political left, there were strong pressures for high levels of state ownership of basic industries, an end to private monopoly, and a greater focus on reducing unemployment and redistributing the nation's wealth.

By the later years of the Occupation, and even more vividly with the consolidation of the Liberal Democratic Party and the Japan Socialist Party in 1955, these competing agendas had been reduced to two: a relatively consolidated conservative camp was pressing for the revitalization of the Japanese economy through a combination of private initiative and government assistance. Nationalized administration of the economy was explicitly rejected, although private oligopolies and cartels were seen as desirable in many sectors. Macrolevel economic improvements were to result in the natural improvement of living standards for all; economic redistribution per se was rejected (see Reading 2-1). The political opposition, on the other hand, continued to call for the nationalization of banks and key industries such as coal and power, tax reductions, elimination of "special tax privileges for the rich," and increased expenditures for social welfare, housing, and the stabilization of small and medium-sized industries (see Reading 2-2).

This basic conflict was steadily reflected in the party platforms of the two major parties, providing much of the grist for postwar parliamentary debate. But with the opposition never gaining more than one-third of the seats in parliament, the consequences of this debate were usually more rhetorical and theatrical than practical. But the polarities of the two agendas facilitated greater unity in the camps of each one's opponents. The opposition's vigorous hostility also continually reinforced the clarity of paths not taken by the government, creating as well a different normative context by which to evaluate government successes and failures.

The immediate postwar political and economic context meanwhile added glue to conservative unity. World War II had destroyed the country's productive capacity and had left Japan much further behind the victorious powers than it had been at any time since World War I. Catching up with the world's industrial leaders again became the central and easily agreed-to target of national economic policies. Starting with the years immediately after the war but continuing through the bulk of the postwar period, the major organizations of big business, the Liberal Democratic Party, and the relevant government ministries were largely in accord concerning Japan's need to reconstruct, rationalize, and modernize the nation's industrial structure so as to maximize its international competitiveness. There was also widespread agreement on the need to do this through a combination of government assistance and private initiative rather than through an exclusive reliance on one or the other. This goal of structural reorganization through cooperation between the government and private sectors dominated the agenda of the conservative camp from its first articulation in the long-term government economic plans of 1950 and 1955. It has been a focal point of all government economic plans, although the specific industries targeted in such plans were continually upgraded. The bicycle industry, once thriving, was replaced by the motorcycle industry; both in turn gave way to the automobile industry. Cameras and binoculars were replaced by fiber optics. Electrical household appliances such as toasters gave way to electronic appliances such as calculators and, later, computers.

In 1960, an additional, highly specific goal was added to that of sectoral development with Prime Minister Ikeda's Plan to Double the National Income in Ten Years. This plan, in addition to supporting the established policies of structural reorganization, put the government's official weight behind a series of tightly linked policies aimed at achieving extremely high rates of growth (see Reading 2-3). In Japan, overall growth in national income took on the character of war by other means.

Numerous subsidiary "agendas" grew out of these two major goals of structural development and high growth. The development of export markets and the increasing of Japan's share of world trade were essential. So was some measure of domestic protectionism for industries targeted for special nurturing. Technology and raw materials had to be acquired at the world's most competitive prices, and large quantities of investable capital had to be generated. All had to be acquired without surrendering too much political control, and all had to be allocated within the country in accord with some clear set of priorities. To avoid the costliness of what many Japanese refer to as "excess competition," oligopolies would naturally be encouraged in certain key areas.

At a further remove, other goals flowed logically from these. To assist exports, it was desirable to maintain a low international value for the yen, to further develop the Japanese shipping industry, and to become accepted as a member of international economic arrangements such as GATT (the General Agreement on Tariffs and Trade), the IMF (International Monetary Fund) and the OECD (Organization of Economic Co-operation and Development). Trading companies in Japan would prove a valuable asset both in marketing exports and in gaining international access to raw materials and technology, making their nurturing important. Holding down military and security expenditures and restraining domestic consumption would aid capital formation, boost savings rates, and allow monies to be transferred into projects directly related to structural transformation. Importing technology without its typical partners, foreign capital and foreign management, also became a logical goal. To the extent that export industries and export markets were a critical part of the conservatives' broad strategy, it was especially necessary for Japanese goods to be of high quality, not just of low price. The label "made in Japan," which had once been a sign of short-lived, low-quality merchandise, would have to connote just the opposite if Japanese products were to develop markets not only at home but also in the advanced economies of North America and Western Europe. These and many other component goals became part of the conservative agenda.

As might be expected, the more specific the goal, the lower the level of full-scale conservative agreement. Although it was relatively easy to gain agreement on the desirability of targeting key sectors for development, not all in the conservative camp were agreed on whether automobiles were more or less key than textiles, or whether machine tools were more or less key than electronics. When it came to the aircraft industry, even though there was agreement on the desirability of its development, there was vigorous disagreement over whether the industry should be developed under the guiding hand of the Ministry of Transportation or of the Ministry of International Trade and Industry (MITI). Nor was there harmony on questions of whether Sony or Toshiba should gain privileged access to the technology needed for transistor products, or whether Kawasaki or Sumitomo should be encouraged or discouraged from increasing their world market shares of steel. Similarly, although exports were to be fostered, should they be fostered at the expense of fiscal stability or political ties? On this point, the Ministry of Finance, MITI, and the Ministry of Foreign Affairs usually disagreed.

In a like manner, while high growth was (after heated debate) finally accepted as a general goal (Itō, 1968, pp. 446–67), many questions arose as to how much growth was to be achieved through increased government spending for public works and how much through export drives in selected products. In achieving high growth, how should fiscal restraint be maintained, what levels of inflation should be tolerated, and how much of a role should be played by monetary versus fiscal policy? These and numerous other questions led to vigorous intraconservative camp disagreements on many occasions. All these conflicts over the specific goals of economic policy must be weighted heavily against belief in the popular notion of "Japan, Incorporated," which presumes that a far more monolithic and uncontroversial political agenda was operating in Japanese government and business circles throughout this period (Kaplan, 1972). Reaching consensus was always easier on abstractions than it was on specifics.

At the same time, these debates over the specific targets and instruments of Japanese economic policy, important and frequent as they were, should not obscure the fact that on the broadest goals of economic policy major conservative actors were in substantial agreement. This was particularly true of sectoral transformation and high economic growth which formed the core of the explicit conservative economic agenda. Nor is it possible to ignore the strikingly different agenda of the left, which was so starkly rejected.

The conservatives' explicit agenda of transformation and high growth also contained a latent political objective: to defuse the political appeal of the left. Most conservatives felt that the dual policies of transformation and growth, if successfully and quickly achieved, would not only provide short- and long-term economic benefits but would also assure longer–term political conditions for continuing the nation's entire political–economic system. If these policies achieved their economic purposes, they would bring with them political stability and continued conservative dominance.

In looking at the Japanese economic agenda during this period, it is also instructive to recognize that certain goals, beyond those called for by the political left, never acquired precedence. Concern with controlling inflation, for example, was minimal, and during the period 1959–76 the consumer price index rose 7.5 percent annually, one of the highest rates among industrialized countries. In this regard, Japanese goals were remarkably different from those of West Germany since 1945, for example. Nor was the creation of a better-developed social infrastructure of much consideration, as it was in Britain or Sweden. Rather, government-inspired sectoral development, industrial rationalization, and high growth dominated the policy agenda, much as they did in France under the Gaullists. And although Japan clearly pursued an economic policy that relied heavily on the openness of world markets, the Japanese market itself remained hermetically isolated from foreign imports of capital and manufacturing goods, while Japanese industries were discouraged from moving their operations abroad to take advantage of cheaper labor, better markets, or proximity to sources of supply. In this regard, Japan's economic agenda differed sharply from that of its closest economic partner, the United States.

The most serious challenges to Japan's agenda for economic success were the dramatic domestic and international shifts that took place in the early 1970s. As a consequence of these, old verities concerning the desirability and the possibility of achieving continuous high-growth rates through the practices of the past lost hold. The most dramatic indication of this came with the formulation and cabinet approval of a five year basic economic and social program in February 1973. Optimistically entitled For a Dynamic Welfare Society, the plan called for a de-emphasis on maximizing growth and for increased attention to the development of social overhead investments such as housing, roads, parks, and regional development. Attention was also directed toward such problems as environmental pollution, urban overcrowding, conservation, inflation, income distribution, and equalization of educational and employment opportunities. The plan also called for less economic nationalism and for more economic cooperation with the other industrial powers.

The government shift away from high growth-rates was only partially matched by a shift in the agenda of sectoral transformation. Rather than abandon sectoral transformation altogether, the government and big business shifted their attention to those technology and capital-intensive sectors that would not consume huge amounts of energy, would require less human drudgery, and would have less detrimental environmental consequences. Hence, the chemical and heavy industrial sectors were to give way to knowledge and research and development (R and D) intensive industries such as fiber optics, computers, telecommunications, fashion design, atomic-powered industries, industrial robots, integrated circuitry, automated warehouses, and the like (see Reading 2-5). To catch up with or, more correctly by this point in time, to take a commanding position in the world economy, still remained an essential goal in Japanese economic policy. The policy shift of the early 1970s simply meant that doing so would require a focus on different industrial sectors.

The new goals of slower but sustained growth and a greater reliance on different industrial sectors were spelled out concurrently in the New Economic and Social Seven-Year Plan adopted in

1979. In addition to recognizing the altered targets of economic policy per se, the plan blended in additional elements such as policies to deal with energy constraints, the need for international economic cooperation, and the development of what was called a Japanese-type welfare society (see Reading 4-6).

This altered agenda for economic policies emerged as a result not of failures of past policies but of their successes. Japan by the early 1970s was no longer the feeble, semiagrarian society of the 1940s but an economic giant with the second-largest economy in the world. Accepting lower growth-rates in Japan still meant sharing a reasonably pleasant dessert, not accepting the inevitability of millet for dinner, as seemed probable in Britain. Shifting sectoral policies from steel to computers was an indication of sophistication in the international marketplace. It contrasted sharply with the United States government's rescue of one of that marketplace's most colossal rejects, the Chrysler Corporation.

Process

The agenda of economic policy in Japan was the conservative agenda of big business and the central economic ministries. Actually formulating the policies to achieve this agenda meant hammering out intraconservative camp agreements on numerous specifics and then ensuring that these agreements, once reached, could be implemented. These illustrate powerfully the consensual-conflictual mix in Japan, though they also reveal that Japanese economic policymaking was rarely harmonious. They also help to explain the vaunted successes of Japanese economic policy and demonstrate the importance of public-private coordination. Finally, they show the extent to which Japanese institutions are well-suited to achieving creative consensus within the conservative camp, particularly under conditions of normalcy, while these same institutions, so good at reacting to stimuli, are poor at anticipating them.

Consider, for example, Japanese sectoral policies. In hindsight, Japan appeared to move steadily and unswervingly toward the development of ever more sophisticated industries. Automobiles replaced motorcycles, supertankers replaced fishing boats, thermal power replaced hydroelectric power, and so on. It was as though a master plan were being implemented by an omnipotent engineer using precision instruments. Though not completely false, this is at best a partial picture.

Consider, as an example, the automobile industry. Autos appear to many as a prototypical manifestation of Japan's successful and foresighted sectoral policy. Yet, as late as 1951 the Ministry of Finance and the Bank of Japan were contending that Japan could not and should not even attempt to develop a domestic automobile industry, while the Ministry of Transportation was arguing that Japan should welcome the importation of foreign, largely United States–made, automobiles. After a protracted debate, and as the Korean War brought in large truck contracts to Japan, the potential of auto manufacture to stimulate the rest of Japanese industry was fully realized. Finally, MITI secured intragovernmental agreement of the other agencies for capital and technological assistance to the industry, and for the quotas, tariffs, and commodity taxes designed to protect the industry from United States competition.

Capital assistance from government to the auto industry was important although not comprehensive. The Japan Development Bank provided 9 percent of the industry's capital during the critical period 1951–55. At the same time, such action undoubtedly signalled private banks of the government's priorities, thus facilitating their aid. Neither, however, did government capital come cheaply. An early Bank of Japan loan worked out in conjunction with two private banks, for example, was given only after Toyota agreed to separate its sales and manufacturing units.

Much of MITI's ability to reorganize targeted industries was vested in the wide scope of its administrative powers and also its vast authority to approve or disapprove industrial loans from a variety of government agencies (Johnson, 1977, pp. 256–57). These powers were often the force behind "consensual" decisions. But MITI's powers were far from complete. During 1962–63, for example, MITI was completely unsuccessful in securing legislative agreement for a proposed law that would have vastly expanded its powers to bypass the Antimonopoly Law and encourage mergers in a variety of internationally weak industries (Honda, 1974, p. 26). The political left, the Fair Trade Commission, and numerous industrial and trade associations were successful in their opposition. At least as vital to sectoral policy was MITI's ability to cooperate with industry and other agencies through joint institutions. Thus, when the auto parts industry struck both major manufacturers and MITI officials as excessively complex, diffuse, and economically irrational, an *ad hoc* committee was created with representatives from MITI, other government agencies, various parts manufacturers, trade associations, and senior officials of the auto makers' Automobile Industry Association (Kaplan, 1972, p. 117). The committee organized numerous mergers within various auto-parts industries in a series of five-year plans lasting through 1971. Low-interest, long-term loans from the Japan Development Bank and the Small Business Finance Corporation stimulated many of the desired actions. But MITI never achieved its goal of reducing the number to 45; in 1980, Toyota alone had some 250 primary contractors and 5,000 subcontractors.

Mergers in the auto industry itself also necessitated cooperation with industry, and here personal connections and intermediation proved more important than formal joint committees. Although an essential catalyst, MITI again proved less than invincible. Faced with the liberalization of capital and imports in 1964, MITI sought to rationalize the industry into two or three internationally competitive firms. Industry successfully resisted several MITI plans. Greater consolidation only took place following a long series of personal interventions and negotiations involving the heads of MITI, Sumitomo Bank, the Japan Development Bank, Prince Auto, and Nissan, as well as numerous intermediaries (Kaplan, 1972, p. 125). Yet government powers were starkly revealed when the auto industry was forced to accept voluntary restrictions on exports to the United States in 1981.

Finally, some of the success of the automobile industry in Japan must be attributed to intraindustry processes. Taking advantage of the elaborate subcontracting network in Japan, Toyota was the first to introduce the *kamban* system of delivery. By insisting that parts needed for the assembly line be delivered by subcontractors to just the right spot, in just the right quantity, and *kamban* ("just in time"), Toyota drastically reduced its warehousing, space, and inventory costs, while overall productivity increased sharply. Quality control at the plant level is extremely good. Moreover, the auto industry, like Japan as a whole, has been a major utilizer of industrial robots. In the late 1970s, Japan had some 40,000 such robots in use, five times as many as the United States and the EEC combined. By 1982, nearly 1,000 such robots were to be on line at Toyota plants alone, further stimulating the industry's international competitiveness.

The auto-industry experience was mirrored to a large extent in many other industries targeted for sectoral assistance, reorganization, and rationalization. MITI, the Bank of Japan, the Japan Development Bank, and other government agencies provided aid in the form of scarce funds, tax breaks, technology, raw materials, international protection, freedom from anticartel legislation, and the like. These mechanisms often, but not always, stimulated the desired private sector behavior. But intervention through formal or *ad hoc* mechanisms was usually also needed, and cooperation was often difficult to achieve in the face of resistance from other government agencies or the political left. Finally, coordination with the private sector was always essential to, but no guarantee of, success.

Japanese policymaking instruments and their role in forging cohesion out of conflict are also well revealed in the area of achieving high growth. One of the most important dissenters from initial suggestions that Japan could and should attempt to follow this pattern came from Ministry of Finance bureaucrats. One of their major concerns was that high growth would generate undesirable inflationary pressures, particularly through vast increases in government expenditure. Not at all incidental to the ministry's opposition, the proposal was generated in the Economic Planning Agency (EPA), not in the Ministry of Finance (MOF), and it would be implemented primarily through EPA and MITI. Thus, in 1959, the ministry allegedly refused to even provide the basic economic and financial data necessary to operate the plan (Itō, 1968, p. 457).

Within about a year, the Ministry of Finance's opposition changed to staunch support. Two things had happened in the meantime. First, Ikeda Hayato had become prime minister. Formerly the highest-ranking bureaucrat in the Finance Ministry (1947–48) and, after election to the Diet, the finance minister (1949–52), Ikeda's credentials as a Finance Ministry loyalist were unimpeachable. Furthermore, his powers over the career and postretirement mobility of his former subordinates were extensive. When Ikeda became convinced that his plan to Double the National Income in Ten Years, was economically feasible and politically essential to the long-range fortunes of the LDP, he was able to exert considerable leverage over recalcitrant MOF officials.

MOF resistance was further weakened when it became clear that Ikeda had every intention of allowing it to play a major role in growth policies by making the budgetary process the central vehicle for high growth and by protecting the ministry's autonomy over the annual budget from other agencies such as EPA, and, at least partially, from the highly expansionary pressures of LDP officials (Itō, 1968; Campbell, 1977, pp. 227–35).

Although the 1961 budget was the first one aimed at stimulating high growth, it began a pattern, followed ever since, in which the ministry imposed a rigid limit on budget requests from individual government agencies. At the time, it refused to consider requests that were more than 50 percent higher than an agency's previous budget. In subsequent years, these limits were reduced to 25 percent and later 10 percent. This mechanism thus forced individual agencies to set internal priorities and to internalize a large portion of the conflict resolution over resource allocation.

With much of economic politics transformed into budgetary politics, many important economic decisions within Japan were also moved from the "yes" or "no" category of politics to the "how much?" category. Since money is almost infinitely divisible, many potentially unhappy but important political actors could be satisfied by slightly higher amounts of money without fundamentally shifting basic governmental priorities. With the Ministry of Finance setting tight controls over agency increases, proposals congruent with overall government economic policies obviously stood a better chance of approval than those which did not, thus further helping to ensure greater coordination across all areas of government than in countries where no such guidelines were present.

Typically, the Japanese budget was overbalanced with expected expenditures less than expected income. So long as growth was high, corporate taxes could be kept low and business kept happy, while total government revenue from income taxes rose automatically as individual incomes rose. Thus, the government could triumphantly announce politically popular cuts in personal tax rates at no threat to its economic objectives.

The budgetary process also insulated much of Japanese economic policy from the electoral process and from the opposition. The Diet must approve the budget annually, but the bulk of the budget is drafted in negotiations between the Ministry of Finance's Budget Bureau and individual agencies. Only after the major outlines are established does it become possible for politicians to press for additional monies for their pet projects, and this process is limited to members of the LDP. The opposition is free to rail against the budget and its implications in the Diet, but at no time between 1955 and 1979 was it capable of forcing any significant shifts in its basic character. As one LDP member, Kobayashi Takeji, gloated in 1971:

> We [in the LDP] are working closely with the government in preparing the budget without sleep and without rest. During this time, what are the gentlemen of the opposition parties doing? I suppose they are back home [keeping] their feet warm or taking a nap. That is to say, the gentlemen of the opposition have nothing to do with the preparation of the budget. . . . The Diet is a place where people make a lot of noise, but it is powerless as far as budget-making is concerned. [Quoted in Campbell, 1977, p. 117]

Finally, the budgetary process proved invaluable in defusing the potential political conflicts injected into Japanese economic policies by the drastic shifts of the early 1970s. Rather than having to forestall desired projects and to make hard "either-or" decisions that would alienate political supporters and the general public, the conservatives opted to extend the practice of deficit spending begun in 1965 (see Reading 2-7). By borrowing from the future, they could buy the time needed to reorient economic policies without suffering the short-term political consequences of slower growth. By 1980–81, the government was politically strengthened and able to begin stringent fiscal measures aimed at reducing the margin of deficit.

It is also instructive to examine how Japanese institutions have dealt with major threats to Japanese economic policy from abroad. When foreign governments have raised the specter of tariff or quota restrictions aimed at preventing a Japanese "invasion" by a specific export product, the Japanese government has typically been able to ward off these threats by generating effective "voluntary export restrictions." These have been enforced mostly by private Japanese trade associations dealing in the products involved. Thus, when conflicts arose with the United States over Japanese textile exports in 1955, MITI refused to recognize any new export contracts until details of an export policy toward the United States could be worked out (Lynch, 1968, p. 102). Once the general quotas were set, the private textile-exporters' associations subdivided these totals among their members by product and region. The widespread powers of the association over its members, together with their vulnerability to the banks and the requirement that export licenses be granted by MITI, assured that there was little cheating by individual firms. Although the process was more controversial in the 1969–71 "textile wrangle" with the United States, the mechanisms for resolution through voluntary restrictions enforced by the Japan Textile Federation remained the same (Destler et al., 1977).

Orderly marketing replaced the potential for cutthroat competition for market shares among Japanese manufacturers as well. Firms disadvantaged by the quotas were stimulated to develop new products or new domestic or foreign markets not covered by the quotas. Much the same has been true for restrictions of auto exports to the United States and Britain, of ball bearings and televisions to the EEC, and of an ever-increasing range of industrial products.

Finally, Japanese institutions were incapable of predicting the rapid rise in oil prices that occurred in 1973. For several months, government and business leaders scrambled frantically and at cross-purposes in an effort to cope. Dependent for about 89 percent of its energy on imported sources, Japan was affected more than any other industrialized country, with only France and Italy approaching Japanese oil-import levels. Following the initial shock and chaos, however, government and business representatives jointly formulated extensive energy plans designed to conserve oil at home and to develop alternative energy sources. Using tax incentives and low-cost loans, the government introduced the Sunshine Project and the Moonshine Project to stimulate private and governmental R and D on alternative sources of energy and energy-saving technologies.

Starting in 1978, idle Japanese supertankers and crews were utilized in an oil-stockpiling program aimed at stabilizing short-term supplies of oil while reducing economic pressures on the stagnant shipbuilding industry.

Meanwhile, the Energy Conservation Law of June 1979 gave MITI strong powers to coordinate industrial energy use, while at the same time industrial federations pressed their members to take creative steps at the plant level. In response, the steel industry increasingly adopted the continuous-casting process of producing crude steel, thus using two-thirds less energy than in traditional ingot-making. Furthermore some gases from blast furnaces are reheated to generate electricity, while recovered gases are reused for heating. Installation of suspension heaters for limestone kilns increased efficiency and cut energy consumption in the cement industry by 16 percent. Japanese autos were manufactured with 21 percent lower electricity and fuel bills through heat recovery in painting as well as improved insulation and better control in steel forging, while mileage ratios of engines were improved 11 percent. Gross capital formation and overall growth fell as a result of the oil shock. But rather than becoming a catalyst to vicious competition for scarce oil and a complete brake on the economy, the oil crisis, because of the way it has been handled by Japanese government and industrial organizations, also stimulated industrial savings, lowered costs, and made Japanese products more internationally competitive.

Consequences

At the macroeconomic level, Japan's economic policies succeeded beyond any reasonable expectations in reaching the goals set out. In 1950, approximately one-half of the country's work force was employed in the primary sector. By 1980, this was down to about 12 percent, and barely more than 10 percent of Japan's farm households were engaged in full-time farming. The country's share of world exports more than tripled between 1955 and 1978. During 1961–68 alone, there was a 39 percent structural change in the national economy in favor of heavy and chemical industries, a figure over twice as great as that of France, the OECD member with the next highest percentage, and nearly four times greater than that for the OECD countries as a whole. The GNP rose nearly eightfold between 1952 and 1978, with an annual average growth rate of about 11 percent during the 1950s and 1960s. Even during the "slow growth" period of the 1970s, GNP growth was almost consistently higher than in any other industrialized country. Japan entered the decade of the 1980s with the second-largest GNP in the capitalist world; the yen represented one of the world's strongest currencies;

there were comparatively low levels of inflation; the economy was exceptionally competitive internationally; most pundits predicted a relatively rosy economic future. In brief, the transformation in the national economy was phenomenal in its scale and speed.

Even though they never rose at rates comparable to that of the GNP or labor productivity, living standards too shot up during this period. Items such as air-conditioners. telephones, color televisions, and packaged foods, all rarities during the 1950s, became commonplace in nearly all Japanese homes, while automobiles, imported fashions, microwave ovens, expensive ski equipment, and overseas travel were commonplace among the middle or upper-middle classes. Clearly, the prosperous international economic giant entering the 1980s bore little resemblance to the impoverished, devastated economic pygmy of the 1940s; few, if any, Japanese would have opted for a return to earlier conditions.

At the same time, Japan's high-growth policies, based on the premises of rapid growth and sectoral transformation, carried with them the presumption that the benefits of growth were not to be evenly distributed throughout society, nor were they to be squandered on consumption. For most of the period, improvements in living standards came as a result of a trickle-down effect. As will be examined in more detail in the next chapter, workers' wages improved only after corporate profits were assured. Small and medium-sized industries frequently languished as a result of the government's policies and, as will be examined in Chapters 4 and 5, macrolevel growth did not result in substantial increases in social-overhead expenses. Finally, as will be seen in Chapter 6, the policies of structural transformation and rapid growth were accompanied by devastating environmental effects. Mainly as a consequence of these problems, during the late 1960s and early 1970s numerous consumers' groups challenged the high-growth policies and their environmental consequences.

The curious domestic political consequences of the government's economic-management policies were twofold. In one respect, the overall macrolevel successes deradicalized much of the anti-capitalist political appeal of Japan's left. Substantial improvements in income and lifestyle became satisfactory substitutes for the wholesale redistribution demanded by the progressive camp. The strength of labor and the left was inversely proportional to economic growth, and both unionization rates and votes for the JSP dropped sharply during the period.

At the same time, the high levels of macroeconomic success raised for many, both inside and outside governmental circles, the inevitable question of "growth for what?" The low levels of social-overhead expenditure during the period of high-growth resulted in Japan's ranking at or near the bottom on most comparative measures of social well-being. Pressures built in the late 1960s and especially in the 1970s for a reorientation of Japan's economy to devote more substantial attention to such matters. Books and articles with titles like "Why is the Price of Beef So High?" "Toward a Concept of Net National Welfare," "Making Citizens' Voices Heard," and "Toward Meaningful Higher Education" topped popular reading lists. Substantial challenges to the underlying economic premises of conservative rule appeared, weakening its electoral grip and forcing a reexamination of basic economic goals and priorities.

Beyond this problem with the public, the government, like Dr. Frankenstein, faced difficulties with the monster it created, Japanese industry. Rationalized and oligopolized sectors gained in domestic and international strength and no longer needed their governmental facilitator as much as they had when weak. An increased ability to raise capital, to purchase, and to sell abroad all reduced the leverage that could be exercised over them by the Ministry of Finance, MITI, and the Bank of Japan. Yes, uniformity of economic goals and the power of government to enforce them that is associated with the image of "Japan, Incorporated" has clearly been overrated in the popular press. But whatever validity the notion may once have had has surely been reduced by the very success of past government policies.

Economic success generated new problems in Japan's international situation as well. Japan's overall growth and success made the rest of the capitalist world increasingly skeptical of Japanese economic nationalism. Increasingly, the United States pressed for concessions involving the liberalization of imports, capital transfers and investment, as well as "voluntary restrictions" on certain Japanese exports and a constant demand that Japan increase its low military budget. Similarly, success led to the rapid increase in the international value of the yen, which in turn made it more and more difficult for Japanese products to undersell the competition in other parts of the world.

Thus, the moorings of the high economic growth policies have been strained. No longer can domestic protection, an undervalued yen, and continued export growth be assured. In turn, this reduces the capability for continuously increasing productivity, which was the very cornerstone of past economic policies. Furthermore, domestic inflation, deficit financing, advances in the technological sophistication of Japan's main products, manpower shortages, and a host of other domestic factors have combined to undercut many of the conditions favorable to past economic policies. Finally, political consensus on the desirability of growth for its own sake, which prevailed for at least two decades after the end of World War II, has been eroded. Thus even if domestic and international economic conditions were more favorable, past policies would in all likelihood have been questioned for political reasons. All the same, both domestically and internationally the strength of Japan was vastly superior in 1980 to that of earlier decades and Japanese economic leaders have begun to exploit such strengths abroad (see Reading 2-9).

But the dilemma for the Japanese government is to devise new economic policies geared to lower macrolevel targets. If high economic growth is not sustained, the domestic political question becomes whether the dominant conservative coalition will be capable of retaining its political base, thereby continuing its long rule and probusiness policies. Entering the 1980s, Japan appeared to have made the shift rather well. Nevertheless, even if the present government fails on a variety of these counts, past successes have clearly left the Japanese business and financial communities in positions of tremendous domestic and international strength, positions they are unlikely to lose, as might have happened during the more tumultuous and uncertain period of the 1950s.

Readings

2-1. THE LIBERAL DEMOCRATIC PARTY'S POLICY ORIENTATIONS*

The following excerpts from the initial party platform of the Liberal Democratic Party indicate both the general and specific economic orientations of the party and provide a backdrop to all its policies. Also of note is the tone of hostility toward the opposition and its basic principles. The reverse can be seen in Readings 2-2 and 2-4.

There is a school of thought in our country represented by, among others, the Marxist-oriented Socialist and Communist Parties, which stresses the supremacy of class warfare. In total disregard for the difficulties it would cause to the bulk of our people, this school of thought would have us destroy one another in the interests of a revolution. . . . This is something completely incompatible with the spirit of conservatism [which we espouse]. . . .

Our party is a political party which seeks to develop a wealthy country.

Our party rejects [the notion of] a socialist economy based on nationalized administration and bureaucratic control over land and the means of production.

In addition it is opposed to monopoly capitalism. Along with strengthening production through comprehensive economic planning based on free enterprise and respect for individual initiative and responsibility, we seek to strengthen social security policies, to bring about full employment and a wealthy country.

2-2. THE JAPAN SOCIALIST PARTY'S ECONOMIC CONSTRUCTION PLAN†

When the Japan Socialist Party's left and right wings recombined in 1955, the party issued a broad outline of its policy goals. Below are

*Tsuji Kiyoaki, ed., *Shiryō: Sengo Nijūnenshi,* vol. 1, "Seiji" (Tokyo: Nihon Hyōronsha, 1966), pp. 124–25.

†Japan Socialist Party, "Seisaku Taiko" [Outline of Policies], October 13, 1955, as reprinted in *Nihon Shakaitō, 20 nen no Kiroku* [Twenty Year History of the JSP] (Tokyo: Nihon Shakaitō, 1965), pp. 166–70.

excerpts from the sections dealing with the economy. In addition to the inclusion of what might be seen as typical socialist measures, the proposals are concerned with severing Japan's economic links to the United States and using fiscal measures to cut back on military expenditures.

This plan aims at establishing a self-supporting economy, expanding employment, increasing the national income, and raising the living standard through modernization and the expansion of production. This plan is to be carried out in 15 years.

The goals of the first five years are:

a. To develop industries and improve the economic structure so that international accounts may be balanced and that economic self-support may be attained without the support of the United States.

b. To employ jobless persons in comprehensive land development and expanding industries.

In the next ten years, the plan will seek:

a. To establish full employment.

b. To improve the people's living standard.

c. To improve cultural facilities.

The above measures, however, presuppose the nationalization of the country's main banking institutions and key industries.

Concrete measures for economic construction are as follows:

a. Development of trade and industry.

 (1) To rectify the current dependence on the United States, to establish trade relations with China and the Soviet bloc by abolishing the COCOM restrictions, to conclude payments agreements and trade mission exchanges, and also to promote trade with Southeast Asia and Africa by settling reparations questions promptly.

 (2) To bring about the socialization of the power and coal industries and to improve chemical and mechanical industrial techniques.

 (3) To establish a land development corps to improve roads, bridges and harbors and carry out reforestation, land clearing and land reclamation.

b. Expansion of employment and stabilization of living.

c. Modernization of rural communities and fishing villages and stabilization of management.

    d. Stabilization of medium and small enterprises.

    e. Fiscal and Monetary Measures.

       (1) A peacefully sound fiscal policy.

In addition to balancing the national and local budgets and stabilizing the currency and prices, we will carry out the reconstruction of a peaceful economy and stabilize and improve the lives and development of citizens.

Among the fiscal items we will carry out are:

—reduction of taxes

—elimination of special tax privileges for the rich

—elimination of the commodity tax and establishment of new luxury taxes

—shrinking of defense-related expenses

—reduction of reparations and other foreign outlays to an appropriately low level

—shrinking a wide array of unwanted and unneeded expenses

—increasing expenses for social welfare, housing, comprehensive development, and scientific and technological development

—developing a comprehensive national economic plan

      (2) A planned . . . and democratic monetary administration

2-3. THE PLAN TO DOUBLE THE NATIONAL INCOME IN TEN YEARS*

The government's most important effort in directing the economy came in 1960 with the Plan to Double the National Income in Ten Years. Excerpts from the plan, given below, are designed to show the plan's general goals, and the roles of government and private industry.

Problems of the Plan

1. *Principal Targets of the Plan*

The eventual target of this plan is to make an advance toward marked improvement of the people's standard of living and the attainment of full employment. In order to achieve this goal, the

*Japan, Economic Planning Agency, *New Long-Range Economic Plan of Japan (1961–1970)—Doubling National Income Plan* (Tokyo: The Japan Times, 1961), pp. 8–9, 12, 31–2, 63, 71–73, 89.

Japanese economy must be developed and stabilized to the maximum extent possible.

From this viewpoint, the following problems have been taken up as the focal points of the plan, with emphasis placed on economic growth as the axis and stability as the necessary condition of achieving the target.

First comes the repletion of social-overhead capital. The rapid economic growth in postwar years was made possible because of the external conditions accumulated in the past. However, as the economic scale exceeded the prewar level in or about 1953 and the economy continued to grow at a high rate, the development of social capital including roads, ports and harbors, land for housing, and service water lagged behind that of production capital, and this has caused a bottleneck in the way of economic development.

Therefore, it will be a problem of great importance to seek improvement of the social capital, both in quantity and quality, by means of public and other investments. It is also imperative that the government should take a step forward from simply supplying goods as an emergency countermeasure, and should exert its efforts for the development of social facilities such as transportation, land for housing, service water, education and life environments.

The repletion of the social capital mentioned above will serve not only to strengthen the foundations of living and industry, but also to expand employment and income, thus to contribute to the economic development of the country.

Next comes an introduction to a highly industrialized structure. An increase in purchasing power, attendant on economic development, creates demand for goods and services. The rate of increase in demand is higher in the products of secondary industry and services of the tertiary sector than in the production of primary industry.

As for secondary industry, the demand for heavy and chemical products is inclined to become greater than other products.

Meanwhile, considering the tempo of technological innovation, the trends in population and the labor force, and the switch to the liberalization of trade in the future, it is imperative to raise the productivity of the national economy as a whole.

In order to meet this demand, it will be necessary not only to increase the productivity of each individual enterprise or industry but also to switch the relative importance of industrial structure from industries of low productivity to those of high productivity.

In other words, there is a strong demand that the level of industrial organization be greatly raised and an inducement in this direction is one of the big problems of this plan.

Then comes the promotion of international trade and economic cooperation. The limitation of the balance of international payments in postwar years has so far restricted the growth of the Japanese economy. It is possible that the rate of the restriction may decrease as the competitive power in export is strengthened as a result of improvement in productivity in the future. However, it is expected that the restriction will remain big in view of the character of the Japanese economy in which lack of resources always makes indispensable a considerably large scale of imports.

In this sense, an increase in foreign exchange revenues centering around exports will provide an important key to the achievement of this plan.

2. *Target of the Plan*

In order to achieve the aforementioned objectives, the plan sets the goal of doubling the scale of the national economy in terms of real value in about 10 years.

It is considered necessary and possible that the aforementioned problems facing this country will be settled in the process of realizing the above goal.

Role of the Government

1. *Economic Growth and the Government's Role*

The object of this plan is centered on the government sector which is subject directly to the government's measures and policies. The similar plans mapped out in the past had much more to do with private fields of business than this plan. Compared with them, therefore, this plan has a narrower scope for the government to intervene in the private sector, but, under it, the government is most responsible for what it does within the narrow scope.

The Government is at all times responsible for positively cultivating factors for economic growth and eliminating adverse elements while maintaining a correct appraisal of the latent growth potential of the Japanese economy. The Government is also responsible for keeping the value of currency stabilized, maintaining economic growth, and minimizing business fluctuations through proper application of fiscal and monetary policies.

(1) Improvement of Social Overhead Capital This will serve to strengthen the nation's economic basis and promote public welfare as well as to ensure the satisfactory conservation and effective utilization of land. Moreover, flexible operation of public investments in this section will serve to regulate business fluctuations.

(2) Improvement of Human Ability and Promotion of Science and Technology under Educational and Training Programs The training of personnel to meet the requirements of this new age coupled with similar private activities, is necessary to expedite the nation's economic growth.

(3) Improvement of Social Security and Welfare It is the responsibility of the government of a modern country to build it into a welfare state.

(4) Guidance of Private Industries in Sound Directions The Government should not step directly into private business activities but instead should lead them in desirable directions by helping improve the basic environments of private industries. In this connection, there are two phases in this type of government activities i.e. positive pursuing of the so-called structural policy on one hand and supervisory protection functions such as price policies and consumer protection on the other.

Means for Implementing Policy

In trying to achieve the economic policies contained in this plan, it is desirable for the Government to count on the originality and devices of private enterprises and individuals. It should refrain, as far as possible, from taking direct control measures.

At the same time, the Government should avoid taking protectionist policies aimed directly at particular enterprises. What should be done is to take policies which will help them operate on a fully commercial basis.

Therefore, efforts should be made to do without the conventional material or exchange control policy and thus to achieve the desired targets by such indirect means as financial and monetary policies and appropriate inducement-measures designed to help private enterprises develop in a desirable direction.

Basic Direction for Fiscal and Monetary Policy

The basic task of the fiscal and monetary policy under this present plan is to insure a smooth and proper supply of funds required for economic growth, while maintaining the stability of the value of currency and minimizing the magnitude of business fluctuations.

Role of the Private Sector

Economic Growth and Tasks of Private Industries

This new plan is based on the recognition that private enterprise bodies carry out rational economic activities on their own initiative, operating through the free enterprise system and market mechanism. The plan, thus, presents a sort of forecast for private economic sectors. Private enterprises are expected to make their own long-range plan, based on the projected trend in national economy and various information in the present plan. They are urged to cease depending excessively on the Government and to stand on their own.

Under the envisioned system, private enterprises are expected to make the most of their potential energies for expansion and thereby contribute to the development of the national economy. Such activities on the part of private firms will eventually result in an expansion of the national income and a rise in the standard of living.

Guiding Policy of Government

The role of the Government vis-à-vis private sectors is to create and develop such basic conditions that will enable private enterprise to operate freely and insure that the results of their unrestricted activities conform to rational economic laws.

Obstacles to such free activities or bottlenecks should be removed by the Government. It is also the responsibility of the Government to stimulate, encourage and guide private economic activities in order to have a highly stabilized growth of the national economy.

Following this basic line of thinking, the Government will abolish what still remains of direct control on industries as soon as possible and hold to a minimum the area of administration directly interfering in the activities of individual enterprises. Even if Government interference in the market economy is necessary for some compensatory purposes that action should be made as economically rational as possible.

First, as to such industries as electric power, gas, transportation and banking, some forms of Government interference are called for in view of their monopolistic character and the public interests involved. The current railway fares and price rates enforced by public utilities industries impede in certain cases an economical distribution of resources or a smooth economic circular flow.

Necessary corrections should be made in the present public utility price-structure to insure economic efficiency parallel with the improvement of the management of enterprises in such industries.

Secondly, foreign exchange transactions should be liberalized, while direct control should be replaced by indirect control with regard to distribution of rice. The indirect control on foreign exchange and rice will remain in force for some time to come as an exception to the free economic setup as they present fundamental problems yet to be solved in the maintenance of economic stability.

The progress in the liberalization of trade and foreign exchange and intensifying competition are expected to accelerate changes in the nation's industrial structure. The primary concern of the Government in this process is to ensure smooth and proper economic activities in private sectors and a free and fair competition. The Government will also see to it that the interests of ordinary consumers and the third parties involved will not be hurt.

It has also the responsibility to provide a business environment, making possible the entry of new-comers into various industrial areas. Efforts should be made by the Government, however, to save private industries from the damaging effect of excessive competition. Only when such conditions are created are private economic activities placed on a rational basis and the interests of consumers adequately protected. Unfair competition, monopoly through unfair practices, unjustified price-lifting through price agreements, and the formation of cartels injurious to the interests of consumers must be rejected in principle. On the other hand, we must not forget the need for the formation of a new industrial order designed to foster the competitive power of Japanese industries and encourage modernization of the industrial structure under the conditions of liberalized trade.

The tariff policy is going to assume a great significance under liberalized conditions. It is necessary to improve and adapt the present tariff system to the expansion of organic and rational economic exchange with other countries, the future domestic economic growth, and strucutral changes. While it is advisable to give protection to those incipient industries which have potentialities for development from the standpoint of comparative advantage for a limited period of time, the Government should refrain from giving relief to declining ones.

Attention should be paid rather to unemployment problems in the declining industries. Such Government attitude as outlined above would be felt as rather severe on industries and enterprises. But only by going through such a phase will Japan be strong enough to compete in the world market and gain a solid basis for economic growth.

Establishment of New Industrial Order The problem of industrial order must be taken up as an important aspect of the question of advancing and modernizing manufacturing industries. The reasons for this are as follows: First, the Japanese economy, despite its small market, has many weak and small enterprises. Therefore, the mass production formula does not work, and many small enterprises have to manage along insecurely [sic] on the basis of low wages. Secondly, the progress of technological renovation is bringing a rapid change in both production structure and consumption structure. Third, the shift to trade liberalization has made it all the more necessary to study the problem of industrial order. Especially, the fact that Japanese enterprises face direct competition with foreign firms has made an indispensable condition for economic growth to establish new industrial order as part of the policy to strengthen competitive power in the international market. The "order" in this sense does not mean the status quo but the establishment of a new structure based on economic rationality.

From the above-mentioned viewpoints, the following problems should be considered in studying a new industrial order in a long-range perspective.

The first is the expansion of enterprises to put up with international competition. For this purpose, consideration must be given to concentration, merger and grouping of enterprises, and establishment of the system of specialized production. Secondly, strong measures must be taken against economic recession. Efforts must be made to narrow gaps in business cycles through flexible customs policy and promotion of cooperation among enterprises. Third, close cooperative relations must be established between large and small- and medium-size enterprises. Fourth, an orderly import of raw materials from abroad must be secured through expansion of joint purchase and joint development of overseas resources. In this connection, it is necessary to give due consideration to the prevention of excessive competition in overseas markets.

Measures for the maintenance of proper order have special significance in the transitional period of trade liberalization. They must be designed mainly for (i) prevention of confusion in the transitional period, (ii) protection and encouragement of new industries and "growth" industries, and (iii) smooth transformation of waning industries.

2-4. THE JSP AND HIGH ECONOMIC GROWTH*

The following is an excerpt from a statement included in a JSP handbook of policies. This book, published in 1969, took the form of two-page outlines of JSP policy designed as answers to broad questions. In this case the question was, "How does the party view the country's high economic growth?"

The policy of high economic growth carried out by the LDP government and monopoly capital has been an ephemeral growth which has put productivity first. It has given priority to large-scale industry and the rich while sacrificing the livelihood of the people. This has brought about a collapse of human sensibilities and an

*Shakaitō no Seisaku [Policies of the JSP], (Tokyo: Nihon Shakaito, 1969), pp. 88–89.

increase in individual alienation. Japan has become second in the capitalist world in GNP, but we remain a lowly twenty-first in income per capita.

Capital's exploitation of the laboring classes has been greatly strengthened. In contrast to the increased shares going to capital, labor's share of national income has fallen from 36.2% in 1955 to 33% in 1966, while individual consumption expenses have slipped from 63.2% of national expenditures in 1955 to a projected 51% for 1969. The exploitation of labor is particularly manifested in first, the great rise in consumer prices and heavy taxation . . . ; second, the widening of economic differences and inequalities . . . ; and third, the expansion of traffic accidents, pollution, and natural disaster, as well as an increase in the instability of daily life. . . .

2-5. INDUSTRIAL POLICY AND SCIENCE AND TECHNOLOGY POLICY*

The government indicated a marked shift in the orientation of its economic policies in its Basic Economic and Social Plan for 1973–77. The following excerpts concern the efforts to shift industrial policy.

1. A Shift in Industrial Policy

(5101) Until now, Japan has built an increasingly involved industrial structure centering upon heavy industrialization and has strengthened remarkably its internationally competitive position.

As the circumstances and conditions surrounding Japanese industry have greatly changed, it is now necessary for Japan, coping positively with these changes, to develop new patterns of industrial growth realizing national welfare and promoting international harmony. In effect, this is basically the problem of achieving harmony between industrial activity and such demands of national welfare and international unity as preventing pollution, considering the finite nature of our land, water, and other resources, shortening working hours, including adopting the five-day workweek and raising the compulsory retirement age, improving the content of work,

---

*Japan, Economic Planning Agency, *Basic Economic and Social Plan, 1973–1977* (Tokyo: EPA, 1973), pp. 84–85, 88–89.

shouldering some of the burden for social security guarantees and other welfare costs, ensuring product safety, respecting the sovereign rights of the consumer, and implementing technology assessment. In this, it will be necessary for industry, while anticipating future changes in patterns of consumption and increased use of information, and resolving steadily these problems to build a desirable industrial structure and regional balance through working untiringly, for structural development making fullest use of its inherent vitality and heightening efficiency.

(5102) Responding to these demands, past policies which have promoted heavy industrialization primarily for greater export competitiveness from the premise of market principles must be first reviewed. As well as implying the rationalization, including reorganization and abolition, of the various industry-related special taxation measures, the continued promotion of policy-re-orientations for governmental finance institutions' lending policies, shifting the emphasis to social development, pollution prevention, technical advances, and other fields suited to the new age: this also means a basic re-examination and determined re-alignment of subsidies and other measures to promote export growth.

3. Realization of a Desirable Industrial Structure

(5301) In order to effect the shift to a desirable industrial structure, it is necessary, at the same time as pollution prevention, industrial relocation, and other such measures are being promoted, to formulate a concept of the desirable industrial development in light of the new demands being made on industry and then to promote movement in that direction. The major orientation here is thought to be toward knowledge-intensification of industry. While it is the accumulated efforts of industry itself toward creative development that are the driving force for making Japanese industry more knowledge-intensive, the Government for its part is to implement the following policies with constant attention to urban development, housing, medical care, education, leisure, anti-pollution, and other social development areas having a major effect upon that industrial knowledge-intensification and directly linked with the welfare of the people.

(1) While the basic directions which industry should take for its knowledge-intensification are those noted below, the Government is also to define its concepts more clearly.

(5311) 1) At the same time as all industries should be induced to become more knowledge-intensive through (1) promoting a higher degree of processing and higher product quality, (2) even when the finished product itself remains the same, attempting to make the processes of its production and distribution information-intensive, labor-saving, and pollution-free, and (3) trying to systematize vertically several industries from material procurement to processing and distribution or to establish horizontal systems unifying diverse functions.

2) The point is to work to make the industrial structure more knowledge-intensive through creating and developing such knowledge-intensive industries as fashion designing, high-quality merchandise, sophisticated processing, information-related industries, and such social development industries as housing and urban needs.

(2) Policies to Promote a Knowledge-Intensive Structure

(5321) 1) Encouraging Technology and Research and Development

Although technology and research and development are crucial to creating a knowledge-intensive industrial structure, the great number of problems which require massive investments for research and development and still defy easy solution means that the Government, while hoping that private initiatives will be actively pursued, is also to take the appropriate measures to promote Government-directed development and to assist corporate technology and research and development.

2) Providing Conditions

Measures to be taken to promote a more knowledge-intensive structure include providing legal protection for software, setting standards for quality controls and the like, and developing designs. At the same time, study is to be given to personnel-training policies.

3) Nurturing Infant Knowledge-Intensive Industries

The appropriate assistance measures are to be taken for those infant knowledge-intensive industries which are deemed both basic and indispensible to the Japanese economy and society and which it is felt necessary to develop.

2-6. THE 1979 ECONOMIC AND SOCIAL PLAN*

The following excerpts are from the 1979 economic and social plan developed by the government's Economic Planning Agency. Its broad goals and specific objectives reflect the drastic shift from those of 1960 that began in the 1973 plan. There is much greater sensitivity to the international conditions affecting Japan's economy, and there is also much greater attention to stabilizing the domestic economy and providing a basis for more secure individual living.

Given the changing external and domestic conditions, notably, developing trends towards higher prices and supply instability, there are now strong calls for fostering an appropriate level of economic growth while dealing with these changes, and also strong demands that this economic growth be changed to one which is linked more directly with a qualitative improvement of the national life and which is in harmony with the rest of the international economy and society. Switching Japan's economy to a new stable growth-path of this kind will be important in regaining confidence in the future in households and business, thereby making the most of the potential vitality of Japan's economy. It will also be of importance in making an active contribution to the development of the international economy and society.

For this reason, the Government has so far directed its full efforts to the rectification of economic imbalances through active effective demand-measures centered on public investment. The effects of these measures have recently begun to appear and Japan's economic situation is now moving toward improvement. With a recovery trend in plant and equipment investment by enterprises and relatively steady household behavior, private demand has gradually firmed up and the international balance of payments is showing a marked trend toward equilibrium.

Nevertheless, the future of the world economy under the process of structural change remains in a state of flux. Particularly notable is the increase in uncertain factors with respect to energy supplies. Domestically, too, there are still imbalances among the various sectors of the economy, and drastic structural changes are called

*Economic Planning Agency, *New Economic and Social Seven-Year Plan* (Tokyo: EPA, 1979), pp. 9, 15.

for. Under these circumstances, although a variety of policy efforts to foster a proper expansion in demand are necessary, the situation is such that solution by these policy efforts alone is difficult. It is becoming necessary to implement structural policies in a longer perspective. . . .

In view of this, this plan shall tackle the problems with a new approach and renewed determination, with three basic directions as the basis for management of the economy. These directions are:

1. Rectifying imbalances among economic sectors
2. Promoting industrial restructuring and overcoming energy constraints
3. Working for the realization of a new Japanese-type welfare society.

In conformity with the basic directions discussed in Part One, the Plan sets as its objectives:

1. Attainment of full employment and stabilization of prices;
2. Stabilization and enrichment of national life;
3. Cooperation in and contribution to the development of the international economy and society;
4. Ensuring economic security and fostering the foundations of further development; and
5. Reconstruction of public finance and new monetary responses.

2-7. THE EIGHT-POINT PROGRAM TO PROTECT THE YEN*

During the middle of 1971, the Japanese government came under extreme pressure from the United States and other OECD countries, due to Japan's huge positive balance of trade. Among the major targets of the pressure was the country's allegedly overvalued currency that enabled Japanese exports to penetrate foreign markets more easily. The value of the yen had been maintained at ¥360 to $1.00 (United States) since the United States Occupation, and Japanese government officials announced a series of steps designed to meet foreign criticisms while still retaining the fixed value of the

*Program adopted by Cabinet Council of Economic Ministers, June 4, 1971.

yen. Their efforts proved unsuccessful several weeks after this proposal was issued.

1. Stepped up liberalization of imports
2. Enforcement of preferential tariffs for developing nations, possible from August 1
3. Acceleration of cuts in import tariffs
4. Promotion of capital investments, including the further promotion of incoming investments and a complete liberalization of outgoing investments
5. Progress in the elimination of non-tariff barriers
6. Promotion of foreign economic aid
7. A review of export promotion tax reliefs and the introduction of orderly marketing
8. Flexible manipulation of fiscal and monetary policies

2-8. DEFICIT SPENDING*

In the midst of several years of deficit spending by the government, designed to stimulate the economy and meet pressures for continuing various domestic programs, then Finance Minister Ōhira delivered a fiscal policy speech before the Diet. In the speech he indicated both the general opposition to deficit spending and the government's desire to continue with the policy during the coming year.

In forming the budget for fiscal 1976, in view of the role to be played by government finance in helping business recovery and notwithstanding the very severe situation of fiscal resources continuing from fiscal 1975, it has been decided to cope with the situation by [again] issuing a large amount of public bonds including those authorized under the special law, as in the Supplemental Budget for fiscal 1975. Strictly speaking, however, this is after all an exceptional step to cope with the immediate situation, and it goes without saying that the cardinal point of fiscal operation should be to avoid an easygoing reliance on public bonds and to return swiftly to a fiscal position not reliant on exceptional bond issuance. The Government is determined to devote its efforts to achieving as

---

*Fiscal policy speech for fiscal year 1976, delivered by Finance Minister Masayoshi Ōhira at the 77th session of the National Diet, January 23, 1976, (mimeo).

swiftly as possible the normalization of public finance throughout the national and local governments.

2-9. THE BUSINESS PERSPECTIVE*

In mid-December 1977, Toshio Doko, the head of Japan's most prestigious business organization, the Federation of Economic Organizations, spoke at a United States –Japan Symposium in Tokyo. Excerpts from his speech provide a good sense of the increased self-confidence and internationalization of major Japanese businesses.

All of you know that both our Governments are making every effort to deal promptly with the immediate problems simply because those involved in the consultations do share the same grave concern that a simple faux pas might cause us to lapse into the nightmare of the 1930s, when we suffered seriously from the vicious circle of protectionism and depression.

. . . First and foremost, I believe that the international economy should be as open as possible. The free-world countries that manage their economies by placing their trust in the market mechanism based on democracy, in particular the U.S., West Germany and Japan who have stronger free enterprises, have been more successful than the socialist countries who prefer controls and plans in their economic management. This can be clearly shown by comparing only a few indicators, such as the rate of rise in their respective living standards and income and their capabilities of developing new technology and enhancing productivity.

Anyone can easily discern which regime of society abounds in greater vitality and creativity. The greatest merit of free trade is that, through international competition, creative and ingenious nations earn prizes and diligent workers are rewarded. I know that America is a country where inventiveness is a highly respected virtue. It has always been my belief that Japan has to emulate your country in building a society which encourages creativity.

Controls on trade do not stop on the shoreline; they invite further controls within nations. We Japanese industrialists remember very

*Japan Information Service, *Japan Report* (Feb. 16, 1978). 24, no. 4.

well the long days of oppression under widespread bureaucratic controls.

The current efforts for liberalization, expansion of quotas, tariff reductions and other measures to widen access to imports, as well as the push we are giving to domestic reflation, are based on our hope and conviction that these will help keep the international economy open and that a liberal move will generate a liberal response.

Limited Resources

Secondly, the world economy has entered into an era where, like it or not, we must be constantly aware of the limitations of resources. This is the very reason why, despite our wish to see domestic demand boosted, we are not asking for a Keynesian prescription of mere enlargement of government expenditures.

We are strongly urging, rather, that increased outlays be made on infrastructural improvement which will promote more efficiency in our economy, housing investments which lead to enhancement in the quality of life, and R&D projects in energy and other fields which promise to bring us a technological breakthrough against constraint from limitation of resources.

It is, accordingly, highly welcome that President Carter is doing his utmost to see his energy package legislated as soon as possible. This, I expect, would favorably affect the U.S. balance of payments.

. . . The fact that resources are limited means that adherence to the principle of free international trade which ensures the most efficient allocation of resources on this planet has become even more important.

If we take the example of steel, the Japanese steel industry consumes the lowest amount of fuel and raw materials in the world to produce one ton of steel. I have to stress the importance of efficient utilization of limited resources through free competition.

In this connection, though I am fully aware of the theoretical advantages of the floating exchange-rate system, we somehow feel that the dramatic exchange-rate change has, by a single fiat, forced our long and assiduous efforts for cost savings back to the starting-point. The floating rate should not be used as a tool to nullify the fruits of input-saving efforts and to give a competitive edge to those who do not emulate such efforts.

Self-Help Required

I believe that increasing interdependence in the world economy even more strongly predicates self-help efforts by the respective governments and the enterprises of each member of the international community.

The "oil shock" has produced a bipolarization of the world between the oil-producing countries with their ever-increasing inflow of surplus international liquidity, and the rest of the world which has, as a group, a large current account deficit.

The U.S. has proposed that the "stronger economies", namely those of the U.S., Japan and Germany, should expand their economies in order to assist the "weaker economies", including a part of the advanced countries and non-oil-producing developing countries.

I would venture to maintain that deficit nations should make efforts to increase their exports of goods and services to the oil-producing nations while making efforts to minimize oil imports, thereby reducing as much as possible the current account deficits of the entire oil-consuming world vis-à-vis the oil-producing world. As to the amount of deficits which will still remain with us, the "strong economies" should render assistance to the "weaker economies" for a period of time.

As the surplus nations, such as Japan and Germany, should boldly expand their domestic demand, deficit nations should strive to enhance productivity and to explore overseas markets.

To state it frankly, it is my impression that stagnant imports and the low ratio of manufactured items in our total imports are due mainly to the present stagnancy in our internal demand, but they are also partly due to lack of efforts on the part of exporters to push their sales in our country.

The Japanese market consists of over 110 million people with an annual per capita income of over $5,000, all very curious about "*hakurai-hin*" or "vessel-carried goods" (meaning imports), crowded into a land smaller than the state of California. Nowhere else is there such a market.

I welcome the ongoing programs of "Exports to Japan" seminars being held in various parts of the U.S., sponsored by the JETRO [Japan External Trade Organization] and the U.S. Commerce Department. I also welcome the fact that another import promotion mission to the U.S. is now being organized by MITI. But I feel that there is room for more efforts by the U.S. Government and U.S. enterprises to support the learning of Japanese which, after all, is the language in which we conduct business in Japan, surveys of local distribution systems, market-survey tours to Japan by small and medium enterprises, or improvements in the use of the sole-agent systems and so on.

Restraint and Discipline Needed

. . . In the face of too-sudden increase in imports or too-violent fluctuations in exchange-rate changes, I consider it only natural that businessmen and workers should be given some time to make adjustments. In some cases, it may be necessary for exporting countries to exercise self-restraint to help the adjustment efforts of importing countries for an agreed period of time. Such restraints have been implemented by Japan in regard to color TV and special steel.

What is important in this respect is that businessmen and workers should make the most of the period of grace thus accorded them either by the government of the importing country or by the exporting industry and unite their ingenuity to raise productivity, diversify business lines, or in respect of manpower, government and business should combine their efforts to retrain the labor force and shift them to more viable sectors of industry.

. . . Also, as to the items under "residual import restriction," which involves difficult problems in meeting international competition, our government should show a clear perspective and remove import barriers at our national border as much as possible by adopting domestic adjustment measures to help the affected sectors.

We think it highly significant that the "Solomon Report" on steel trade included such domestic measures as special reductions, extension of federal credits and guarantees, relaxation of environmental controls, assistance to local community and workers, relaxation in the application of anti-trust laws in dealing with mergers and joint undertakings. These will serve as helpful suggestions.

The last but a very important point about the international economy is that the U.S. and Japan should force strict discipline upon themselves, and take a considerate and understanding attitude towards developing countries. If our two countries lapse into protectionism, the upward path for the developing world will be closed. Our international economic society should welcome the participation of new and dynamic economies, constantly rejuvenate itself, and expand with the new vigor contributed by the new entrants.

South Korea, for example, which lacks resources and is devoid of capital just as Japan not so long ago, has exported this year as much as Japan did ten years ago, and its foreign exchange holdings are twice what Japan had at that time. In the so-called "Olympiad of skills", an international contest of skills and dexterity, South Korea has eclipsed Japan and become the No. 1 in the world in June last year.

Japan should reorganize its own industrial structure and make way for such countries as much as possible. I will not be surprised to see the day when steel and color-TV exports from Korea and Taiwan to the U.S. should drive us out of the market, just as they have with transistor radios and monochrome TV receivers. We can not stop the march of time in the world economy. I expect that these emerging economies will, in turn, render their helping hand to the yet newer entrants to the international economy, and contribute their share to the lasting expansion of the world economy.

. . . America and Japan enjoy a truly close relationship. Believing that the proof of intimacy is how candidly you can talk with your friends, I have availed myself of this opportunity to bare my thoughts in all candor and friendship. Thank you.

3 Labor-Management Relations: Between Action and Passivity

Japanese labor-management relations present a curious puzzle. In the wake of the world oil crisis of the mid-1970s, Japan absorbed oil prices that had quadrupled, major fluctuations in exchange rates, vastly lower rates of economic growth, and mild inflation. Yet during the same time, unemployment rates remained at or below 2 percent. Meanwhile, West Germany struggled to hold its unemployment below 5 percent; Britain's hovered around 6 percent; and the United States' figures were officially just below 8 percent. This obvious Japanese success is difficult to understand, given the fact that Japanese labor federations and the Japanese left have been politically weak and stridently hostile to the dominant conservative regime. Why did labor fare so well in a situation of crisis, especially compared to countries where labor is politically stronger?

There is a second, related, puzzle. Japanese labor-management relations have become the subject of awe and fascination to managers in Western Europe and North America. Workers are prompt, efficient, rarely absent, and highly productive. They work longer hours and take shorter vacations than their Western counterparts. During inclement weather or transportation strikes, they bed down in their offices or plants, rather than taking advantage of the confusion to stay home. They sing company songs, and rarely complain when they are replaced by new labor-saving technology (see Reading 3-1). At the same time, although not nearly as high as in Britain, the United States, France, or Italy, Japanese strike-rates are higher than those in Sweden and West Germany. And when Japanese workers go on strike, their tactics are often confrontational to an extreme. Management officials are frequently surrounded by workers and held as virtual captives for many hours with the hope of wrenching out a favorable settlement. Before the union presents its demands, there is a long preparatory period of snake dancing, meetings, harangues, songs, cheers, red flags and headbands, posters, and derisive cartoons of management (Gibney, 1975, p. 183). How does one explain this apparent gap between harmony and conflict?

Finally, how does one explain the combination of passivity and activism that characterizes government actions in the field of labor-management relations? Throughout the postwar period, Japanese economic policy saw government playing an active and catalytic role. Government has been far more passive in most phases of labor-management relations. Government's role in most private sector labor-management problems has been minimal. During the 1960s and 1970s, governments in Britain, Sweden, and even the United States experimented with or actually implemented wage settlements based directly on government-enforced guidelines or on wage negotiations in which the government was an actual participant. Japan's wage settlements, in contrast, have been largely the function of bargains struck at the level of the individual enterprise. The government has intervened only in a limited number of instances when such agreements appeared to be incapable of resolving fundamental threats to the regime as a whole, such as those that took place during the recession of the mid-1970s. In most other instances, government passivity was sufficient to ensure the success of conservative goals. Yet government has played a direct and consistent role in labor-management relations involving public sector unions in which government is the employer and in which political threats have been more pervasive.

The answers to these puzzles lie in the strength of the conservative regime in Japan and in the effective institutions of labor-management relations that have been developed, particularly at the plant level, over the past several decades. But to understand the apparent incongruities, it is also necessary to recognize the very different institutional levels of conflict and conflict-resolution involved in Japanese labor-management relations. In particular, one must understand the gaps between national and company level and between public and private sector union activities.

Context

At least three important features form the contextual background of Japanese labor-management relations. First, there is the historical legacy of labor's weakness. Second, there are important structures encouraging plant level rather than class loyalties among workers. Third, there are noteworthy differences in the politics of public sector versus private sector workers.

The Japanese labor movement has always lagged behind the country's industry, finance, and management in organizational coherence and strength. Many Japanese firms were strong domestically and some were even internationally competitive by the turn of the century. But while sporadic efforts at unionization began during this period, Japan's first important proto-union, the Yūaikai, did not come into being until 1912. Modelled after the moderate Friendly Societies in England and the American Federation of Labor, it initially brought together a small number of very low level blue-collar workers for mutual help and "the cultivation of virtue." In this early form, the Japanese labor movement was relatively free of the class consciousness and socialist, syndicalist, and revolutionary ideologies which informed the International Workers of the World in the United States and most unions in continental Europe.

By the end of World War I, Japanese unions had begun to develop along more radical ideological lines. Syndicalism, socialism, and bolshevism prevailed. For a short period, the movement spread rapidly: in 1919, there were 71 unions with 30,000 members; in 1922, over 1,000 unions with about 132,000 members. But this growth was soon stunted. At the union movement's highpoint in 1936, 420,000 union members represented less than 7 percent of the total workforce. And at no time during the prewar period did Japanese unions secure the passage of national legislation legitimizing their formal status and granting them the basic rights of organization and collective bargaining.

Many factors contributed to this retardation in growth. Up until World War II, Japan was still about 50 percent rural, and the agricultural sector continued to supply a large pool of residual labor during periods of expansion. Receptivity to paternalistic appeals and the temporary nature of much of the industrial workforce posed additional difficulties to union organizers. Moreover, the union "movement" in prewar Japan was rife with the kinds of internal factionalism that have haunted the political left in all countries.

Overt political repression exacerbated labor's difficulties even more: The Public Peace Law of 1900, for example, banned all actions designed to "force" participation in groups engaged in collective actions related to labor conditions and wages. Strikes could not be "forced" on workers nor could employers be "forced" to make any concessions regarding labor conditions and wages. Although in principle voluntary unionization, strikes, and negotiations were not prohibited, the judgment of any particular strike's voluntariness or force was entrusted entirely to a police force entirely unsympathetic to the unions or the left. Later, the Peace Preservation Law enacted in 1925, revised in 1928, and revised again in 1941, made it a crime to join or lead any organization or activity aimed at ending private ownership. It created a Special Police Force aimed at further weakening "radical" organizations. The law provided a maximum penalty of death for violators.

During the military-dominated 1930s, repression of the left accelerated. By 1938, military and right-wing labor leaders had created the Industrial Patriotic Movement which absorbed the labor movement into the collective national war effort against China. All autonomous unions and their national associations were dissolved and reorganized into the Industrial Patriotic Association in 1940. All union activities independent of the association were prohibited.

Drastic changes took place under the United States Occupation. Beginning as they did with a tradition of free collective bargaining and frequent but relatively calm protest, Americans imposed three important pieces of legislation to encourage union formation, to legitimize negotiation of labor disputes, and to establish minimum working conditions. Unemployment insurance and unemployment relief projects were begun, and an autonomous Labor Ministry was created. The results were dramatic. The number of unions shot up from zero at the end of the war to 509 in 1945 alone, to 17,266 in 1946, and to 34,688 by 1949. Union membership soared to 381,000, to 3.7 million, and then to 6.7 million during the same period. By 1949, membership was about 50 percent of the workforce, well above that in the United States or even Britain at the time. This trend signalled to many the approach of a new national regime based on a different socioeconomic coalition, as well as a drastic alteration in the structure of labor-management relations.

The drastic reversal of United States policy altered this course of events. Starting in 1947, General Headquarters (GHQ) banned several important strikes. Many others were subject to semiofficial expressions of dissatisfaction. Sanbetsu Kaigi, the main federation of industrial unions, was dismantled. Economic policy shifted to an emphasis on stability and economic recovery, and there were sharp provisions against allegedly inflationary wage hikes. The major labor laws were revised; the Trade Union Law became less like the Wagner Act and much closer to the Taft-Hartley Act. The National Public Service Law and the Public Corporation and National Enterprises Labor Relations Law banned collective bargaining and strikes by most public sector unions. Prolabor personnel in the Labor Division of GHQ were removed; a "red purge" removed key Japanese labor leaders; and cutbacks in the number of public service personnel reduced the strength of public sector unions, particularly in transportation and communications. (Takemae and Amakawa, 1977; see also Chapter 7).

Labor's weakness in much of the postwar period was also fostered by the fact that from the Korean War through the mid 1960s the country's labor supply was more than adequate to meet growing industrial demands. Returnees from overseas colonies; demobilized soldiers and sailors; members of the rural sector freed from much of the time and labor-intensive work of farming by new machinery and fertilizers; women anxious or forced by family or economic circumstances to enter the workforce either permanently or temporarily; and then, later, the offspring of the postwar baby boom—all swelled the size of the labor pool from which industry could draw. During the decade of the 1950s alone, approximately three million workers shifted from the agricultural to the industrial or service sectors. Japan was thus unlike Sweden, Britain, France, or Germany which faced notable labor shortages during the postwar period. The Japanese government consequently was not called upon by business to take measures such as importing foreign labor, enforcing an incomes policy, or retraining or relocating vast numbers of workers. But this surplus also held down the political and economic powers of Japanese workers. The labor surplus began to decline only in the late 1960s and early 1970s. By then, the successes of Japanese economic policies in sectoral transformation and in achieving high rates of growth had long since undercut much of the early organizational potential of the union movement.

Labor's inherent historical weakness was furthered by several organizational steps taken by government and business to structure the labor movement into politically and economically less threatening directions. The advantage of being a historical latecomer allowed the prewar regime an element of preemptive foresight. As Kaneko Kentarō, then Vice-Minister of Agriculture and Commerce noted in 1896, "The advantage of being one of those who follow is that it gives one the opportunity to take note of the history of those who have gone before and to avoid taking the same path." Some of Japan's more prescient economic and political leaders attempted to follow a course of business paternalism aimed at ensuring worker loyalty rather than class hostility. Essential to this goal were multiple unions formed within the single enterprise rather than a union movement developed along more cohesive craft, industrial, or geographical lines.

The enterprise-union principle began with the national railways in 1906 and spread to the private sector, in particular Japan's largest firms. At the plant level, many joint worker-management councils were established by employers. Typically separate from any union structure and purely advisory in nature, these proved effective in defusing plant level labor-management tensions and the union movement. The national organizational manifestation of this paternalism was the Kyōchōkai (The Association for Harmony and Conciliation), a body designed by the government and private business to take the lead in harmonizing relations between labor and capital (Marshall, 1976).

The prewar legacy of union organization at the plant or enterprise level was continued under the Occupation. A national peak association of business, the Japan Federation of Employers' Associations was formed in April 1948 to provide a unified business voice on labor-management problems. Among its primary concerns was the encouragement of enterprise unionism. Individual firms were quick to support friendly unions when unionization appeared inevitable.

Enterprise unionism was also fostered by the extreme poverty prevailing at the end of the war. Fledgling unions saw little reason to use strikes to stop production. Instead, they relied on "production-control struggles," which required the unified cooperation of blue- and white-collar workers within the single enterprise. Similarly, the postwar emphasis on "democracy" was taken by many workers as an invitation to reduce invidious status-distinctions among various categories of workers (Kuriki, 1977). Thus, the basic unit of the union movement in Japan remained the enterprise union. Blue- and white-collar workers regardless of work assignment are members of the same union. Links to those with comparable skills in other firms are minimal.

Loyalty to the firm is actively encouraged by a number of practices at the firm level. Permanent employment for regular employees, the bonus system, liberal allowances above low-base salaries, company vacations, marriage-counselling services, regularized drinking among coworkers, company songs, and a host of other practices all create a psychological link between the worker and the individual firm for which he works. They militate against the development of the horizontal class links that were so much a part of the historical labor movements in Britain, France, West Germany, and Sweden (see Reading 3-2).

Some enterprise unions are federated along geographical and industrial lines. But fragmentation, not unity, and enterprise autonomy, rather than federational solidarity, have been dominant. Only one-third of the Japanese work force is unionized. Nearly 40 percent of the 12,500 unions in Japan lack any affiliation with a national federation. Sōhyō, the largest of these bodies, represents only 38 percent of the unionized work force, while Dōmei, the second largest, represents a scant 17 percent. In Japan, only six unions have memberships as large as 100,000, the size of the average number of members per union in the United States. Over 2.1 million of the 12.4 million unionized workers in Japan are in unions with fewer than 300 members. Meanwhile, workers in small and medium-sized industries are largely unorganized.

Finally, it is important in the case of Japan to distinguish between workers in the public sector and those working for private industry. Public sector employees constitute approximately 11 percent of the total regular labor force in Japan. Approximately 28 percent of all union members are employed in the public sector. Legally, they are in a completely separate category from those employed in the private sector. As is becoming increasingly true throughout the industrialized countries, the political and economic problems associated with public sector employees are different from those facing industrial relations in private industry. The role played by public policy in labor-management relations differs considerably, depending on the group in question. Most importantly, public sector workers lack the legal right to strike. But the absence of this right has not prevented them from taking strike and other actions that have given them a more militant character than their private sector counterparts.

The picture of postwar Japanese unions, therefore, is one of relative impotence, both economically and politically. Plant-level relations have been largely quiescent. The picture changes when public sector unions have been involved, or when labor-management confrontations have been at the national level, pitting the peak business and labor associations against one another. Then for most of this period, labor-management relations in Japan have resembled the conflictual processes of France, Italy and, to some extent, Britain more than those in countries which have developed structures and ideologies for conciliation and harmonization, such as Sweden and West Germany. Only by the mid-1970s did signs of a consensual interaction emerge at the national as well as at the plant level.

Agenda

In contrast to their local member unions, the national labor federations in Japan have not been advocates of bread-and-butter unionism. Their ultimate goal, and that of the parties they support, has been to bring about fundamental alterations in Japan's entire socioeconomic system (see again Readings 2-2 and 2-4). In reality, through the mid-1970s, despite the rhetoric of class warfare and working-class solidarity, targets set by the federations were usually unambiguously directed at items that would benefit union members: a nationwide minimum wage, guaranteed employment, substantial unemployment benefits, minimum standards for health and safety in the workplace, limited hours for women and children, and the like. The main instrument to achieve these targets was to be a unified working-class movement, and for most of this period unification of labor was itself a goal.

In contrast, the bulk of the Japanese business community actively encouraged, or at least tacitly agreed with, the government's long-standing policies of sectoral development plus rapid economic growth, which were examined in the previous chapter. In their view, these would provide for long-term economic improvements that would benefit those at the lower end of the economic spectrum, union and nonunion alike. For such long-term gains to materialize, however, labor and management would have to coordinate their efforts to improve productivity, while labor would have to show wage restraint.

The hostility between business and labor at the national level has been mitigated by cooperation and coordination at the level of the individual firm. Individual unions in many private sectors of manufacturing have been principally concerned with the two traditional goals of most unions: economic benefits and job security. The latter has been particularly important for the unions, and most of the important strikes in private industry have revolved around worker dismissals. Conventional labor interests transcending the firm—such as national standards for union rights, minimum wages, or safety—have been less compelling. Broad goals of foreign policy or alterations in the political economy have usually seemed even more remote. Japan's larger, more capital-intensive, technically advanced, and economically successful private firms have often found it easier and more economically feasible to provide wage increases and job security to their regular workers rather than to face the threat of a strike or the need to rehire and retrain skilled workers.

Private sector unions, even though they are organized at the plant level, have thus helped ensure wage increases and have been important barriers against the arbitrary dismissal of workers that occurred frequently during the nonunionized prewar period and in several major instances immediately after the war. They have also made it difficult for employers to treat blue- and white-collar workers vastly differently, as they previously did, particularly in such matters as the allocation of bonuses. The power to strike has been the ultimate threat behind what limited powers these private sector unions possess.

This has not been the case with public sector workers. Civil service personnel in both national and local governments, as well as public school teachers, have the right to organize and negotiate, but they can not conclude collective-bargaining agreements, nor can they strike. Public service personnel in the various government corporations and enterprises (mint, agriculture and forestry, postal service, national railway, telephone and telegraph service, and the like), as well as local-government officials in similar positions, can bargain collectively but they too are denied the right to strike. Given the highly politicized character of many of these workers and their unions, and given the fact that the government is their employer, it is not surprising that one of the primary goals they have often sought has been the legal granting of the right to strike (Hanami, 1979; Harari, 1973).

The Japanese government has thus had a twofold set of problems. With private business in a relatively strong position vis-à-vis labor, especially at the plant level, government has not been forced to become heavily and actively involved in private sector labor-management relations. Passive maintenance of the status quo was in most cases adequate to ensure conservative ends. As will be seen in Chapter 5, the government was active in shifting certain policies in higher education to increase the number of scientists, technicians, and engineers. In 1963, it began to phase out the public sector unemployment-relief projects, a reduction which not only added to the pool of privately available labor but also cut sharply into the strength of one of Japan's larger unions, the Dayworkers Union. But firm intervention by the government into labor-management relations by a comprehensive manpower policy, by an incomes policy, by becoming the employer of last resort, or even by overseeing private collective bargaining, was given little systematic thought prior to the labor shortage in the late 1960s and the soaring inflation and international economic crisis of the mid-1970s. In this regard, Japan's government policies were quite different from those of Britain, Sweden, West Germany, and even the United States.

Yet when the economy was thrown into confusion during the mid-1970s, and when the private sector seemed faced with a choice between the terribly expensive retention of surplus labor and politically threatening dismissals, the government was ready to step into private sector labor-management relations. But as will be seen, its actions were designed largely to provide an economic buffer until private sector arrangements could be stabilized.

On the other hand, the government has had to get involved continually in problems of wages, job security, and working conditions that affect the 11 percent of the nation's work force that it employs. Since, unlike the procedure in Britain, virtually all agreements affecting public sector workers are subject to budgetary scrutiny by the Ministry of Finance and by the Diet, an additional element of politicization is added. And finally, as the executor of national laws the government is forced to take an active position whenever public sector workers violate the legal prohibition against strikes.

As a consequence of the government's dual role as activist and subdued bystander, the politicization of labor-management relations in Japan has been uneven. Problems of public employees, their bargaining power, and the legality or illegality of their right to strike have been politicized at the national level since the early years of the United States Occupation. Conversely, private sector labor management relations remained depoliticized for most of the postwar period, at least at the plant level.

Process

Since the status quo from the end of the Occupation until the early 1970s clearly favored business and government interests, pressures for changes in labor-management policy during this period were more frequently generated by labor. Throughout most of the postwar period, the government's major involvement in labor-management relations, however, involved only the public sector workforce. The mechanism for setting national government wages is straightforward. The National Personnel Authority (NPA), patterned very much on the United States Civil Service Commission, annually surveys the wage structure within the government and private industry. If private sector wages exceed those in the public sector by 5 percent or more, the NPA then makes recommendations to the Diet and cabinet for adjustments aimed at bringing government wages into line. Local public-service commissions perform a parallel role in determining salaries for local government employees, and the National Enterprise and Public Corporation Labor Relations Commission does so for those employed by public corporations. The government, however, retains the authority to determine whether or not to put the national level recommendations into effect. For much of the period since 1949, the NPA recommendations were not automatically implemented by the government. More typically, proposed wage increases were reduced or delayed for several months beyond the date recommended for implementation. Public sector wages thus invariably have lagged behind those in the private sphere.

This lag in public sector wages has exacerbated the demand by public sector unions that government return to them the right to strike that was lost under the Occupation. The left has long contended that Article 28 of the constitution guarantees the right to organize and to strike and that any subsequent restrictions on such rights are unconstitutional. And despite their illegality, railway, telecommunications, and postal-service unions in particular have carried out many "job actions." The official response has been to dismiss union leaders and, not infrequently, large numbers of participants. Between 1953 and 1975, over one million members of public corporations were dismissed for illegal union activities. In many instances, such punishments generated further labor actions and further punishments.

In 1958, several unions shifted the battleground over the right to strike by appealing to the International Labor Organization. They contended that government restrictions on public sector union activity violated the ILO's Convention No. 87 granting freedom of association and the right to organize (see Reading 3-4). After a long series of union appeals, ILO criticisms of Japanese labor practices, governmental promises, and procrastination, the ILO sent a mission to Japan in 1964, which among other things urged the Satō government to ratify Convention No. 87 (see Reading 3-5). Outside pressure led the government to an active reconsideration of the status quo. Eventually the government ratified the convention, and several of the legal provisions most offensive to labor unions were revised, but the right to strike was still not granted to public sector employees (Harari, 1973).

Instead, a series of government councils and advisory commissions were created, starting in 1965, to attempt to arrive at a politically acceptable formula for dealing with public strikes. Normally such bodies have been effective consensus-builders in Japan, but the range of viewpoints represented proved too divergent to coordinate. Thus, neither of the first two councils were able to come to unified positions on the problem, and the third council in late 1974 merely suggested the alternatives that existed: no changes in present laws and regulations; granting the right to strike to employees in some fields; granting the right to strike under certain conditions to employees of all public corporations and national enterprises. The government promised to reach a definite conclusion by autumn of 1975, but after a year and a half and thirty meetings by still another informal advisory committee the government was no closer to a decision.

At this point, public sector unions adopted another new tactic. Until then, most public sector "strikes" had really meant working strictly by rules (*junpō tōsa*). In 1975, led by the national railway union and other transportation unions, a ten day "strike for the right to strike" was called. Although the strike lasted for only eight days, its disruption succeeded in forcing another reconsideration of the issue by the government. Further study of the issue was promised, and in June, 1978 a government committee recommended converting certain government enterprises such as the national railways and the alcohol and tobacco monopoly to private enterprises and granting their employees the right to strike. But by 1980 these steps had not been taken.

Throughout the period, the government showed its tremendous ability to forestall change on a highly conflictual issue generating strong pressure from the political left. The study commissions that had frequently been so useful in reconciling differences within the conservative camp could not reach any consensus that would reconcile the diverse views of government and opposition.

The courts have also been an important force in upholding the legal restrictions on public sector strike activity. The closest the Supreme Court ever came to supporting an alternative position was in the Tokyo Central Post Office Case of 1966. There it held that, although the right to strike did not permit violence, the prohibition of all forms of strikes was overly inclusive and a literal interpretation of the ban was against the spirit of the constitution (see Reading 3-6). Following several changes in personnel, the court later reversed itself and, in 1973, reaffirmed the constitutionality of the total prohibition on public sector strikes. This position was repeated in a May, 1977 decision. As of 1980, all public sector strikes remained illegal, illustrating the important powers of the court system to reinforce the status quo.

The process of dealing with private sector union demands provides a more complicated mixture of consensus and conflict. Most settlements on wages and working conditions are made through negotiations at the plant level, which Dore (1973, pp. 171–76) has aptly characterized as an "ambivalent co-partnership" between labor and management. Collective bargaining is far less centralized than in Sweden, West Germany, or even the United States. Strikes are not at all impossible and Japanese law is liberal on matters of labor-union tactics in the private sphere. But paternalism, enterprise-consciousness, the threat of breakaway unions, and a host of other factors combine to weaken the bargaining position of most plant-level unions (Cole, 1971). In 1955, Sōhyō, in an effort to consolidate labor's power, introduced a new tactic which was to revolutionize much of the bargaining process in labor-management relations. The spring offensive (Shuntō) was to be a concerted campaign by workers in all industries to negotiate with business at the national level. In its first year, the spring offensive involved only eight industrial union federations, but in 1956 public employees joined and participation was about three million. Subsequently, Sōhyō was joined by Japan's third-largest labor federation, Chūritsu Rōren. In 1960, even Dōmei followed the same pattern, although it refrained from calling its activities Shuntō. During the spring offensive, a unified set of labor demands is drawn up by the participating unions and federations. These are presented to the national business federations by a national coordinating committee; then there are joint strikes and coordinated bargaining. Although the actual negotiations of contracts still take place at the level of the enterprise, unions try to coordinate their demands and tactics, usually refusing to negotiate until agreement has been reached by the most powerful unions, which are chosen to lead the year's bargaining. The conditions of this initial settlement then become the basis for subsequent settlements in other plants. Negotiations typically proceed rather quickly once the first several agreements have been reached.

Although spring offensives were effective as a tactic their impact was largely confined to wage increases. With the introduction in 1974 of The People's Spring Struggle (see Reading 3-3), demands of a more political and socioeconomic character were made nationally. However, these were rarely pressed effectively in negotiations by individual unions at the plant level. Hence, little progress was little progress was made in areas such as unemployment compensation, a national minimum wage, a five-day week, or the improvement of social welfare programs (see Chapter 4).

In the period of high economic growth and an increasing demand for labor that characterized the 1960s, Japanese workers fared increasingly well in wage negotiations. Real wage increases averaged 3.6% annually from 1960 to 1965, 8.8 percent from 1966 to 1970, and went up 7.4 percent, 10.6 percent and 10.6 percent in the following three years (Japan Labor Bulletin, Aug. 1, 1976, p. 5). The recession that began in the wake of the oil shock, however, forced a reassessment of past practices by union, business, and government. Faced with tremendous drops in demand, rising labor costs, and the prospect of major losses in market shares, many businesses pressed simultaneously for government assistance and for low wage increases. In the 1976 spring struggle, for example, the Japan Federation of Employers' Associations, the main opponent of the union federations, announced the united business position: zero or, at most, single-digit wage increases (see Reading 3-9), a far cry from the 33 percent rise in nominal wages that had been won in 1974.

While many plant-level unions greeted the demands for wage restraint with some sympathy, the national federations were extremely reluctant. The spring offensive had been having tremendous nominal success, and wage gains seemed essential to offset the rapid rise in the cost of living. But as productivity declined even in the advanced sectors of the economy, it became increasingly difficult for a divided labor movement to present a credible united front to demand high wage increases. During the 1975 spring offensive, there was a great deal of division along sectoral and firm lines. Several union leaders, such as Miyata Yoshiji of the Japan Federation of Iron and Steel Workers and Amaike Seiji of Dōmei, began proposing various forms of voluntary wage restraint.

By the 1976 spring struggle, labor's lack of unity was even clearer. The Private Railway Workers Union tried to break away from the "scheduled struggle" and to engage in "independent bargaining." Miyata this time went even further, suggesting a heretical proposal drawn from the British experience: wage increases would remain below the rate of increase in consumer prices in exchange for a government tax cut to improve the real income of workers. Although such actions were roundly criticized by many other leaders, particularly by those of the public sector unions, in fact the new wage-policy carried the day, and wage demands in the spring offensive shifted to demands of "maintaining employment" and "guaranteeing real wages."

Because contracts in Japanese firms are typically negotiated annually, and at approximately the same time in all major industries, such a solution also made it possible for Japan to avoid the inflationary spiral that plagued countries with longer term contracts and contracts that expire at different times in different industries. There, unions seeking to maintain parity must make demands based on living costs and settlements made with unions in other industries several months earlier. This provides a continually escalating spiral of demands, with industries passing on these increased labor costs to other industries and the consumer, triggering further wage demands aimed at maintaining purchasing power. The annual settlement in Japan, in contrast, makes it possible for business and labor in all major industries to reach agreements that are not only anti-inflationary but that do not necessitate a loss in the purchasing power of union members.

The trade-off of high nominal wage increases for tax cuts required the cooperation of government. Increasingly the government had shown some willingness to intervene in private sector bargaining and in 1974 passed the Employment Insurance Law. This was a comprehensive national policy to improve employment, to develop the abilities of individual workers, and to reduce the tendency of the unemployment system to provide the bulk of its benefits to the young, and to temporary, seasonal, and female workers. The bill also granted substantial subsidies to private businesses to prevent them from laying off workers. In particular, it provided money to employers who kept employees on paid furloughs rather than discharging them.

This new legislation helped tremendously to keep down Japan's macrolevel unemployment figure. But within the firm as well, there is a great deal of slack which can be taken up during economic downturns. The thought of skilled Sony craftsmen sweeping the plant or of middle-level Sanyo managers holding classes for unskilled workers idled during slowdowns reinforces the popular notion of permanent employment as a vital feature of Japanese labor-management relations.

Japanese firms used many measures to reduce labor costs during the recession: overtime was cut; employees were transferred within the firm, often to totally new skill-categories; work was shared; old activities in the plant were curtailed and new projects begun ahead of schedule; contracts of temporary or seasonal workers were stopped; early retirement was encouraged; and some workers were actually dismissed (see Reading 3-8). In the first two quarters of 1975, for example, over 50% of the firms surveyed by the Ministry of Labor had curtailed overtime, and only a slightly smaller percentage had reduced or stopped the hiring of mid-career workers; 20% were transferring workers internally and nearly 20% were giving temporary layoffs to regular employees.

Large Japanese firms whose unionization rates are high were quicker than medium-sized firms to use internal transfers, restrictions of overtime, and dismissal of temporary workers, while they were much slower in soliciting early retirements and in selective designated dismissals, options designed to be less objectionable to unions (Shimada, 1980, p. 26). Early retirements and dismissals were more frequent in the typically nonunionized small- and medium-sized firms.

Moreover, the Japanese employment system as a whole has a greater capacity to abosrb workers who are dismissed or forced into early retirement. One dimension of this is indicated in Table 3-1. The high level of self-employment in family businesses in Japan indicates a good deal of absorptive capacity if and when an individual is laid off or dismissed. For many, the alternative is to open one's own small shop or enter the family business. These alternatives are much less viable in the other major industrial countries. Moreover, because of the low level of unemployment benefits

TABLE 3-1   Employment Structures in Major Industrial Countries (1978)

	Japan %	U.S. %	Britain %	West Germany %	France %
1) Self-employed	17.8%	8.4%	7.7%	10.0%	18.6%*
2) Family workers	11.8	0.9	—	5.5	—
3) Employees	70.4	90.7	92.3	84.5	81.4

*Combines 1 and 2.
Source: Nihon Kokusei Zue, 1979, p. 102.

available in Japan, there is added incentive to find some form of employment very quickly.

The low Japanese unemployment figures are not a hoax by any means. Japanese firms are typically more reluctant than their Western counterparts to lower the ax at the first sign of a falloff in sales. But these firms do adjust their labor costs rather quickly during economic downturns. This becomes clear if one examines not only unemployment figures but also data on employment, overtime, job openings, women in the workforce, and movement into family enterprises or self-employment. Certainly shifts in these areas were dramatic in the mid-1970s; moreover, it is worth noting that many of the strategies followed in reducing labor costs during the recession of the mid-1970s, such as closing old facilities and developing new plants ahead of schedule, had by the beginning of the 1980s proved to be economically much sounder than layoffs.

Consequences

The most striking consequence of policies in the area of labor-management relations is the limited rights, privileges, and benefits which labor has managed to secure. The legitimacy of unions and union activity is explicitly recognized in law and by all parties to negotiations at both the plant and the national level. This legitimacy is a marked improvement over the status of unions during the prewar period and even over that in the Occupation period and the early 1950s.

Beyond this, it is clear that labor-management relations were an integral component of the government's economic policies. The success of the high-growth policies depended on preventing labor from crippling the conservative coalition; dividing the labor movement; restricting the right of public sector unions to strike; holding down wages and consumer purchases; and ensuring a talented and ample supply of labor.

But national economic success did not bring with it practical, long-term union achievements. The spring offensive, for example, improved real-wage levels during a period of economic boom and a tight labor market. But the fragility of the tactic is clear when one looks at labor-management relations and wage policy since the mid-1970s. The evidence demonstrates the problems of obtaining substantial increases in income during a period of much slower growth than during the previous twenty years.

If there have been severe restrictions in the power of organized labor to win real wage increases, the constraints have been even greater in other areas. Unionization rates have been constant or declining since the mid-1950s. Public sector employees still lack the basic rights their counterparts possess in most other industrialized countries. At the beginning of the 1980s, Japan had not passed a national minimum-wage law. National unemployment and pension benefis remained low and varied greatly among firms. Unions and union federations had gained virtually no formal role in the economic planning machinery of the country. Labor-management councils were rare at the industrial, regional, or national levels. Those that existed at the plant level are almost exclusively advisory in nature. In only one firm, Matsushita Electric, did labor participate in managerial decisions (Japan Labor Bulletin, Sept. 1, 1978, p. 4). And as will be shown in detail in Chapter 4, the unions were never able to increase social welfare benefits in the manner characteristic of Western Europe. From the standpoint of Japanese conservatives, all these features are marks of tremendous success; to labor, they are indications of failure.

At the same time, the life of the Japanese worker is by no means an oriental duplication of the unrelieved misery of those who worked in the "satanic mills" of 18th or 19th century Britain. Perhaps most significantly, for a large segment of the working population unemployment is not a major threat. Neither the Japanese government nor most large firms have needed to resort to extensive layoffs in periods of economic slowdown. Official Japanese unemployment figures undoubtedly conceal many pockets of underemployment, but there is no reason to suspect that the Japanese figures are any less credible than those of other countries.

Furthermore, non-wage benefits, particularly in the areas of social welfare, have been high for employees in many larger firms. The government has not been forced by the national labor federations to do for all its citizens what individual firms have often been forced or have voluntarily chosen to do for their permanent employees.

At the same time it will not do to suggest, as have many in the West, that benefits provided by the state are interchangeable with those provided by the employer. The histories of Germany, Britain, Sweden, and the United States show that while unions have pressed for state action primarily to benefit their union members, the benefits, once made available, have eventually spread to the general population. But in Japan private social welfare benefits have more typically accrued to unionized members of the most advanced firms, and these benefits have not been given to the population at large (see Chapter 4). Moreover, dispersed benefits are associated with the firm and the enterprise union and thus deradicalize the working class as a political force. Cooperation between management and labor at the plant level focuses primarily on particularistic benefits and avoids demands to restructure the entire economy or polity. Labor's wage-restraint in exchange for job security and tax cuts in the late 1970s is but one example of this.

One of the major factors impeding the development of Japanese unions has been the compact time-frame within which they developed. Since unions were illegal or suppressed during the prewar period, it seems logical that the movement had its beginning in the year 1945, far later than in Europe or North America. Japanese workers have not had the long process of socialization into a working-class ethic or of unionization consciousness such as existed, say, in Britain or France. Successive generations have not grown up imbued with labor consciousness. Furthermore, during the period since the end of the war, Japan's economy, like that in most capitalist countries, has undergone substantial changes. Large numbers of workers have moved out of the generally highly unionized industrial sector and into the typically much less highly unionized services and tertiary sectors. The interesting historical question is whether, given the timing of labor's unionization, and given the present complex nature of the Japanese economy, the long-term impact of labor on the social, economic, and political shape of Japan can ever be anything like that of the union movements in other industrialized countries.

Readings

3-1. MATSUSHITA WORKERS' SONG*

Japanese workers are traditionally loyal to the firms where they work. An example of this loyalty can be seen in the following company song which is sung by workers daily. It is not at all untypical. It may be worth noting, however, that following the economic shifts of the mid-1970s the emphasis on production for its own sake was dropped, and Matsushita developed a new song focusing less on productivity and more on harmony.

> For the building of a new Japan,
> Let's put our strength and minds together,
> Doing our best to promote production,
> Sending our goods to the people of the world,
> Endlessly and continuously,
> Like water gushing from a fountain.
> Grow, industry, grow, grow, grow!
> Harmony and sincerity!
> Matsushita Electric!

3-2. "UEDAGIN" UNION OFFICIAL'S SPEECH†

A further example of union loyalty to the firm can be seen in this speech by a union representative to new employees. Throughout the speech, the stress is on harmony, rather than on conflict, which is stressed by the national union federations.

We have three major goals before us: to create a bright and pleasant work place, to create a work place that has a passion for work, and to create a work place that is satisfying. All of you are automatically members of the union, and we hope you will cooperate with us and with the bank to achieve these goals. The history of

---

*Herman Kahn, *The Emerging Japanese Super State* (Englewood Cliffs, N.J.: Prentice-Hall, 1970), p. 110.

†Thomas P. Rohlen, *For Harmony and Strength* (Berkeley: University of California Press, 1974), pp. 179–81.

our union is part of the general story of postwar labor-union expansion. As you probably know, the American Occupation encouraged the establishment of unions, and throughout the land this was taken as a directive. The era of Japanese democratization and social modernization thus began, and labor consciousness developed rapidly. Unlike American unions however, most Japanese unions are company-centered. Our own organization, which was formed in 1946, shares in this general history. But many unions have acted politically and have, in some instances, failed to give cooperation to their companies. There are enterprises where a very large gap has developed between management and labor, to everyone's detriment in our opinion. As a rule, the more disruptive unions have been the least successful in raising wages and improving working conditions.

We might say that a company's management is a mirror that reflects the character of the company's union. That is, successful management and a well-run union are closely interrelated. If the union is cooperative, then so will management become cooperative, and vice versa. The reality of modern economics clearly indicates that companies grow and succeed as the workers grow and improve individually. Companies that succeed are places where their members enjoy their work and therefore work well. Wherever companies succeed, wages are higher and the general condition of life and work is better. . . .

Our procedures for negotiating any increase in base pay begin at the office level, where everyone is to discuss what amount the increase for the year should be. The results of these discussions pass from regional meetings to the central committee, where they are combined with the information collected by the union about wages in other comparable banks, increases in the cost of living, and the conditions of bank business. All of these serve to define our position for negotiations with management about increases in base pay, bonus, retirement pay, and other problems. Management has been very cooperative to date, and our rate of wage increase has been better than the other cooperative banks. Recently we have also been working with management to reduce the number of overtime hours so that we all have more time to ourselves. In conclusion, let us say that this union is your union. If you have problems of any kind please consult us. We exist for your benefit and for the benefit of all Uedagin people.

3-3. ON THE PEOPLE'S SPRING STRUGGLE AND THE UNITED STRIKE*

Until 1974, spring offensives concentrated on achieving additional benefits for union members. In 1974, there was a major shift, and the struggle became "The People's Spring Struggle." Its goals, while by no means unfavorable to union members, included many objects of a broader nature, designed to appeal to the general public.

March 24, 1974   Socialist Party of Japan

After the second central action, centered on the March 26 united strike, the spring struggle of 1974 is going to climax in a decisive battle scheduled for the first [ten days] of April. The second united strike, scheduled for March 26, is expected to be participated in by the Council of Government and Government Enterprise Workers Unions, transportation workers, local government workers, and private-industry workers' unions, which will press for people's demands, for institutional reforms, and for higher wages to the government and monopolies, with strikes and other mass action.

This year's spring struggle is developing in such a way as to justify the name "People's Spring Struggle," as will be clearly seen from the first central action from the end of February to the beginning of March, particularly from the March 1 united action and the March 3 people's rally against inflation, which were marked by an unprecedentedly high upsurge of people's struggle. If we examine the mobilization of workers and other peoples for these mass actions carried out under the leadership of the Joint Spring Struggle Committee, we will find the following fact. Usually in the past, the turnout of workers and other people were 30–40 per cent of the targets set, but this year, the actual turnout exceeded expectations, and the workers' actions were greatly expanded, as they held negotiations not only with the Government and government agencies concerned but also with the Federation of Economic Organizations, and other organizations of employers and enterprises. Further, during the March 1 strike, retails stores called a strike in protest against inflation, and large numbers of pensioners, farmers, physically handicapped persons, and people engaged in welfare work took part in the February 27 central rally held under the spon-

Japan Socialist Review no. 295 (March 15, 1974), pp. 3–5.

sorship of our Party. These facts show that this year's spring struggle is enjoying the support and sympathy of ordinary people.

The significance of this year's spring struggle lies in the fact that not only workers but also broad sections of people, including the low-income people who are hardest hit by inflation, are fighting in solidarity for their respective demands in order to defend their living. We consider that we should pay special attention to the following as this year's "people's spring struggle" develops.

First, we should not make the struggle for the defense of the living of low-income people and socially weak sections of the society a temporary or limited one. The Government has already made clear its intention to pay anti-inflationary allowances of ¥2,000 per head. Even if we succeed in winning anti-inflationary welfare-allowances of ¥30,000, as the Joint Spring Struggle Committee demands, this does not mean a solution of the problem. More important than this is to provide a social framework incorporating a sliding scale system, minimum wage system, and other measures, which will enable low-income people to increase their resistance to inflation, and this is precisely a struggle for institutional reforms. In short, it is possible that the government and monopolies may make certain concessions if they consider that if they pay a temporary allowance only this year, there would be no need to pay any more. Actually, the government and monopolies are arguing that political matters cannot be separated from economic questions and are adamantly refusing to make any concessions on sliding scales, minimum wage system [or] other institutional questions, or concessions which would be binding on them in the future, because they recognize the importance of such concessions from their own standpoint. Therefore, it is all the more important for our Party to clearly understand the importance of our struggle for a sliding scale and a minimum wage system, attach strategic importance to it in the people's spring struggle and strengthen struggles for them.

Secondly, it is important that workers, mainly transportation workers, demanded a change in the government's transport policy in the March 26 united strike. Transportation difficulties today are a headache even to the government and monopolies. The present situation is such that the principle of private enterprise based on economic rationalism is not sufficient to solve transportation problems in remote areas, not to speak of [overcrowdedness] in commuters' transportation in urban areas. It is one of the most important tasks imposed on the people's spring struggle to maintain transportation as a public enterprise for the benefit of ordinary people. It is necessary for our Party to powerfully encourage the transportation workers in their struggle and to strengthen our struggles for a change in the government's transport policy in urban areas and in the countryside, firmly uniting ourselves with local citizens.

Thirdly, it is necessary to pay special attention to the struggle to win back the right to strike for government and government enterprise workers. The question of winning back the right to strike is posed as an important task for this year's spring struggle. If, in spite of this, workers tend to avoid this question as different in nature from their economic demands, they are completely wrong. Even though we call this year's spring struggle the people's spring struggle, our struggle is essentially aimed at defending the living and rights of the working class. Furthermore, the right of government and government enterprise workers to strike is essential for the working class to win not only workers' demands but also people's demands. If there is a tendency to regard emphasis on the right of workers to strike as a selfish attitude of workers in the people's spring struggle, we cannot but say that they are playing into the hands of the government and monopolies. In replying to questions put by Socialist Diet members in the Diet, Prime Minister Tanaka said in order to divide workers that the Government considered the question of workers's right to strike as inseparable from enterprise form. It is necessary for us to repel such attacks on workers and further strengthen our struggle to win back the right to strike for government and government-enterprise workers.

Our Party has formed problem-by-problem project teams of Diet members concerning all the major tasks of the spring struggle and is developing struggles in the Budget Committee. It is necessary for our Party to make increased efforts for the victory of the people's spring struggle by further strengthening our endeavors in the Diet and successfully carrying out the March 26 united strike.

3-4. THE KAWAKAMI LETTER TO THE ILO*

In 1958, Sōhyō called upon the International Labor Organization to investigate the condition of public sector unions in Japan.

Japan Socialist Review no. 36 (April 15, 1963), pp. 60–66.

Although the ILO began some studies, its policy has traditionally been not to refer a case to its Fact-Finding and Conciliation Commission without the consent of the government concerned. As of 1963, the Japanese government had not given the needed permission. But it had begun to consider adopting ILO Convention 87 governing public sector union rights. This letter from the head of the Japan Socialist Party explains the party's opposition to the government's position, which it sees as giving rights with one hand and removing them with the other.

10th April, 1963

Mr. David A. Morse
Director General
International Labour Organisation
Geneva, Switzerland
Dear Mr. Morse:

As the Chairman of the Central Executive Committee of the Japan Socialist Party, I beg to avail myself of the opportunity presented by the visit of Mr. Toru Ohara, M.P. to express my deepest appreciation for the strenuous efforts you and your organisation are making on behalf of the workers of the world to secure their legal position, improve their working conditions, develop a good social security system and, generally, to achieve a higher standard of living.

At the same time, I want to express my admiration for the efforts made by your Secretariat in trying to solve very difficult problems and in studying the legal structures of the countries of the world. Such study is complicated by the very different historical and social conditions in each country.

My Central Executive Committee officially requested Mr. Ohara, Vice Chairman of the "Special Committee for the Early Ratification of the ILO Convention," to explain the position of my Party on the problems of getting ratification in Japan.

I earnestly hope that his report and my letter will be useful to you in your continuing efforts to settle questions still before you, because the Japan Socialist Party, as the largest opposition party representing the workers, is vitally interested in expediting the solution of the "Japanese Problem" in the ILO.

First, I would like to explain the current differences between the Socialist Party and the Liberal-Democratic Party which is now in power and occupying two-thirds of the total seats in the Diet. As you are already aware, the Government was forced by public opinion in Japan as well as from abroad to present a bill to ratify ILO Convention No. 87. But, in order to counterbalance the effect this Convention would have on labour relations here, it also presented some bills to review certain existing labour statutes. These the government attached to the ILO ratification bill as one package.

In order to conform to the Convention, the Government agreed to delete Section (3) of Article 4 of the Public Enterprises Labour Relations Law and Section (3) of Article 5 of the Local Public Enterprises Labour Relations Law. However, the Government intends at the same time to revise statutes covering employees in Government offices and public enterprises and to alter even the National Railway Management Law so that workers would be subject to harsher punitive actions. If the Government-proposed amendments were approved by the Diet, the following regressions would occur:

(1) Workers could not work as full-time union officers without losing their job status;

(2) Union dues could no longer be checked off, though this practice has existed for years;

(3) Instructions by union headquarters to go on strike would not be binding on the members;

(4) Employers could unilaterally decide those eligible for union membership;

(5) The scope of and participation in negotiations would be very limited;

(6) Employees' political activities would be restricted;

(7) The functions of the National Personnel Authority would be transferred directly under the Government. (The National Personnel Authority was established as an independent body to compensate for the denial of the right to civil servants to bargain collectively.)

The Socialists argued against the restrictive aims of the Government. They insisted that the Convention must be ratified immediately with changes only in the articles of the laws which contradicted the Convention. They felt that the Government's plan to take advantage of the ratification bill to amend other laws in a way unfavorable to workers violates the very essence of the ILO Convention.

I can assure you that the Japanese Socialists are willing to cooperate with the ILO in every way as the ILO strives to fulfil its historic mission. The Japanese Socialists well know that the guarantee of rights for workers is not only a barometer of a people's good and stable life but is also the foundation for prosperity for all people and the basis for world peace by eliminating unfair competition in International Trade. These beliefs, I think, are fully in keeping with the very spirit of the ILO as well as the Japanese Constitution.

With my sincerest greetings,
Yours faithfully,
Jotaro Kawakami
Chairman
Central Executive Committee
Socialist Party of Japan

3-5. FREEDOM OF ASSOCIATION FOR PUBLIC SECTOR EMPLOYEES*

With the permission of the Japanese government, the ILO sent a fact-finding mission to Japan to investigate the conditions of public sector unions. Headed by Erik Dreyer of Denmark, the group filed a massive 500-page report. The following excerpts illustrate the mission's criticisms of both government and union rigidities, but in particular they show the ILO's criticism of government policy up until that time. Both the failure to recognize the legality of some unions and the rigidities surrounding the settlement of wages in the public sector were particularly noted.

Right to Strike in the Public Sector

2134. The fundamental divergence of view which continues to dominate labour relations in the public sector in Japan relates to the right to strike. The General Council of Trade Unions is pledged to continue to pursue its goal of the *total restoration* of the right to strike for public employees; the Government's view as expressed to the Commission during the hearings was that the *absolute prohibition* of the right to strike should be maintained indefinitely in the public sector.

*International Labour Office, *Official Bulletin* 49, no. 1 (January, 1966): pp. 490–93. Footnotes have been deleted.

2135. The Commission regards both these views as unduly rigid and unrealistic. It believes that in Japan as in other countries a reasonable compromise is both possible and necessary in the matter.

2136. In those areas of the economy which are truly essential and in which strikes would disturb critically the normal life of the nation, special measures may be necessary to protect the public interest. The general public demands and expects this. In such cases strikes may be prohibited, provided that adequate compensatory means of settlement or redress are established and function in practice in a satisfactory manner. On the other hand, it cannot be accepted that the activities of all public corporations and national and local enterprises are equally essential. In those which are less essential, the public interest does not require that all strikes be equally prohibited.

2138. While the Government has tended to treat all acts of dispute as illegal, the unions have adopted the converse attitude of assuming all such acts to be legal. This conception that all such acts are legal the Commission must utterly reject. The Freedom of Association and Protection of the Right to Organise Convention, 1948 (No. 87), specifically provides that, "In exercising the rights provided for in this Convention, workers and employers and their respective organisations, like other persons or organised collectivities, shall respect the law of the land". While the Convention adds that "The law of the land shall not be such as to impair, nor shall it be so applied as to impair", the guarantees provided for therein, this qualification does not impair the obligation of respect for legality. In the view of the Commission, acts of dispute do not become either legal or illegal because they are acts of dispute. Their legality or illegality depends on their nature.

2139. The future of labour relations in Japan will depend in large measure on the wholehearted acceptance of this principle by Government and trade unions alike. There is no Convention, Recommendation, or other decision of the International Labour Conference defining the extent of the right to strike in public services, but the Governing Body Committee on Freedom of Association has formulated a series of principles on the matter which has won general acceptance. These principles are essentially—

   (a) that it is not appropriate for all publicly owned undertakings to be treated on the same basis in respect of limitations of the right to strike without distinguishing in the relevant legislation between those that are genuinely essential because their interruption may cause serious public hardship and those which are not essential according to this criterion;

   (b) that, where strikes by workers in essential services or occupations are restricted or prohibited, such restriction or prohibition should be accompanied by adequate guarantees to safeguard to the full the interest of the workers thus deprived of an essential means of defending occupational interests;

   (c) that impartial machinery should be established for this purpose, the decisions of which should be fully and promptly implemented once they have been made.

The Commission endorses these principles; they are not yet accepted in Japan.

Compensation Measures in Cases where Strikes Are Prohibited

2142. The Commission has considered with special care how far the prohibition of strikes is accompanied by satisfactory alternative arrangements for settling questions relating to conditions of work or redressing grievances. It is far from satisfied that the present arrangements for this purpose are adequate.

2147. The principle that awards and collective agreements should be binding on both sides and should be fully and promptly implemented is most imperfectly applied. Under both the Public Corporation and National Enterprise Labour Relations Law and the Local Public Enterprise Labour Relations Law collective agreements, and in certain cases, arbitration awards are voidable by action or lack of action on the part of either the Diet or local public bodies. Awards of the Public Corporation and National enterprise Labour Relations Commission which call for the expenditure of funds not provided for in the current budget of the corporation or enterprise must be submitted to the Diet for the additional appropriation before they can be implemented. Collective agreements and arbitration awards under the Local Public Enterprise Labour Relations Law which contravene a local public body's by-laws or call for the expenditure of funds not available from the budget or funds of the local public enterprise are not implemented until the by-law is amended or the appropriation made. The complainants contend that many agreements are rejected on these grounds and that the mere existence of such provisions means that only dis- advantageous agreements are concluded. The Government has not given any indication that it is willing to make substantial changes in the existing procedures.

2148. In the view of the Commission the existence of these legislative provisions and the practices which they have induced cannot help but undermine confidence in the equity and utility of collective bargaining and arbitration procedures; the Commission accordingly recommends early and thorough reconsideration of the position in this respect, in the light of the recommendations made by the Committee on Freedom of Association.

3-6. THE TOKYO CENTRAL POST OFFICE CASE*

In 1966, the Japanese Supreme Court ruled that public sector unions were entitled to take certain job actions bordering on strikes. The basis of their decision was Article 28 of the Japanese Constitution which guarantees "the rights of workers to organize and to bargain and act collectively." During the labor offensive of 1958, officials of the National Postal Service Union urged employees of the Tokyo Central Post Office to leave work and to hold a rally. Following the walkout, those who left and their leaders were charged with violating the Public Enterprise Labor Relations Law. Although lower courts ruled in favor of the government, the Supreme Court held in favor of the appellants.

1. Article 28 of the Constitution guarantees the fundamental rights of workers, that is, the right to organize and to bargain and act collectively. These guarantees derive from the fundamental idea of Article 25 of the Constitution which provided that "all people shall have the right to maintain the minimum standards of whole- some and cultured living." On the premise that a life worthy of human beings is to be guaranteed to workers, the Constitution guarantees, on the one hand, the right to work in Article 27 and, on

---

*Hiroshi Itoh and Lawrence Ward Beer, *The Constitutional Case Law of Japan* (Seattle: University of Washington Press, 1978), pp. 90–91.

the other hand, in Article 28 the rights of workers to organize, to bargain collectively, and to resort to dispute activities, as the means to secure substantive freedom and equality to workers standing in a disadvantageous economic position.

A statute curtailing the fundamental rights of workers should be construed reasonably in light of the Constitution, which provides for the guarantee of these fundamental rights so as to be in conformity with the spirit of the constitutional guarantee. Under the Constitution, which guarantees the right to maintain minimum standards of wholesome and cultured living as one of its fundamental concepts, and which, along with the guarantee of the right to own property, enumerates the guaranteed rights of workers to work, to organize, to bargain collectively, and to resort to dispute activities, a legal interpretation of the substantive law curtailing fundamental rights of workers must be both sound and reasonable when interpreting the statute so as to maintain harmony and balance between these two groups of rights.

The fundamental rights of workers are guaranteed not only to employees in private enterprises but also, as a rule, to employees of public corporations and for workers engaged in national or local public services; for these public employees are not different from the workers mentioned in Article 28 of the Constitution. So it is not permissible, in our opinion, to deny these fundamental rights to public employees by relying on the provision of Article 15, which states, "all public officials are servants of the whole community and not of any group thereof." As will be explained later, the fundamental rights of workers engaging in public services or in public enterprises involve restrictions different from that of private enterprises only according to the nature of their duties. . . .

3-7. THE LABOR ECONOMY OF 1976*

One of the major concerns of the Japanese Ministry of Labor has been ensuring an adequate labor supply for business' needs. The aging of the workforce, coupled with Japan's traditionally early retirement ages, meant that a large potential workforce would be left untapped. The following excerpts from the 1976 Labor Ministry

*Rōdōshō, *Rōdō Hakusho 1976* (Tokyo: Ōkurashō Insatsukyoku, 1977), pp. 153–65.

*White Paper show the ministry's concern over this problem and some
of the steps being encouraged to take advantage of the availability of
older workers.*

Problems in the Labor Economy under Stable Economic Growth

The Aging Society and Workers' Lives

The change in the economic environment resulting from the shift
from high growth-rates to stable growth and the growing advancement in the age of the workforce will have a great influence on the
lives of working people.

As workers age, the demands they make rise accordingly. So far,
the seniority-based wage system has been able to cope with these
rises. In addition non-wage benefits, facilities, and institutions provided by private companies have also contributed to satisfying lives
for working persons.

However, since 1965, the wage-by-age curve has flattened rapidly; company facilities and institutions for welfare have begun to
manifest certain changes. In the meantime, working-people's lives
have also begun to change with their changing needs. Given that the
future will see a shift to the aging society, what kind of policy is
necessary to give stability to working-people's lives? We should
begin any investigation of future problems by investigating the
changes that are taking place in the life-structure of people of
middle and advanced age.

*Responses of Employers and Labor Unions to the
Aging of the Workforce*

With the aging of the workforce likely to expand in the future,
companies will be forced to take measures to cope with the needs of
the increasing number of middle-aged and older employees.

According to the "Survey of Trends in the Labor Economy"
conducted by the Ministry of Labor (February 1977), 79 percent of
all enterprises in manufacturing and 59 percent of the wholesale and
retail businesses are showing increases in the average age of their
employees. Thirty-three percent of all manufacturing industries
and 25 percent of the wholesale and retail businesses have started to
take some measures regarding the aging of their respective work
forces. Thirty-five percent of the manufacturing industries and 32

percent of the wholesale and retail businesses have not yet begun any concrete measures but are studying possible measures.

Far more large companies and companies in the heavy and chemical industries employ increasing numbers of older employees and have started to enforce some countermeasures for the problem than is the case in medium- and small-sized companies or in light manufacturing. Big companies and those in the heavy and chemical industries thus appear to be more conscious of the problem of aging. This is probably because the phenomenon of an older workforce has appeared there more recently than in the medium- and small-sized companies and in the light industries and also because of the heightened sense of crisis to the age-advancement of the workforce in those sectors. This latter is due largely to increasing costs caused by the seniority-based wage system and by difficulties in reducing the number of middle-aged and elderly employees under conditions of low economic growth.

Among the measures currently enforced by big companies, the most numerous involve "extension of the retirement age, reemployment and the extension of employment." These constitute 56 percent of all measures. "Transfer to related companies" (51%), "personnel reshuffles" (35%), "introduction of a merit-based wage system" (24%), "flattening the seniority-based wage curve" (21%) and "retraining" (22%) are measures also frequently implemented. There is almost no mention of "voluntary retirements or dismissals."

Thus, the larger companies retain their middle-aged and older workforce by extension of the retirement age, reemployment, and personnel reshuffles. At the same time, they try to make positive use of such employees through retraining and through improvement of job methods suitable for the older employees. On the other hand, they are, for the present, also trying to cope with the problem by transferring personnel to related companies and by developing the abilities of these older employees to change jobs.

According to the Labor Ministry's "Employment Control Survey" of January 1976, 47 percent of the companies with a uniform retirement age set the age at 55 while 32 percent set it at 60. From 1971 to 1973, 59% of the companies which extended their retirement age raised the level from 55 to 60 but between 1974 and 1975 this figure was only 17 percent. The retirement ages of the companies vary according to the company size. In case of companies with 30 to 99 employees, 37 percent have a retirement age of 60. Corresponding figures for companies with more than 5,000 employees and for those between 1,000 and 4,999 employees are 18 percent and 19 percent respectively.

Only 0.4 percent of the companies which have different retirement ages for male and female employees, set 54 years or less as the retirement age for their male employees while in contrast, 68.6 percent set their retirement ages for female employees below 54.

Although the number of companies whose retirement age is still 55 fell below one-half of all companies in 1976, many difficulties remain in further extending the retirement age.

Recent trends show that the tempo has slowed down under the conditions of low economic growth. Eleven percent of the companies with uniform retirement ages extended their retirement age during the three years between 1971 and 1973, while only 4 percent did so during the two years between 1974 and 1975.

According to the Ministry of Labor's "Fact-finding Survey on the Employment of Older Employees" (June, 1976), 18 percent of all enterprises did not employ, as permanent employees, those over 55 years of age. Moreover, fifty-six percent of the enterprises have not yet attained the target of 6 percent older workers set in the "Provisional Law on the Promotion of the Employment of Middle-Aged and Older Persons."

When employment ratios are examined according to company size, it is clear that many of the medium- and small-size enterprises employ relatively large numbers of older workers. In contrast, more than 70 percent of the companies with more than 300 employees have fewer than 6 percent aged employees.

Seventy-one percent of all enterprises retain employees who have passed the retirement age, of which 10 percent grant both "extension of employment and reemployment" while 39 percent grant "extension of employment" and 31 percent "reemployment." Among larger firms, the percent of companies which receive reemployed persons is rather high.

Many obstacles to the extension of retirement age remain, among which are problems of personnel mobility, the simple difficulties of personnel reshuffle, and wage-related problems such as increase in wages and retirement allowances.

In the future, to promote an extension of the retirement age it will be necessary not only to strengthen existing policies but also to make changes in the wage- and retirement-allowance system and the seniority-based personnel management system. Such proposals were advanced in two reports submitted to the Minister of Labor by private sector groups: "On the Extension of the Retirement Age and Wage System" by the Wage Study Group (December 1972) and "Employment Policies for the Ten Years 1975–85" by the Investigation and Study Group on Employment Policy (December 1975). An increasing number of companies have started to implement measures in line with the points of view expressed in these reports.

Although one of the biggest obstacles to the extension of the retirement age is the delay in the revision of the wage system and the retirement-allowance system, there have been recent examples in which the total wage is divided into two portions, one based upon seniority and one based upon merit. The seniority-based portion of the wage is then kept unchanged after a certain age is reached. And according to one Labor Ministry Survey, 21 percent of all enterprises have already started to implement policies designed to "flatten out the seniority-based wage curve." Another 29 percent plan to enforce such policies in the future.

Of the personnel-management problems cited as hampering the extension of the retirement age, the most numerous are that "the jobs or work-environment are not suitable for older employees and that "personnel mobility is hindered." Big companies are especially conscious of such problems posed by stagnation in personnel mobility. To counter such problems, some companies have adopted a "specialized-job system" or a "retirement-age system for managerial personnel." Some companies have also established "centers for middle-aged and older employees" to enforce general policies designed to open up new jobs for older employees, and to aid them in making preparations for their retirement through the establishment of adult schools and by granting aid for extra-company correspondence education and the encouragement of physical exercise.

On the other hand, since 1970, labor unions have begun to diversify their demands to include things other than wage increases. They have been especially interested in demands related to problems of the older workforce, including demands for increases in the retirement allowance and for extensions of the retirement age.

According to the Labor Ministry's "Fact-finding Survey on Wage

Increases," the number of labor unions demanding increases in the retirement allowance rose from 22 percent of all unions in 1971 to 41 percent in 1976. In 1974, 11 percent of the demands presented were accepted as presented. This percentage dropped slightly, to 6 percent in 1976. In that same year, 33 percent of the demands were accepted after being partially revised. Demands for an extension of the retirement age increased from 16 percent of all demands submitted in 1971 to 27 percent in 1974 and to 25 percent in 1975 and 1976. In 1974, 22 percent of these demands were accepted without change, while 25 percent were accepted with some revisions. The corresponding figures for 1976 were 8 percent and 14 percent. On the other hand, in spite of the increase in these demands, there were many cases in which no agreement was reached or in which the demands were submitted to further negotiations. The difficulty of the problem of extending the retirement age can be seen from the fact that 38 percent of the cases did not reach any agreement, and another 35 percent had to be submitted to further negotiation in 1976.

Although many aspects of intracompany welfare have been developing, especially in big companies, policies for the older workforce are still inadequate. This is partly because the number of the older employees is relatively small in big companies. However, the aging of the workforce is expected to continue in every sector, and both employers and labor unions must try to cope with the problem more seriously.

Wages and fringe benefits will be heavily influenced by the tempo with which the aging of the workforce occurs, by the needs of the employees of older age and by employer and labor union policies.

3-8. RECESSION DICTATES ADJUSTMENTS IN EMPLOYMENT LEVELS*

During the economic downturn of the mid-1970s, many Japanese firms sought to retain their permanent work staff rather than to cut costs by layoffs. The Ministry of International Trade and Industry undertook a survey of alternatives that were followed. Below is an official description of the survey's findings.

Japan Report 24, no. 4 (Feb. 16, 1978): 4–5.

A recent survey of the Ministry of International Trade and Industry (MITI) showed that a "Japanese" way of adjusting employment levels has emerged as a response to current low-growth economy. The survey was conducted by the Labor Mobility Research Council, an organization within MITI, and supervised by Professor Shizuo Matsushima of the University of Tokyo. Questionnaires on labor mobility during the last three years were sent to some 900 companies listed on the Tokyo Stock Exchange; 485 replies were received.

According to the survey, 90 percent of the companies sampled were either carrying out or planning to carry out some sort of employment adjustment by reducing the number of new workers hired, by not replacing workers who retired or by relocating workers within the same enterprise. It was also learned that 25 percent of the companies surveyed were studying the possibility of transferring surplus workers to affiliated companies and thereby modifying the principle of lifetime employment.

A paternalistic lifetime-employment system, in which a worker once hired stays employed until mandatory retirement age, has been a distinctive feature of employment practices in Japanese companies. This system has kept Japan's unemployment rate within the 2 percent level even during the most serious recession. Since the oil crisis of 1973, however, business managers have come to realize that the days of high economic growth are over and a time of low growth has arrived. As a result, an increasing number of companies are resolutely pushing retrenchment drives, and MITI's labor-mobility survey reveals how employment is being affected.

The survey determined that the number of workers employed by the companies surveyed declined 2.2 percent from fiscal 1974 to 1975 and by 2.8 percent from fiscal 1975 to 1976, thus registering two consecutive years of decline. Employment cuts have been most notable among female workers. Not replacing workers who retire and reducing the number of new workers are the principal means of decreasing employment. In fiscal 1976 in particular, 67.4 percent of the companies either stopped recruiting new workers or reduced the number of new workers. As a consequence, the average age of employed workers has been rising yearly, and reached 33.2 in fiscal 1976.

Many other types of employment adjustment are also being

enforced. By fiscal 1976, one out of every three companies had carried out intracompany relocation of workers from one department to another. The ratio rises to 90 percent when companies planning such relocations are included. Most worker relocations are between production departments. This is followed by shifts from managerial and administrative jobs to sales departments and from production jobs to sales departments. The companies cite falling demand and shrinking production as the major reasons for worker relocation, followed by the streamlining of corporate organizations.

Although the average age of workers is rising, 45.4 percent of the companies said they did not plan to extend the mandatory retirement age. In June 1976, the Government established a corporate guideline extending the mandatory retirement age to 60 and reemploying those who retire at 60 for another four years. Asked about this guideline, 37.3 percent of the companies replied that is was the Government's responsibility to guarantee the livelihood of senior citizens.

In connection with the survey, MITI officials interviewed representatives of 98 companies in the textile and machinery industries. The interviews showed that recession, layoffs of non-regular workers, reduced-pay furloughs for regular workers and reducing the number of new workers hired were carried out before such actions were taken in other industries. It was also found that encouraging workers to retire early by offering them incentive-severance pay was very helpful in adjusting employment levels. In the electric-appliance manufacturing industry, employment adjustment appears to have been less extensive than in the textile industry, since the recession in the electric-appliance field is expected to prove to be only a cyclical downturn.

3-9. BUSINESS'S OPPOSITION TO ANY WAGE INCREASES*

Following double-digit wage increases throughout most of the late 1960s and the early 1970s, the Japan Federation of Employers' Associations in the recession of 1976 called for unified business

Nikkeiren News 55 (March 1976): 1–4.

resistance to such big jumps. The following reading gives their rationale.

How Wage Settlements Ought to Be Reached in the Immediate Future

1. Three Basic Points of Recognition

The Japanese economy has entered a new stage but it is still in the process of adjustment. A new stable course has yet to be charted. It is difficult, therefore, to present here a long-range vision of Japanese wages. Yet it is clear that whether future wage increases are reasonable or not is a major question that determines the long-range course of the Japanese economy. From such a point of view, wages should be determined in the immediate future along the following lines:

Firstly, it must be kept in mind that the funds required for wage increases can be made available only through improvement of productivity, which means, in macroeconomic terms, real growth of the economy and in microeconomic terms, expansion of the paying capacity of individual enterprises. Only when these conditions exist is it possible to improve real wages without undue difficulties. Unless these conditions exist, real wages will not be increased even if nominal wages are increased. Therefore, productivity is the key to wage increases. However, difficulties are expected to increase in this area, so that further cooperative efforts between management and labour are called for. It must be also kept in mind that if the economy's real growth rate declines from previous levels the real rate of increase in wages must also decline.

Secondly, the continuing growth and development of the Japanese economy always requires the maintenance and strengthening of its international competitiveness. If wage increases lead to the decline of industry's international competitive position, the existence of enterprises will be threatened, with a resulting increase in unemployment. Such a situation must be avoided at all costs. However, this point has not been taken into full account in the Japanese wage increases awarded in the years following the oil shock, despite the fact that the international economic environment had drastically changed. As a result, the competitiveness of Japanese industry declined.

Thirdly, inflation must be avoided. The Japanese economy is becoming increasingly vulnerable to inflationary pressures, what with the constraints imposed on its growth by the limited availability of natural resources and the decline in its growth potential. Therefore, a resurgence of inflation must be avoided now that it is coming under control. If inflation rises again, the vicious circle of wages and prices will begin again, destroying the national economy and ruining the lives of the Japanese people and social welfare.

2. Reviewing Wage-Determining Factors

What about the paying capacity of individual enterprises? In Japan business failures have sharply increased during the past two years. In this bleak situation corporations are enduring persistent deficits on the books while they are under constant pressure to meet their payroll needs. It is therefore necessary, first of all, to raise productivity and thereby improve business performance and increase the paying capacity. In other words, the standard theory of productivity formulated earlier by Nikkeiren must be confirmed anew. In the past, however, this theory has not been observed because wage increases have been awarded on the basis of those in high-productivity industries. In the background, of course, was the fact that the Japanese economy was faced with a chronic labour shortage. Thus, even in low-productivity sectors it was impossible to secure fresh labour unless similar wage increases were granted. The upshot of this, if considered in the context of the national economy was to increase upward pressures for consumer prices. The present situation, however, is completely different in that enterprises are saddled with surplus employment and plagued by continued deficits. Individual enterprises should consider wage increases to an extent commensurate with their paying capacity, particularly their paying capacity based on the improvement of physical productivity. If wages are increased beyond that extent, the very existence of present employment may be endangered. . . .

3. How 1976 Wage Increases Ought to Be Determined

The Committee to Study the Outcome of Large Wage Increases, in the report published on 5 November 1974, declared: "As an interim step leading to moderate wage increases, the average rate of wage increase for fiscal 1975 should be kept below 15 percent through talks between management and labour in both the public and private sectors. For fiscal 1976 and thereafter, a wage guidepost limiting increases to a one-digit percentage figure should be observed."

Thereafter, the committee continued to study wage increases for fiscal 1976, and results of that study have confirmed the committee's belief that there is no need to change the basic recognition set forth in its original report. To put it more specifically, the commiteee believes that wage increases should be considered in the light of widening wage-gaps that exist in different industries and regions. In some industries it may be necessary to even suspend wage increases. And where wage increases are possible the rate of increase will have to be limited to the one-digit level.

4 Social Welfare: The Tentative Transition

"Social welfare" defies precise definition. It usually refers to a broad array of efforts designed to promote the well-being of individuals deemed in need of assistance. Most typically it includes programs designed to aid the elderly, the injured, the sick, and the poor. A wider perspective would include education, housing, corrections, and even agricultural assistance. Taken to its logical extreme, the concept becomes broader still. As William Graham Sumner wrote in 1881, ". . . the human race has never done anything else but struggle with the problem of social welfare. That struggle constitutes history, or the life of the human race on earth" (Tratner, 1979, p. xii). Although "welfare" is a flexible term, in this study it will be restricted to its more common usage, namely, efforts to alleviate the most pressing and destructive miseries of the poor, especially the elderly, the ill, and the injured.

A nation's efforts in the area of social welfare are, perhaps next only to the conditions of its penal institutions, one of the most insightful indicators of its approach to questions of humanity and social justice. Increasingly, most advanced industrial societies are adopting certain common minima in areas of social welfare (Heclo, 1974; Wilensky, 1975). Yet a country's overall commitment to such minima and the composition of the programs to achieve them differ drastically from one country to another.

What is most striking in the case of Japan is the historical importance of private rather than public efforts to cope with most problems of social welfare. The Japanese government began its programs later and funded them at much lower levels than most other industrialized countries. With the exception only of health insurance, introduced in 1922, Japan had little public commitment to social welfare programs until the 1960s. Even then, efforts were small scale. In most respects, the government's approach to social welfare was the logical corollary to its policies in economics and labor-management relations: it did little in social welfare that might interfere with industrial development, economic growth, and the power of employers over employees. As a result, through the 1960s Japanese government spending for social welfare was by far the lowest in the industrialized world. Monies not spent for welfare were, therefore, available for the support of private enterprise, development of an industrial infrastructure, and high economic growth.

The success of national economic policies and the high levels of macroeconomic growth achieved by Japan in the 1950s and 1960s led to public and some bureaucratic questioning of national priorities. What was the purpose of all the growth? Should industrial expansion occur for its own sake? Was there no need to give increased attention to improving the quality of life within the country? A widescale reevaluation of the country's past approaches to social welfare grew out of such questioning, and programs were introduced by a wide range of bureaucratic agencies. Yet commitment in principle did not completely alleviate the tension between social welfare measures and government economic policies. Throughout the 1970s there was a good deal of political battling over the extent to which increased social welfare efforts were economically feasible or industrially desirable, as well as over which agencies should supervise welfare programs.

Throughout the world, most social welfare efforts have involved programs that, once begun, have been difficult to eliminate or reduce. Thus, the question that haunts Japanese political leaders is whether a full-scale commitment to social welfare programs will undercut long-term economic goals. While more welfare may appear politically astute in the short run, there is reluctance to let Japan imitate the European welfare state. The official fear is that a rejection of the long national tradition of minimal state involvement and reliance primarily on private assistance will lead to programs which develop political constituencies and an economic momentum of their own, as happened in Europe and North America. If this occurs, the result could be expanding public expenditures, less flexibility in the selection of economic goals, and a fundamental change in the government's essential priorities. Yet failure to move in such a direction may eventually reduce the political support for the dominant coalition, a reduction which could well result in many of the same consequences.

Context

Until the turn of the century, in most western societies it was historically the duty of the individual to provide for his or her own welfare. Gainful employment was, of course, the most obvious way to do so. Providence in spending and sensitivity to the creation of a nest egg were considered logical guarantors against the rainy day when old age, invalidity, or unemployment might eliminate one's ability to provide. While churches, charities, philanthropists, and local agencies often took it upon themselves to assist the most needy individuals, care was usually taken to prevent such assistance from eroding the incentive to self-help, hard work, and diligence. Although approaches differed from country to country, England's Poor Laws and work houses were a typical combination designed to discriminate between the "deserving" and "undeserving" poor (Heclo, 1974).

Toward the end of the 19th century, some of the more industrialized countries of Europe began to act contrary to this fundamental principle. Faced with persistent unemployment, more visible poverty, and illness, plus in many instances pressures from a growing labor movement, the governments of Germany, Austria, Britain, and Sweden developed social insurance and relief programs in the late 19th and early 20th centuries. With time, such programs expanded in scope and moved beyond the coverage of isolated individuals to provide assistance for entire categories of society presumed to need collective help, such as the elderly and the sick. Along with this, the conception of which groups needed public aid and the standards for receiving aid also expanded. Not long after World War II, most of these countries were well on their way to providing the "cradle-to-grave" protection associated with the modern welfare state. In such countries, contemporary social welfare measures seek to ensure that all of society's destitute and needy will enjoy living standards approaching the average standards of the community.

In Japan, social conditions and government actions were different. As has been noted, Japan's industrialization began relatively late and was carried out under the dominance of a conservative political coalition. While many Japanese leaders sought to pattern their country's development on the experiences of Germany, this emulation did not extend to copying Bismarck's efforts in social policy.

Six years after the Meiji Restoration, the government issued a relief regulation that made public financial assistance available to those under fourteen, or over seventy, as well as to the chronically ill. But, in 1890, the lower house of the Diet defeated a bill to expand the country's limited relief efforts, contending that any expansion would simply encourage indolence and would strain the government's budget at a time when the threat from abroad was great. Such penury characterized the official approach to social welfare throughout the prewar period. The only significant exceptions were the relatively generous benefits provided to servants of the state—the civil service and the military (see Reading 4-3). Public neglect toward the misfortunate was only partially relieved by reliance on local and private voluntarism.

Setting the pattern for such efforts was a system begun in Okayama Prefecture in 1917. There, eminent local citizens served as voluntary welfare councillors, each one supervising a single welfare district. Following a series of violent disturbances by the poor over the rapid rise in the cost of rice in Osaka in 1918, the local government put together what has aptly been dubbed "an ignominious marriage of authoritarian government and the charitable spirit of local leaders . . ." (Chubachi and Taira, 1976, p. 425). Under this system, the welfare commissioner kept card-files on the living conditions of all the poor in his district. These files were then shared with police for surveillance purposes.

Although the United States Occupation advanced numerous reforms in many areas of social policy, it raised no serious challenge to the country's reliance on private assistance and limited financial contributions from the national treasury. This should not be surprising, since the United States itself was at the time adhering to comparable principles. As a result, the prewar pattern of minimal government activity in this area continued through most of the immediate postwar years. Most social relief was taken to be, not the responsibility of the state, but of the voluntaristic paternalism of families or employers.

Without a doubt, Japan's late industrialization and the conservative character of its ruling coalition contributed to this orientation. Germany, Austria, and to some extent Sweden, shared both of these conditions with Japan; yet all followed a path of early and expensive commitment to state-run programs of social welfare. What accounts for the difference? Two factors are important.

The first, while difficult to evaluate comparatively, appears to differentiate Japan. From the Meiji Restoration through World War II, and with a strong residue thereafter, Japan maintained an ideology of familism and of filial piety. These attitudes undoubtedly played a role in social welfare. Families were socially and legally required to care for elderly parents, for the ill, the enfeebled, and the unemployed. The three-generation family living under one roof was not unusual. Hence, a worker injured or laid off from a job in the city could expect to be received in his village and cared for by his rural kin, however reluctantly. The political impact of such beliefs is difficult to pin down explicitly. It is also difficult to separate cause and effect in this area, since the absence of effective social welfare programs undoubtedly left many individuals with no alternative but to rely on the family. Yet, a series of Japanese governments consistently endorsed and reinforced such attitudes through the educational system as well as through propaganda concerning the family's role in the emperor system and in the "national essence" (*kokutai*). With the possible exception of efforts in Germany during World War II to propagate the belief in "Küche, Kirche, Kinder," in none of the other countries does such an ideology seem comparable.

The second element, the structure and weakness of organized labor in Japan, is more concrete. Government and business leaders effectively resisted most union-formation throughout the prewar period, and numerous legal restrictions and overt efforts at labor repression mark the entire period. Only enterprise unions were favored and this as a means of undercutting the class-based force of the labor movement and strengthening the ideology of familism in the work place. Thus, as was discussed at greater length in Chapter 3, only about 6 percent of the Japanese labor force was unionized at any time during the prewar period, a figure far below that for any of the European countries, which were spending relatively large sums on social welfare programs. Whereas in these countries the union movement had provided a stimulus, direct or indirect, for governments to act positively on social welfare problems, in Japan there was no such political incentive.

Even when unionization increased dramatically in the years immediately after the war, enterprise unions remained the dominant organizational form. When seeking specific programs to cover the sickness, retirement, or injury of their members, unions, therefore, had no incentive to take their battle to parliament and to seek legislation. Labor's efforts were directed almost exclusively at wresting benefits from the enterprise itself. Consequently, many of the larger Japanese firms, in which unionization is strongest, introduced social welfare packages or programs of their own. From the national standpoint, such privatized benefits reduced the pressures to create national programs paid for and run by the state.

As a result, the scope and scale of Japanese social welfare programs remained quite limited. Unemployment insurance, accident insurance, and health insurance schemes were all put into effect in the early years after World War II. By 1961, social insurance programs for medical care and pensions had been made nationwide. But the qualifications for most of these programs were rigid while benefits were small. Even by the late-1960s, the Japanese government's expenditures for social welfare constituted a very small percentage of GNP, about one-half that of the United States and one-third that of France or West Germany. Only in the area of health insurance was the Japanese government's effort comparable to that of these countries, and this program stemmed chiefly from efforts to maintain a healthy workforce rather than from a concern for the nonworking needy. Pensions, child allowances, and other programs that provide assistance for the two extreme ends of the life cycle lagged considerably behind the efforts made in other countries.

This situation presented an undeniably stark contrast to the successes being achieved in industrial reconstruction and macrolevel economic growth. As such, it provided fodder for critics of high-growth policies and for advocates of greater concern with improvement of all forms of social overhead.

This contrast was particularly noteworthy in the case of Japan's elderly, because by the 1960s the country was becoming conscious of a major demographic transition. Compared to most European countries, Japan in the 1950s was a nation with a small proportion of its population over the age of sixty-five. Improvements in health, sanitation, and medical care, however, led to a steadily increasing life expectancy, while at the same time the country witnessed a declining birth rate. The result was that Japan began moving quite rapidly toward becoming a society of the elderly. Although Japan's population is still young compared to that of most other industrialized countries, the shift toward greater numbers of elderly citizens was widely noted in government and private circles. Yet pensions and other programs for the elderly were woefully less developed than in other industrial countries, and most of the elderly were dependent on their offspring for assistance.

As such juxtapositions were becoming evident throughout Japan, and as quality of life issues gained public salience, the electoral fortunes of the LDP continued to drop steadily. Though the decline had many more causes than simply the government's small contribution to social welfare, it was clear that the electoral, demographic, and ideological context of Japanese politics had changed significantly from that which prevailed during the period of greatest conservative strength. In this new context many, both inside and outside the dominant coalition, but particularly bureaucrats in the Ministry of Health and Welfare, began proposing measures to demonstrate an increased public commitment in the area of social welfare. Electoral politics and the threatened loss of LDP hegemony provided the ideal political context within which such efforts could bear fruit.

Agenda

The agenda of social welfare policy in Japan has been far more fluid and uncertain than those of economic policy or labor-management relations. For the first decade after the war, any agenda for social welfare that could be said to have existed reflected the bipolarity of national politics. Major business organizations, the LDP, and most government officials, committed as they were to rapid economic growth, were uniformly hostile to any rapid expansion of social welfare measures. At best, these were seen as unaffordable; at worst, they posed a threat to the virtues of hard work, thrift, and self-reliance essential to economic recovery. The organized left did call periodically for more systematic state efforts in all areas of social welfare, particularly in improved pension, health care, and unemployment programs. However, these rarely amounted to much more than ritualized statements lamenting the government's alleged lack of concern for society's needy and promising increased social welfare efforts when the conservative regime was toppled. Consequently, during most of this period social welfare was not a major concern in either the conservative or the progressive camp. Instead, primary attention was devoted to matters of foreign policy, military spending, constitutional revision, and economics. Most conservatives remained content with a nonagenda; most of the opposition did not rate the area as particularly critical to its fortunes. And given the political balance between the two camps, little public effort was made.

The initial pressure for increased public commitment to social welfare was generated by public sector unions of health professionals and social workers, clientele groups such as the elderly and working mothers, as well as by individual bureaucrats in agencies responsible for social welfare problems, such as the Ministry of Health and Welfare and the Ministry of Labor. Yet these groups were politically weak, not only in the broad arena of Japanese politics but also in their respective political camps. About the only political ammunition they could muster was a call for the implementation of the principles of Article 25 of the constitution. This stated: "All people shall have the right to maintain the minimum living standards of wholesome and cultured living. In all spheres of life, the State shall use its endeavors for the promotion and extension of social welfare and security and of public health." Translating such a principle into political commitment, however, involved more than moral suasion.

Electoral losses added incentive. The 1956 upper house elections provided something of a shock to the conservative camp as the progressives broke through the "one-third barrier" for the first time. In the following year's budget message, the conservative government suddenly shifted away from its past position, declaring, "We have by no means disregarded the expansion of the social welfare system up until now, but from here on it is absolutely clear that even though we are a conservative party, we [must] treat the expansion of the social welfare system as an essential item of policy" (Yokoyama, 1979, p. 34). This is almost certainly the first time that social welfare was officially recognized as a policy target by the conservative government. This also signified the beginnings of a shift in the governmental agenda of social welfare.

Although there was increasingly general support for more government involvement in social welfare, the specific agendas of competing actors were much more complex. In principle, parties on both left and right supported "more" government involvement in social welfare. On matters of costs, targets for reform, and specific programs there was wide division. To simplify, it is possible to think of three somewhat overlapping groups involved in the process: the redistributors, the refiners, and the reluctants.

The first group, the redistributors, saw social welfare as a form of income redistribution. They pressed for programs in which the costs would come mainly from the rich through increased corporate and progressive income taxes. Benefits would be evenly distributed to most members of the lower-income brackets. The core of this group was the Japan Socialist Party and the Japan Communist Party, as well as the major labor federations, but the left's positions were complicated by the fact that most labor unions wished to protect the privileges and benefits enjoyed by their members. The radical redistributive position was most prevalent during the 1950s and early 1960s when left-right bipolarity characterized most issues in Japanese politics (see Reading 4-1), although it is a position which has never completely died out.

During the late 1950s and throughout the 1960s, a second identifiable group emerged with clarity, the refiners. For the most part these were concerned with increasing social welfare benefits but doing so in a manner that would not fundamentally challenge the reliance on social insurance schemes. Government bureaucrats, especially from the ministries of Labor and Health and Welfare, were foremost in this group. Occasionally, they were joined by social work and health professionals who, because of their union affiliations, were usually in the first group but who were willing to work with government officials to refine and expand existing benefits. They were joined too on certain issues, by a clientele interest group, the elderly, who were organized into over 6,000 clubs throughout the country, as well as by non-Marxist social welfare scholars.

The final group, the reluctants, were most prominently found in those organizations responsible for funding any increases. Employers were hostile to increased managerial contributions (see Reading 4-2), while the Ministry of Finance and, in particular, officials from the ministry's Budget Bureau were tightfistedly hostile to most reform-proposals that would require increased public spending. In addition, they were frequently joined by businessmen and LDP politicians, especially those of the prewar generation, whose opposition came not simply because of cost, but for fear that a European-style social welfare system would erode the value-structure of Japan. One of the more notorious instances of reluctance was shown in a 1972 speech by Labor Minister Hara, who declared that old peoples' homes were filled with selfish individuals lacking in self-reliance and making themselves a burden to all around them (see Reading 4-4).

In the broad sense, the political agenda and the balance of forces calling for different agendas shifted with the Japanese electoral calendar and with the relative success of the Japanese economy. Thus, expansion of social welfare, both in principle and in specific programs, was significantly easier as elections approached and as the economy demonstrated signs of strength. For example, the Kishi cabinet in 1957 announced that it would institute a system of Health Insurance for the Whole Nation (*Kokumin Kai Hōken*). The LDP also adopted explicit pension-payment targets before several elections: ¥10,000 before the 1965 upper house election; ¥20,000 before the lower house elections of 1969, and ¥50,000 before the election of 1972. When the economy was prosperous, as it was before the 1972 election, the government adopted various slogans suggesting that social welfare would be increased in conjunction with economic growth; during periods of slump, such as that surrounding the 1976 election, there was much greater emphasis on buttressing the work ethic and the family system. The dilemma of choosing between electoral and economic objectives became especially vexing for the conservative camp, once it had made its general commitment to increased welfare spending in the 1970s. For example, Prime Minister Miki proposed, in 1975, an electorally appealing comprehensive social welfare package called the Life Cycle Plan, only to be sharply and successfully opposed by the Finance Ministry (see Reading 4-5).

Such fluctuations, however, became rare, as there rose a tidal wave of increasing conservative acceptance of a wider government role in social welfare. As was noted in Chapter 2, until the early 1960s, national economic plans, for example, concentrated exclusively on economic development. But the 1965 and 1967 plans called in general terms for some attention to the improvement of living conditions. The 1973 plan called explicitly for the realization of a "vigorous welfare society," and that of 1979 devoted a good deal of attention toward directing the economy in such ways as to create a "Japanese-style welfare society" (see Reading 4-5). Throughout the period, the LDP sought for electoral purposes to chronicle its growing concern with the alleviation of social burdens, especially those of the elderly (see Reading 4-7). Most of the detailed proposals for action emerged from within the bureaucracy (Campbell, 1979).

While the social welfare targets were many, during the 1970s pension reform represented by far the most important target in terms of the breadth of the population affected and the potential financial burdens it posed. Retirement insurance had been made mandatory by the government as early as 1959, but many problems remained in the system. One of the more important relates to retirement age. Although they rarely leave the work force at that age, most permanent male employees formally "retire" at the age of fifty-five; most women are retired mandatorily at fifty. Yet under the Employees' Pension Insurance System, which governs employees in firms with five or more employees, individuals have to be in the program for twenty years before they are eligible for pensions. In addition, men can not draw pensions until age sixty and women not until age fifty-five. Under the National Pension System, the age is sixty-five for both. Thus, many individuals are not eligible for benefits until they are officially retired for five or more years. Dealing with this gap led competing groups to propose extending the retirement age or lowering the age for pension eligibility (see readings 3-7, 4-1, and 4-2).

A second problem concerned the limited number of pension recipients. In 1970, there were only 4.8 million pension recipients, representing about 44 percent of the population over sixty years of age. Of these, 57% were recipients of the non-contributory Welfare Pension under the National Pension System, payable to persons over seventy years of age and subject to a means test. An additional 26 percent were retired government officials on good pensions. Only 17 percent were beneficiaries under employer contributory schemes. The low number of recipients was due both to the strict work requirements for qualification (e.g., twenty years of contribution) and to the limited number covered under the original program established in the early 1940s.

In addition to the fact that there was a limited number of recipients, pensions were small (see Reading 4-3). The basis for determining the pension is lifetime earnings, and the high growth and inflation-rates during the 1950s and 1960s meant that a pension was rarely close to a worker's wages at the time of retirement. Furthermore, the bonus and fringe benefits, which provide a fundamental part of most workers' annual salaries, were excluded in computing salaries for retirement benefits. The level of benefits provided amounted to only 10–15 percent of the average annual wage of those employed in manufacturing, in contrast to about a 50–60 percent average in Western Europe. Retirement benefits were even lower than welfare payments and were jokingly dismissed as "candy-money benefits," the implication being that the elderly would use them only to buy sweets for their grandchildren after they had moved in with their children. Finally, retirement benefits contained no inflation-proofing, and in the highly inflationary 1960s the purchasing power of the measly pensions rapidly deteriorated.

During the 1970s these and other problems with the pension and annuity system in Japan were targeted for reforms by bureaucrats in the ministries of Health and Welfare and Labor. By the beginning of the 1980s the issue of cost for the new programs had become more central. Virtually everyone involved with pension reform must confront the ever-escalating cost of improved pensions. Hostility toward expanded pension plans was and remains most vigorous in the Ministry of Finance, most especially in its Budget Bureau. Fixed on balancing the budget and benefiting from a pension fund swollen to about $20 billion which it controlled and could use for favored economic projects, the Ministry showed little sympathy for expanded and expensive programs in the 1960s. Under the severe economic pressures of the mid- to late-1970s and early 1980s, it became even more reluctant to see major expansions in coverage and benefits (Reading 4-5). Even the Ministry of Health and Welfare showed increased sensitivity to these problems, though it remained an active advocate of higher and more comprehensive benefits. Thus, its 1975 White Paper was suitably entitled "Better Welfare and Higher Burdens." Though the reluctants once appeared to be anachronistic defenders of an indefensible past, they gained increased credibility as economic growth rates lost the air of inevitability that they had in the 1950s and 1960s. Moreover, as the population ages, the number of contributors to pension plans decreases relative to the number of recipients. And as benefits themselves increase, the cost of paying for them becomes ever more problematic. This fact has become as undeniable in Japan as it is in all other countries undergoing similar changes. As can be seen in Britain, or the United States, the very nature of pension expansion is such that, once begun, it is difficult to reverse; the manner in which the system operates and the political power of the elderly and their bureaucratic and journalistic allies make it probable that the advocates of fiscal conservatism will be fighting a losing action during the 1980s.

Process

For about fifteen years after World War II, the Japanese government played a minimal role in virtually all aspects of social welfare. The Ministries of Labor and of Health and Welfare were among the government's weakest. In most problem areas, the private sector, families, communities, and employers bore the major financial and organizational burdens of welfare. At the same time, a basic framework for a comprehensive public social welfare system had been established. Work injury laws had begun in 1911; the health insurance system had been in operation since 1922; an Employees' Pension Insurance System had been created in 1941; and unemployment compensation dated from 1947. Although the programs existed, eligibility for most of them was severely restricted, and the benefits they provided were scant compared to need. Therefore, only a limited number of citizens benefited from them. Most were forced to rely on whatever privatized benefits they could command.

In the larger firms, these benefits were frequently quite substantial. Under the provisions of the health insurance laws, for example, firms with over three hundred employees could establish a firm-based Health Insurance Society, to collect health insurance payments and provide health treatments either directly or by paying for the treatment of its members. Actually, most large firms instituted clinics where their employees and families could get free or low-cost health care. Retirement, too, was firm based. Most typically, a retiree would receive a lump-sum payment, often one month's pay for each year worked.

Under such a system of privatized benefits, the individual working for a large firm was frequently able to claim benefits relatively comparable to those provided by the large, state-funded welfare systems typical of Western Europe. At the same time, the system benefited the large firms. Particularly during the period of rapid economic expansion in the immediate postwar years, these firms were heavily concerned with maximizing their investment capital. By paying for costs as they occurred, i.e., by paying lump sums for retirement rather than making long-term contributions to a state-operated retirement fund, the firm retained much greater investment potential. Furthermore, by mandating retirement for employees at an age usually around fifty-five, the firm kept the actual costs of retirement lower. Retirement occurred when the employee was younger and hence making a salary lower than he or she could have expected to receive five or ten years later. Finally, because most benefits, including housing, family, health, and retirement benefits, were channelled through the firm, the system reinforced the bonds of loyalty between employer and firm. It was the firm, not the state, which saw to an employee's well-being; benefits had the aura of employer gratuities rather than that of inherent rights guaranteed by the state and transferrable from one job to the next (Cole, 1971).

Such a privatized system excluded numerous needy individuals and groups, and both redistributors and refiners pressed the government to take on increased responsibility for social welfare needs. This pressure built steadily from the late 1950s on, and between the middle of the 1960s and up until the oil shock of 1973 a number of factors converged to force action. Politically, the LDP was in decline both nationally and locally, and at least one factor in the party's decline seemed to be the gap between its commitment to economic growth and its low level of action on social welfare. The success of many progressive coalitions in local government reinforced this image, as many of them sought to demonstrate the uniqueness and humanity of their administrations by instituting a variety of social welfare schemes (MacDougall, 1976). At the national level, the DSP, Dōmei, and the CGP, in particular, sought to mobilize concern around the social welfare gap.

The media and individual writers and critics were devoting a great deal of attention to the low public concern for social welfare at the same time. In 1972, for example, one of the best-selling novels, *A Man in Ecstasy*, provided a depressing story of a woman's valiant efforts to cope with an aging and senile father. By that time, it is fair to say, Japan was undergoing a combination of a social welfare boom and an old people's boom that provided the ideal climate in which advocates could push specific reform proposals, formulated along lines noted in the previous section.

The Ministry of Health and Welfare was in the forefront of efforts within government to press such reforms. Its major weapon was publicity. In 1968, it conducted a survey of the elderly that showed that some 80 percent of those over sixty-five years of age lived with their children, whereas the figures for Britain, the United States, and Denmark were 42 percent, 28 percent and 20 percent, respectively. Those not living with their children were often found in intolerable circumstances. In 1970, the ministry's Social Affairs Bureau issued a report entitled "Comprehensive Policies for the Problems of the Aged," and, in the same year, it held a well-publicized National Conference on a Rich Old Age (Campbell, 1979, pp. 343–44). Various white papers on the livelihood of Japanese citizens began to appear during the early 1970s from various government agencies. Numerous public commissions began reporting on aspects of the social welfare gap. Clearly, elements in the conservative camp were pressing for more social welfare. Once the national mood and the political climate was conducive, state initiative became a vital catalyst to action.

At the initiative of what Campbell (1979) has called "entrepeneurial bureaucrats," the Ministry of Health and Welfare, along with numerous other agencies developed and pressed through parliament a wide range of new programs. The national health care system was supplemented by a program of free medical care for the elderly (1972); pension benefits were adjusted legislatively every five years or so until eventually they were explicitly tied to the consumer price index (1973). Allowances for children were introduced in 1972. By the middle of the 1970s, the Japanese government provided substantially the same social welfare programs as most other industrialized countries (Yokoyama, 1979).

Once the principle of greater government aid was accepted, and with a social welfare framework in place, increases in the levels of government expenditure meant a process dominated by bureaucratic and budgetary politics. By the early 1970s, virtually every government agency began jumping on the welfare bandwagon, seeking to establish programs that would allow it to relate its overall mission to the goal of improved social welfare and not at all incidentally to retain its "fair share" of the national budget (Campbell, 1977). The Ministry of Construction, for example, developed a program to provide larger mortgage loans to allow a room to be added for aging parents, and the Ministry of Agriculture and Forestry came up with a program to encourage cattle raising by the elderly (Campbell, 1979). Such an incremental budgetary process helped to minimize the degree of intrabureaucratic conflict over questions of which agency should have which responsibilities for which dimensions of the social welfare problem. But at the same time, there was the danger that the long-term implementation of the programs could become extremely expensive, with the annual and geometric expansion of numerous programs that once appeared small. As a result, most new proposals faced strong opposition from the Ministry of Finance. But in the prevailing climate, such opposition proved largely a rear-guard action.

Public support of welfare benefits soared, partially closing the gap between Japan and Western Europe that had previously existed. In 1973, the year of the first big jump, 14.8 percent of the national budget was allocated to social welfare. In 1974, this was 16.9 percent; in 1975, 18.4 percent and, in 1976, Japan broke through the symbolic 20 percent barrier with 22.4 percent. Recession and revaluation brought a downturn to 18.4 percent and 14.8 percent in the next two years (Yokoyama, 1979, p. 136), but in 1979 the figure was back to 20 percent. Yet even with such increases, Japan still provided only about one-half the public support given in France and West Germany and far less than that given in Sweden.

Despite the government's increased role in social welfare, the privatized and localized system that had long prevailed remained vital. Most of the new programs continued to encourage continued reliance on the firm for many particular benefits while providing government aid for those who lacked such private support.

One of the first examples of this approach occurred in the area of health insurance. To bring about the "health insurance for the whole country" that the Kishi cabinet had promised in 1957, the government mandated that each city, town, or village that had not already done so institute, by 1961, a health insurance program in accord with national guidelines. The new system was to complement, not replace, the already-existing system of health insurance societies managed by private firms or by local governments. The national government was to have a minimal administrative role in the system, even in the so-called National Health Insurance System, which contained the largest number of participants. Thus, Japan retains two main medical-care insurance systems. One is an Employees' Health Insurance System in which workers and their dependents are well covered through firm-based insurance. The other is a Community Health Insurance System in which the local governing body serves as administrator and receives partial subsidization from the national government. Charges for health benefits work against those with low incomes; the community public health systems cost more and provide less than most private systems. Private insurance companies and private doctors fare very well under the public system, as in France. For these reasons, the system was strongly opposed by the JSP and the major labor federations when it was introduced, and it has been subjected to additional criticism from redistributors ever since.

When the National Pension System was implemented in 1961, it had a similar arrangement. Similar to that in Britain, the existing Employees' Pension System begun in 1941 was supplemented by a National Pension System. National pensions involve a contributory program for all between the ages of twenty and fifty-nine not otherwise covered by the Employees Pension System and a noncontributory welfare pension program primarily for the unprotected elderly

The government also took certain steps actively to encourage reliance on private pensions. It now allows large firms to opt out of the national programs and to establish their own pension and health care systems in which the risk pool and costs are less and in which any increased benefits are of particular value to the firm and its employees, an alternative not unlike the British merger plans of the 1970s. In addition, employers may contribute additional amounts to the pension schemes for their workers, for which they receive special tax exemptions. Thus, pensions in large firms can be made higher than for the rest of the country at an equal or lower cost to their employers. Finally, the government allows generous tax deductions for individual payment of private-insurance premiums.

Retaining a substantial private component in the pension schemes did not keep the Japanese government from becoming substantially more involved, financially and administratively, in the area of social welfare by the 1970s.

As a consequence, by the beginning of the 1980s, the Japanese government had developed a relatively complete and costly system of social welfare programs. Yet it had done so in a manner that, at least in the early stages, did not fundamentally undercut its principles of minimal involvement by the national government in such areas and of reliance where possible on the private sector. Yet the programs established during this period of welfare expansion may also contain the seeds of abandonment of these principles as the programs mature.

Consequences

Japan's late start in introducing and expanding its various social welfare programs meant that the treasury expended very little for social measures throughout most of the country's modern history. Even by the mid-1960s, the Japanese government's expenditures for social welfare measures constituted a smaller percentage of GNP than in any other industrial nation in the world. Whereas the figure was approximately 15 percent or more for most European countries, in Japan it was only 6.2 percent (Wilensky, 1975, pp. 30–31). Even though many of the qualifications and standards of Japanese social welfare programs were comparable to those in other countries in the 1970s, expenditures remained low because of the long delays between development of a program, such as pension reform, and its full maturity.

Low public expenditure for social welfare meant a comparatively low tax burden on both Japanese citizens and business. It also benefited the government's economic policies by allowing a low and balanced budget, which encouraged investment and employment. Low expenditure for social welfare reduced the drain of resources away from the support of economic growth, the main government concern. Finally, pension funds were administered by the Finance Ministry's Capital Investment Fund and could be utilized for economic development projects with minimal requirements that benefits be plowed back for the use of the contributing pensioners.

The limited overall government effort in these areas also strengthened the work ethic. In the absence of readily available government programs, many Japanese citizens undoubtedly did work longer and harder than their counterparts in countries where retirement, medical care, unemployment benefits, and the like were more readily available. Certainly this was true of the population over age sixty-five. Even in the mid-1970s, over 50 percent of those over sixty-five remained active in the labor force. Comparable figures for France, West Germany, and Britain ranged from 12 to 18 percent (Zusetsu Rōjin Hakusho, 1980, p. 95).

In addition to the impetus they gave individuals to continue working beyond the normal retirement age, low government benefits strengthened private savings and insurance schemes. With public benefits low and difficult to qualify for, most citizens relied on personal efforts to ensure social well-being. Personal savings in Japan through the 1970s remained consistently higher than in any other industrialized country. Citizens saved approximately three times more of their disposable incomes than did their United States counterparts. Private insurance looms large in the Japanese citizen's preparation for the possibly lean days of retirement, medical emergency, or unemployment. There is an inverse relationship between government transfer payments and private-insurance investment. Japan has more life insurance in relation to its national income than any other major industrial country except Canada. All of these factors have stimulated economic policies, as government, banks, private insurance companies and, in turn, private industries were blessed through the 1960s with a substantial pool of available capital that might otherwise have been privately consumed. Even in the beginning of the 1980s Japan's comparative advantage in capital formation is without parallel.

Enterprise-consciousness is also stimulated while the union movement, in turn, is hampered, by the Japanese welfare system. A cornucopia of welfare benefits is provided by Japan's largest employers, those with the highest rates of unionization, while for pensions and health insurance, the national government, as in Britain and France, allows larger firms to establish private programs outside the national system as long as benefits are at least equal. In this way, business can opt out of responsibility for contributing to the programs for the nation's most deprived, while at the same time providing benefits that come from the company rather than from a generous government or as a result of union pressures.

The conservative coalition has probably also benefited electorally from these policies. The LDP's electoral decline was rather steady from the mid-1960s to the early 1970s, but by the beginning of the 1980s the seemingly inevitable downward drift had levelled off and been reversed. Numerous factors contributed. But, through increased social welfare spending, the government appeared to have blunted one of the potential objections to its rule; its introduction of various benefits suggested that it was not more concerned with the profitability of big industry than with the improvement of the living conditions of the country's citizens.

There was risk to this tactic, however. As the government introduced various social welfare programs, it also left itself open to many of the problems inherent in the programs themselves. The social insurance schemes for medical benefits and, more especially, retirement benefits have economic costs that creep up slowly but inexorably.

Such programs contain a potential political backlash for conservatives. Slow as they may be in taking effect, these systems are extremely difficult to dismantle. To lower benefits is to "break faith" with contributors to the program who anticipate specific minimum benefits. The political pressures of the retired and the economic pressures of higher medical costs easily justify ever increasing benefit-levels, and lower standards for eligibility. As the Ministry of Finance continued to stress, the total costs of such programs can easily mount astronomically, as they did in Britain, France, and the United States. But the capacity of the government to exact contributions to cover such increases invariably diminishes. Simply raising the contributions made by non-beneficiaries is politically difficult. Moreover, longer life-spans, earlier retirements, and diminished birth rates increase the proportion of beneficiaries to contributors. An ever-smaller proportion of the population winds up supporting ever larger retirement or medical benefits to the needy. In 1977, for example, official government estimates suggested that there were twenty-five contributors to the Employees Pension System for each recipient of benefits. By the year 2,000, this ratio is expected to have dropped to 4:1. The government and private industry, therefore, by 1980 had begun to raise the retirement age and the age at which pension benefits could be drawn (see Reading 4-8), anticipating the proposals of the Reagan administration by over a year.

Given the political difficulty of either reducing or restricting benefits, or alternatively of exacting larger employee or employer contributions to these programs, governments almost invariably find themselves compelled to move away from self-sufficient social insurance programs and to supplement social insurance funds with state monies, as did Britain, and as the United States was considering. Yet public contributions necessitate tax increases which are never politically desirable. Former Prime Minister Ōhira discovered this when, just prior to the 1979 elections, he proposed a form of value-added tax, and the LDP lost numerous seats.

Thus, at the beginning of the 1980s, Japan was engaged in a major debate over whether to provide the same degree of social welfare coverage as had become typical in the West, and, if so, how to do so in a manner that could somehow avert the threats to fiscal stability and economic growth that such programs have posed elsewhere (see again Reading 4-6).

Readings

4-1. LABOR'S PROPOSED REVISIONS OF THE EMPLOYEES PENSION INSURANCE LAW*

During the debate on possible revisions of the Employees Pension System in the 1960s, five major labor-union federations issued the following joint declaration. Among the points to note are the pressure for the treatment of pensions as a form of income-redistribution, the reluctance to have private pension plans affected by increased state aid, and the calls for substantially higher benefits and for a lower retirement age.

1. The Employees Pension Insurance System was instituted in order to provide insurance benefits for workers in their old age or in the event of death or retirement. It would thus contribute to a more secure existence and improvements in the well-being of both the workers and their surviving dependents.

2. Nevertheless, the existing Employees Pension Insurance system remains inferior both in term of payments provisions and conditions: the social security function for which the system was originally conceived has yet to be realized, not only in the area of old-age benefits but in other categories of benefits as well.

We must move speedily toward a drastic revision of the present Employees Pension Insurance Law. In addition to introducing wide-range improvements in all categories of insurance benefits, including, to be sure, old-age pensions, but with special emphasis on the fixed sum portions, we must press for a thorough investigation aimed at establishing eligibility criteria for the spouses and families of insured workers, and focusing, for the time being, on workers' wives.

3. Moreover, it is widely rumored that there is a move afoot to transform the organization of the Employees Pension Insurance system. It is proposed that in exchange for a few improvements in the existing law, there should be a so-called "adjustment of industrial pensions in line with the Employees Pension Insurance Law." What is required today, however, is a thoroughgoing reform of the Employees Pension Insurance Law in its capacity as a public system conceived for the purpose of providing social security. In other words, it should be made to function, in fact as well as name, as the basic employees pension system it was designed to be.

The "adjustment of industrial pensions" is completely antithetical to the above concerns and we are staunchly opposed to it.

*Tsuji Kiyoaki, ed., *Sengo Nijūnenshi*, vol. 4, "Rōdō" (Tokyo: Hyōronsha, 1966), p. 523.

4. We request that the existing Employees Pension Insurance Law be revised in accordance with the basic principles stated as well as with the following substantive proposals.

Specific requests:

1) Immediately raise the fixed portion of basic pensions from the present ¥ 2000 monthly to at least ¥ 6000. Levy insurance fees according to income and institute a benefits system with a guaranteed minimum. Take measures to impose fixed limits on amounts which are conspicuously high relative to average pension-income earners, and raise overall pension benefits to a level commensurate with the maintenance of decent health care and civilized living conditions for workers and their families.

2) Increase disability pensions to appropriate levels commensurate with the degree of labor incapacitation resulting from the infirmity.

Furthermore, in estimating the amounts for disability pensions, the degree of labor incapacitation should be taken as the base. There should also be substantial efforts to accomodate the requirements of the occupational category of the worker in question.

3) In calculating insurance benefits, cease using the present formula of average standard compensation during the time one is a policyholder and take measures toward a readjustment of pension benefits in line with living expenses, salary levels, etc.

4) Lower the eligibility age for benefits from its present sixty. Also, pay reduced pensions on a gradually increasing scale for employees who have had insurance for fifteen years, even though they may not yet, according to the prescribed criteria, have attained the eligibility age for receiving payment.

5) Make discretionary the continuance of eligibility-status qualifications for those who have reached the eligibility age, and institute benefit payments from the period desired by the insured in question.

6) Lower further the eligibility age for women and special occupational categories.

7) Lower the present twenty-year term insurance requirement to fifteen years.

8) Modify the pension-financing system by eliminating the present installment method and instituting a modified assessment for-

mula combining the fixed-sum portion and proportional compensatory amounts.

9) Make enterprises with less than five employees subject to the same compulsory provisions.

10) Substantially raise the amounts of benefits to those presently receiving pensions.

11) Make the increases in pension allocations the joint responsibility of the government and the employers.

Modify the present formula of equal shares by labor and management even in cases where an insurance premium rate hike cannot be avoided, and make every effort to ensure that the workers do not suffer additional burdens.

12) Remove the pension-fund administration from the Finance Ministry's Capital Investment Fund and set up a distinct mechanism for administering the Employees' Pension Fund (for example a Social Security Fund) on a par with other official pension-reserve funds.

Include worker representatives as participants in the ensuing administrative process and take steps to ensure that it functions democratically. Specify that the top priority of pension-fund operations should be the amelioration of workers' well-being via substantive reforms in the Employees Pension Insurance System and by restoration of the prerogatives of labor unions and labor-welfare groups.

13) Take into account the insured terms of those who have been covered previously by public pensions. Exclude, however, those who are covered by the military Pension Law.

14) Take account of the special conditions and anticipatory rights of female workers; make the severance allowance discretionary and take into consideration the time during which employees were insured.

Sōhyō (General Council of Trade Unions of Japan)

Chūritsu Rōren (Federation of Independent Unions of Japan)

Zenrō (All-Japan Trade Unions Congress)

Sodōmei (Japanese Confederation of Labor)

Shinsanbetsu (National Federation of Industrial Organizations)

4.2 EMPLOYERS' VIEWS ON REVISION OF THE EMPLOYEES PENSION INSURANCE LAW*

During the debate on the Employees Pension Insurance System, the Japan Federation of Employers' Association issued the following statement concerned with holding down costs to industry and taking account of existing private retirement plans.

I. Basic Principles

Under the present circumstances wherein industry is confronted with a number of urgent internal and external economic pressures and is already bearing a heavy burden with regard to the retirement pension system, we must avoid, to every possible extent, any new impositions stemming from modifications in the Employees Pension System. It is also true that, from the perspective of substantively improving social security, there are some undeniably important aspects to be considered in the revision issue. Consequently,

(1) Due attention should be given so that revision does not bring about a precipitous increase in the burden on industry.

(2) Steps should be taken to assure a rational accomodation with industrial pension systems.

The two above points should be made fundamental policy-components of the imminent revision. Should appropriate deliberation not be given to these two items, it will be difficult for the Japan Federation of Employers Associations to support the revision without reservation.

II. Concrete Policy Aims

1. Benefits

In line with these basic principles, we propose the following concrete aims corresponding to the main items of the revision.

(1) While increases in benefits should apply primarily to the fixed-sum portion, there should also be some rise in proportional benefits corresponding to that in fixed benefits. The increase in the fixed-sum portion should be a reasonable sum, taking into account correlations between livelihood protection standards, national pensions, and the like as well as the burden of the insurance premium

---

*Tsuji Kiyoaki, ed., *Sengo Nijūnenshi*, vol. 4, "Rōdō" (Tokyo: Hyōronsha, 1966), pp. 523–24.

resulting from the revision. Priority should be placed on reform of the fixed-sum portion, which functions as a minimum standard-of-living guarantee. However, in light of the proportional weight of the insurance-premium charge relative to compensation, there will inevitably be a need for a corresponding increase in the proportional amount as well.

(2) The earliest age for receiving benefits is in principle sixty, but steps should be taken to allow payment of reduced pensions starting at age fifty-five. The present gap between ages 55 and 60 in the retirement system should be closed. Furthermore, given the likelihood of extension of the retirement age-limit in the future coupled with the increasingly frequent phenomenon of re-employment after compulsory retirement (giving rise in all probability to a widespread continuation of these workers on the insurance rolls), the outlay involved in this measure cannot be expected to grow significantly.

(3) On the severance-allowance system to insured female employees: Eligibility criteria and the amount of benefits should be restored to what they were prior to the revision, and we should institute a system offering a choice between an inclusive old-age pension and lump sum retirement allowance. In view of the limited possibility women have of receiving old-age pensions, due to the particular nature of their social role and the brevity of their terms of employment, it is appropriate that the severance-allowance system be restored to its pre-revision status (Law no.57, 1960).

2. Regarding the matters of standard compensation,
insurance premiums, national treasury charges, etc.:

(1) While increases in the upper and lower limits of standard compensation should be comtemplated, the additional charges stemming from other insurance systems as well as from this increase should be taken into account, and appropriate limits should be set.

(2) For the time being any increase in the insurance premium rate should be restricted to the necessary minimum by substituting a modified assessment formula for the present financing method.

Also, the insurance premium rate for women should be lowered to an appropriate level.

Inasmuch as increases in the upper and lower limits of the standard compensation are also linked with allocation reform, it is imperative that wage conditions also be taken into consideration.

Given the prevalence of fixed-sum benefits, however, any decision involving the setting of appropriate limits will also have to take into account the increased charges. . . .

(3) Care should be taken that the National Treasury share of responsibility at least does not drop below existing limits, and that it is applied to the fixed-sum payment portion. In addition, the combined total of resources used to maintain the real value of pensions and the revised portion of already-determined pensions should be assumed by the government.

The government share should be applied to the fixed-sum benefits, which is the portion having the quality of a minimum guarantee. This is inappropriate with regard to the proportional amount, since it results in an inequitable situation: the higher the compensation the greater the burden imposed on the government.

It should be established as a principle that the maintenance of real value with regard to this basic fixed-sum portion is the responsibility of the government. Accordingly, it is proper that the adjusted resources, including the predetermined portion, are assumed in their entirety by the government.

3. On the issue of adjustments pertaining to industrial pensions

(1) Appropriate measures should be taken to adjust those industrial pensions with specific requisites in line with the proportional-benefits portion of old-age pensions.

(2) The conception of this adjustment should be as explicit as possible; it should be such that the autonomy of the enterprise system is respected and without subjecting enterprises to excessively broad regulation and inspection measures.

(3) The industrial pension system, which is the object of this reorganization process, should be dealt with, insofar as tax law is concerned, in a manner equivalent to that applying to the public system.

Given the historical evolution of the relationship between employee pensions and the industrial retirement-fund system, as well as the fact that the retirement-fund system has in fact funtioned as a proxy for employee pensions, thus placing the two systems effectively in competition with one another, a rational adjustment in both functional and economic terms is necessary. Accordingly, in addition to developing a rational industrial pension system as a post-retirement guarantee (this in preference to a lump-sum payment system), it is appropriate that adjustments of a similar nature be made with regard to the proportional-benefits portion of the old-age pension.

Since the ensuing arrangements are likely to be intricate and controls tend to be strictly applied, adequate care must be taken to avoid difficulties in implementation.

Furthermore, inasmuch as the industrial pension, the focal point of the adjustment, is highly similar to social security in character, it should be dealt with in a manner identical with public pensions from a tax perspective.

4-3. SMALL AND BIG PENSIONS*

The government has long provided generous pensions for civil servants and former members of the military. One of the major complaints about the other pension schemes is their failure to match benefits paid to these two groups. The following letter to the editor of Asahi Shimbun *summarizes the complaint as it appears to one pensioner.*

To the Editor:

My pension amounts to ¥ 100,000 a month, while my friend's to ¥ 200,000. We both paid premiums of similar amounts for the same number of years. Why, then, is there such a big difference?

I paid for the private welfare pension system, while my friend belongs to the mutual-help pension scheme for public workers. This constitutes one of the big gaps that exist between private and public sectors.

The pension system is basically designed to protect elderly people. It should have nothing to do with an individual's status and professional ability.

My pension was calculated on the basis that I had received an average monthly wage of ¥ 150,000 in the last 30 years. In my friend's case, his pension amount is based on the ¥ 300,000 monthly salary he received immediately before his retirement.

*Asahi Evening News, Tokyo, Jan. 21, 1980.

Whether to base pension amounts on the average salary in one's career or the salary at the time of retirement makes a big difference. The government and the ruling Liberal-Democratic Party should clearly decide on which salary to base the pension.

Yuzo Suzuki

4-4. SOCIAL WELFARE AND INDIVIDUAL INITIATIVE*

In a brief address to young adults in 1972, Labor Minister Hara Kenzaburō castigated residents of old-age homes, displaying a hostility toward social welfare not uncommon in conservative circles. The speech generated a good deal of controversy over the possible debilitating effects of social welfare on individual initiative.

Labor Minister Hara Speaks Against Welfare

"Old people's homes are assemblies of self-centered people with no sense of gratitude." Thus did Labor Minister Hara Kenzaburō, a native son of Sumoto City, Hyōgō Prefecture, berate the elderly residents of old-age homes, whom he referred to as a "stagnant pool of self-seekers", in an address he delivered at the Adult Day Ceremony held at Sumoto Town Hall on the fifteenth. The Labor Minister's speech comes at a time when the government is putting forward a large-scale welfare program for the new year, and especially when there is a demand for added construction of old people's homes to improve the living conditions of the elderly. In addition to displaying contempt for the elderly under care, the speech also runs counter to present policy and contains elements which cannot be dismissed as mere bombast. Mr. Hara was unrelenting in asserting that "all people should espouse the important concept of 'self-reliance'." Yet, given the recent dismissal of former Defense Agency Director Nishimura for irresponsible remarks concerning the United Nations last December as well as the fact that the opposition parties will not fail to pursue the matter in the Diet, which is scheduled to reconvene next week, there is every indication that the issue of political responsibility will be raised once again.

*Yomiuri Shimbun, Jan. 16, 1972.

"A Deterioration of Political Responsibility?"

Labor Minister Hara's "irresponsible remarks" reached the public ear on the fifteenth of January at the "All Awaji Adult-Day Ceremony" held at Sumoto's Town Hall. It was before some eight hundred of Awaji Island's "new adults" gathered together for the occasion that the Labor Minister referred to the residents of old-age homes as "a stagnant pool" of egoists.

The Labor Minister, in his discourse on "human ethics," noted that "human beings can be neither happy nor successful if they neglect gratitude." Mr. Hara went on: "Each day of my life, from dawn till dusk, is permeated with a sense of wholehearted gratitude. The type of people who go to old-age homes when they are sixty are the lowest of the low, people who have forgotten what it is to be thankful. Because they are so ready to become a burden to others, because they are essentially self-seekers indifferent to the people around them, they are destined to be unhappy. Egoists who forsake the debt they owe to nation, society, and God are bound to end up in old people's homes." He concluded his remarks by urging his listeners "to strive not to end up in old-age homes."

The address lasted barely five minutes. Among the young adults, accustomed to the Labor Minister's tendency to indulge in "wild speech-making", there were some bitter smiles up until the minister rattled off his views on "old-age homes." At this point, most in the audience appeared astonished, and there was barely a smattering of applause at the end of the talk.

The Labor Minister departed immediately after delivering his address. One of the young adults being honored, Mr. A., a public service employee from Honcho, Sumoto City, had this to say: "It seems to me that there are a lot of people who have no choice and find old-age homes the only source of peace and comfort left open to them. I don't care how trite it sounds, but I'd say that to talk like that is the same as punching those poor people while they are down." One of the visitors to the ceremony, a town leader from Mihara County, was critical.

"I understand what the Labor Minister was trying to say, but his example was badly chosen. After all, even a Cabinet Minister still has to say things that the majority of people will relate to. It's especially pitiful when he puts down helpless old people who really don't have much in the way of facilities."

Words of Encouragement to Young Adults
Cabinet Secretary General Takeshita's Speech
(Matsue, January 15, 1972)

In the evening of the fifteenth, Cabinet Secretary General Takeshita made the following comment with regard to Labor Minister Hara's speech in his native Sumoto: "I can't say anything until the Labor Minister returns to Tokyo and I find out what he really meant. I believe, however, that his speech was intended to encourage young people setting out on the road of life. I would like people to understand that the government considers its social welfare programs, and particularly those pertaining to the well-being of the elderly, to be a cornerstone of its domestic policy."

"I just expressed my convictions"
Labor Minister Hara Kenzaburo's Remarks:

"Yes, that's what I said. I just explained my conviction that people can never be happy without a sense of gratitude. There are too many people these days who express no appreciation even when others help them out. That's why the thrust of my remarks was to tell young people that they were in danger of ending up in an old-age home unless they possess a sense of gratitude. All the young people in the audience applauded me. The reason I used old-age homes as an example is that they are not places one goes to by choice, nor are they facilities whose number should be increased indiscriminately. It is best not to enter such a home but rather to work as best one can and to be self-sufficient. Of course, people who are totally incapable of living independently should be placed in a home. Last year, I visited a facility for the handicapped in the United States; not only did all the people there have jobs, but I was impressed to hear them say that they did not depend on any government aid. In our present Labor Administration, too, I am working toward a situation where everyone can be self-sufficient and not have to depend on anyone else."

4-5. OPPOSITION TO PRIME MINISTER MIKI'S WELFARE PLAN*

In 1975, Prime Minister Miki Takeo proposed an extensive welfare scheme designed to cover all stages in the life cycle. Coming in a period of economic decline, it was sharply criticized by the economic agencies. The following news item summarizes the opposition voiced by the Minister of Finance.

Welfare Spending Plans Hit Snag

Government agencies are searching for new ways to improve social welfare in a period of slower economic growth, but some basic differences in stance of policy are looming up among them.

The Finance Ministry, which is expected to suffer a revenue shortfall of more than ¥ 3,000,000 million for the current fiscal year, emphasizes the need to "reexamine" the present welfare system.

Last month, senior officials of the ministry declared welfare will not be improved "unconditionally" as has been done in the past.

Furthermore, they proposed that the age at which one begins receiving welfare pensions be raised. Predictably, the proposal met strong opposition of the Health and Welfare Ministry and aged people.

Some Finance Ministry officials complained they had received so many protest telephone calls that they were unable to do their routine desk work.

Their tough stance toward welfare spending was based on a progress report submitted by the Financial System Research Council, an advisory body to the Government.

The report said:

—Japan's welfare payments are half those made by an industrialized European nation. But this is largely attributed to a comparatively small number of aged persons.

—The Government's welfare budget has been expanded sharply in the past, because of very high economic growth.

—The Government should not pursue an "inefficient, all-round welfare policy in order to please everybody" by ignoring the "reasonable" limits to budget allocation.

Japan Times Weekly, Sept. 20, 1975.

—Therefore, the Government should refrain from further increasing welfare pensions. Instead, it should try to increase public-health and insurance rates on the basis of the "beneficiary pays" principle.

Encouraged by these recommendations, the Finance Ministry concludes the present welfare system is sufficient to serve aged people, though there remain "technical problems" related to the operation of the existing system.

By contrast, the Health and Welfare Ministry stresses that "despite slower economic growth and resultant revenue shortfall," it is necessary for the government to drastically improve welfare because the number of aged people in Japan is expected to sharply rise in the near future.

The ministry's stand is supported by the Council for Long-Term Social Welfare Policy, an advisory body to the Health and Welfare Minister.

The council recommended Aug. 12 the securing of a stable life for all people "throughout their life;" achievement of social fairness; promotion of independence of aged people and their social activities; and more effective distribution of manpower and material resources for welfare and rational sharing of welfare costs.

The council places emphasis on the last point in the recommendations.

The council also stresses the necessity to maintain the "beneficiary pays" principle.

4-6. GOVERNMENT'S EMPHASIS ON "JAPANESE-TYPE" WELFARE*

Pressure for increases in social welfare were frequently countered by hostility toward the possible conversion of Japan into a socialist state. The government committed itself to improvements in the social welfare system, notably by including improved welfare as one of the main goals in the national economic plan of 1979. At the same time, it sought to reconcile this commitment to more traditional cultural values by stressing the importance of retaining a "Japanese" character in such programs.

*Economic Planning Agency, *New Seven-Year Economic and Social Plan* (Tokyo: EPA, 1979), pp. 11–12.

The national standard of living rose sharply during the process of high economic growth. It has reached the levels in the advanced industrial nations, and regional income-differentials have noticeably diminished. As national economic life has become more affluent, leading to changes in values relating to living, people have come to place emphasis less on "flow" than on "stocks," showing growing desire toward permanent settlement, and a welfare society based on individual purpose in life and warm human relations, where people can live comfortably and with peace of mind, is now being sought. During the recent period of high economic growth, the Japanese people were able to exhibit in full their vitality both as individuals and in the workplace. They tended, however, to lose sight of human links within the family and their neighborhood community. In future, Japanese will no doubt endeavor to restore caring relations to their lives, as well as exhibit outstanding ability in the workplace, and go on to build up full and enriched lives. To achieve this, individual ingenuity and effort will of course be needed, but, on the public side, it will also be necessary to put emphasis on improvement of conditions in various aspects of life such as conditions for building families, and neighborhood and regional communities. Coordination and synthesis of policies to this end will be necessary. A dignified and composed national society has its basis in such caring families, and neighborhood and regional communities. As the foundation for this national society, it will be necessary to combine the high productivity and superior information of the city with natural abundance and caring relationships of the country—the "seedbed" of the Japanese nation—and develop measures aimed at the concept of the healthy and comfortable "Nation of Garden Cities."

Now that its economy and society have caught up with those of the industrial nations of Europe and America, Japan should aim not at seeking models in the industrial nations, but at the realization of a new welfare society, which might be described as the "Japanese-type"—to select and create Japan's own path, which is motivated by the creative vitality of a free economy and society and where an efficient government guarantees appropriate public welfare according to priorities, while regarding the new national society mentioned above as a background, and setting solidarity of families neighborhood and regional communities and self-help efforts of individuals as its basis.

If, in the process, both public and private sectors can fill their roles and functions appropriately in responding to changes in diversifying national needs, the economy can be expected to switch over to a more domestic demand-centered development and create a great deal of employment opportunity.

However, this does not just mean the recovery of human relations within Japan's own society or the exploitation of new domestic markets. There need to be greater exchanges of personnel and information, and closer links and exchanges with the world economy, and [they] should be constructed so that the international division of labor progresses smoothly. In this context the new Japanese-type welfare society should be one that is open to the international society. The realization of this society will be the basis of management of the economy during the plan period and beyond.

4-7. GOVERNMENT'S HELP TO THE ELDERLY*

The LDP has long received much greater support from older voters than have the other parties. The following are excerpts from a 1970 campaign pamphlet chronicling the contributions made by the conservative government to the nation's elderly.

On Behalf of our Senior Citizens

Once again this year the Old People's Welfare Law is actively promoting the happiness of our elderly. Approximately seven million of our senior citizens are over age sixty-five. Of this total, women are in the majority (56%). A vital function of social security is to see that these people are able to spend their later years in health and happiness.

Policies for the Elderly Blind

A new area of emphasis this year has been the development of welfare programs for the elderly blind, who number some 100,000 in the over sixty-five group. This year we are financing 3,000 operations to bring light to senior citizens afflicted with senile cataracts.

In addition, we are engaged in efforts to build special old people's homes for the elderly blind.

*LDP, *Kurashi to Seiji* [Livelihood and Politics] (Tokyo: LDP, 1970), pp. 34–35.

Old-Age Welfare Pensions

Monthly grants of ¥ 2,000 (a ¥ 200 increase as of October) are provided to some 3,020,000 people over seventy who receive no pension at all. The number of recipients of these grants has been expanded this year, thanks to a relaxing of the eligibility requirements.

Budget: ¥ 65,900 million.

Employee Pensions

Eligible for these are men aged sixty and women aged fifty-five who have carried this insurance for twenty years. This year, about 500,000 people are receiving benefits. The insurance is constituted by the accumulated reserves of 3.1% (men)–2.31% (women) of the policyholders' incomes and a reserve of equal magnitude furnished by employers, with the remainder being supplied by the government. Benefits received are calculated in accordance with the worker's wage-scale at the time of retirement and the number of years of actual employment. This year's budget of ¥ 27,800 million is calculated on the basis of ¥ 20,000 pension allowances. There are presently 20 million policyholders.

National Pensions

Individuals having neither welfare nor other types of pensions may pay insurance fees (¥ 250 mo. between ages 20–34, ¥ 300/mo. between ages 35–59; from July of this year, a uniform ¥ 450) and after 25 years may become eligible for pensions of up to ¥ 8,000/mo. at age sixty-five. The government also contributes to help cover the costs of this plan. This year it spent ¥ 36,100 million (an increase of ¥ 1,200 million) on behalf of 24 million policyholders. The program has been in existence only nine years, so there have been no recipients as yet.

Pensions

Former government employees and similar categories (200,000 persons) have received ¥ 32,200 million. This year, as part of an effort to provide increased economic security to recipients, pension payments have been increased and the guaranteed minimum has been raised. Measures such as these are providing support for retired employees and their beneficiaries in their later years.

Military Pensions

A total of ¥ 238,000 million (an increase of ¥ 27,800 million) is being paid out to 2,620,000 military personnel and their survivors. This year saw an increase in the pension amounts as well as an expansion of the number of eligible recipients. The major part of these funds go to support military wives and aged parents. Another ¥ 24,500 million is earmarked for bereaved families abandoned by survivors, which do not receive pensions.

Measures for the Bedridden Elderly

There are some 400,000 bedridden elderly in Japan for whom we arrange health-examination visits. Assistance is provided twice weekly by 4,400 Elderly Home Service personnel. In addition, a number of other services are furnished (including special beds) to speed up convalescence and in general to provide a ray of light to the bedridden elderly.
(Budget: ¥ 440 million).

Measures for the Welfare of the Elderly

Health examinations are provided to the elderly over sixty-five years of age (1,430,000 persons) with a view to facilitating early detection of disease. Visits are made to households where the elderly live alone by 1,700 (an increase of 200) Elderly Household Home Service personnel. In addition, ¥1,500/mo. in activities fees is provided to 65,000 Old People's Clubs.

We are also expanding the number of employment placement bureaus for the elderly.

The number of *old-age homes* and related facilities (952 already built, total capacity, 71,000 persons) is being increased; we are also improving the quality and increasing the number of Special Assistance Old-Age Homes (2,500-person capacity) for the elderly who are deprived of their freedom of movement. The care provided in these institutions is generally free of charge.

In addition, we are ameliorating the facilities of our *low-cost old-age homes* (49 existing institutions with capacities of 3000 people) where admission charges are kept at a minimum (generally in the ¥10,000 range). We have also built thirty additional *Elderly Welfare Centers* (now totaling 129) and are assisting municipalities in their efforts to increase the number of *Elderly Recreation Homes*, presently numbering 178.

The budgeted amounts for these programs comes to ¥18,200 million (an increase of ¥3,900 million).

We thus continue our efforts to secure a comfortable existence for pensioners spending their later years in old people's homes.

One of the still-unresolved serious issues confronting us today is whether happiness in old age lies in being in an old people's home or living out one's role as an elderly person within the family environment. Let us all strive to eliminate the stigma attached to old people as the "world's leading suicide candidates." The issue demands our deepest and nonpartisan reflection.

4-8. OPPOSITION TO PROPOSALS FOR RAISING THE RETIREMENT AGE*

Faced with growing pension expenditures, the government in early 1980 proposed raising the eligibility age from 60 to 65 for men and from 55 to 60 for women. The proposal generated great opposition from labor unions and parties of the left, which have traditionally pressed for earlier *retirement ages.*

In response to questioning by representatives of both the Upper and Lower houses, Prime Minister Ōhira commented yesterday on what has become one of the present Diet session's most controversial issues, extending old-age annuity benefits-eligibility to age sixty-five. At the Lower House Budget Committee meeting of January 31, the Prime Minister indicated that "the government has also received a (favorable) report from the Liberal Democratic Party and is rapidly proceeding with its investigation to see what can be done." He suggested that one possibility would be a deletion of the age-deferral clause from the amendment to the Employees Pension Insurance Law being proposed by the Welfare Ministry to the current Diet.

At the present time, men become eligible to receive their old-age pensions at age sixty and women at age 55. The Welfare Ministry,

Asahi Shimbun, Feb. 1, 1980.

with an eye to assuring the future soundness of pension financing has consulted with the Social Insurance Deliberative Council (an advisory organ of the Welfare Ministry headed by Kanazawa Yoshio), regarding its goal of incorporating the following clause into the Welfare Law Amendment bill it is submitting to the present Diet:

"The starting age for receiving benefit payments shall be raised one year every three years commencing in 1988, such that by the year 2000 men will be eligible at age 65 and women at age 60."

In addition to Ōkōchi Kazuo, chairman of the Prime Minister's Social Security Advisory Council, who has expressed a dissenting view on this issue, there has been widespread resistance on the part of opposition parties, labor, and other groups. In consultation with representatives of the recent Diet plenary session, the opposition parties each in turn urged the government to withdraw its proposal. These circumstances have also led to stirrings within the Liberal Democratic Party itself, where fears have been voiced about the influence of what could be "a repeat of the general consumer tax issue" on the upcoming House of Councilors election. It comes as no surprise, therefore, that on January 30 (LDP) Secretary General Sakurauchi proposed to the Prime Minister that "due caution be exercised" on this issue.

5 Higher Education: Aiding Privatized Expansion

Public policies related to Japanese higher education have had to deal with three fundamental tensions, all more or less present in other industrialized countries. First, there is the tension between higher education for a small number of potential political and economic elites and higher education for larger proportions of the general public. With the noteworthy exceptions of the United States and, to a lesser extent, the Soviet Union, all industrialized societies prior to World War II had higher educational systems designed to serve a very narrow portion of their general populace. Since then, and particularly since the 1960s, there have been dramatic shifts by virtually all of these countries toward much more widely available higher education. Japan has been no exception; in fact, it moved quicker than most to expand the number of student places available within its universities.

A second tension, related to the first, has been that between public and private higher education. American higher education has been heavily private, although boosted with large injections of state and federal funding, particularly since World War II. In Great Britain, although universities are technically all private, the government, through the Universities Grants Committee, provides virtually 90 percent of all higher educational funding. Higher education in most other industrialized countries is public, both in administration and in financing. Unlike the arrangements in these countries the Japanese solution to mass higher education until very recently involved the almost total privatization of costs and benefits. In this regard higher educational policy is closely parallel to that of social welfare, as shown in the previous chapter. Only in the

1970s did the government begin to take an active role in funding private higher education.

The third tension, related to the above two, concerns the problem of university autonomy versus government control. To what extent will higher educational curriculums and student, faculty, and administrative activities be subjected to government supervision? How free shall the university be to stand relatively outside the whirlwind of day-to-day sociopolitical activity and "speak truth to power?" In contrast to universities in Western Europe and North America, which developed in some isolation from the "real" worlds of politics and economics, modern higher education in Japan has been closely linked to industrialization, economic growth, and the labor market. Lacking the liberal and individualistic roots of their counterparts in other countries, Japanese universities have been seen by government, and by many parents and students, largely in instrumental terms: how can the university best be utilized for national or personal needs? Such instrumentalism operates, of course, to some extent behind higher education in all societies, but most often it has lurked as an unspoken motive antithethic to the purer and more long-standing notion that the university should serve intellectual cultivation for its own sake. In Japan, the values have been almost the reverse: higher education for its own sake has been a late-developing motivation always forced to contend with a predominant concern for the pragmatic virtues of higher education. In this spirit, official higher educational policies have been intimately linked to economic and labor-market policies in Japan.

Context

One of the quickly recognized necessities of Japan's rapid industrialization under the Meiji regime was that of having an educated populace. Under close supervision by the Ministry of Education, local areas were required to provide schooling at the primary level for all children. By the turn of the century, virtually all Japanese children between the ages of six and thirteen were in school and the level of literacy was at least as high as that in most Western countries.

This philosophy of mass education dominated at the lower levels from very early on. As one moved up the educational ladder, however, elitism and hierarchy became ever more prevalent. At the pinnacle stood the imperial universities, with Tokyo Imperial at the very top. Between the primary school and the imperial university stood a number of mutually exclusive institutional tracks, each accessible only after passage of increasingly rigid examinations. During the prewar period, for example, only one out of a hundred primary school graduates could expect to enter a university; only one out of two hundred could expect to enter one of the extremely high-prestige imperial universities.

In addition to the narrowness of the educational ladder past primary school, the system was characterized by foundations different from the humanistic values of early European and North American universities. The establishing charter of Japan's first university, Tokyo Imperial, went so far as to state that learning was to be pursued not for its own sake, or in the interest of some broad definition of the educated man or the humane society, but "in accordance with the needs of the state." Most particularly, the early public institutions were designed to train a modern elite for the nation; most essentially, they were to provide well-trained cadres for the state bureaucracy (see Chapter 7).

At the same time, while places in the imperial universities were few, low tuition and the absoluteness of the examination system increased the chances for the bright young farm boy to gain a place in the national elite. Japan's national universities, though difficult to enter, were from the start more diversified socio-economically than their socially elitist counterparts in Europe and the United States.

A higher educational background soon became the necessary, and frequently the sufficient, basis for subsequent elite status. And as the links between educational background and subsequent career success became more and more visible throughout society, demand increased for a larger number of higher educational opportunities. Although the size and number of national universities increased with time through the prewar period, the bulk of the response to broadened demands came from the private sector. Many of these privately administered and autonomously funded universities took political positions critical of the government in their early days but such antigovernmental stances were rather short-lived. In a 1918 ordinance, the government gave official recognition to the private university system. At about the same time there was a noticeable decline in their antigovernmental posture. Most private institutions came to develop into less-prestigious carbon copies of their nationally run predecessors. Typically, they produced graduates who followed careers in commerce, journalism, and the professions. They thereby provided an attractive alternative for those offspring of the country's established families and its nouveaux riches who were academically unable to enter the imperial universities. Thus, during the prewar period, Japanese higher education had something of a bifurcated character. A relatively limited number of public institutions provided relatively meritocratic recruitment channels which almost guaranteed subsequent career success, particularly in national or local public service. Below these in prestige were a somewhat larger number of privately administered schools, more restrictive in both their recruitment and in the careers to which their graduates could sensibly aspire. Yet, despite the fact that there were forty-eight recognized universities by the end of World War II, the channels to a university degree remained narrow and only about 4 percent of the nation's 18–22-year age cohort went on to universities. Prewar Japanese higher education, like that in virtually all other countries at that time with the notable exception of the United States, was markedly restricted. (Nagai, 1971).

Most universities played important roles in the achievement of national goals of social and economic development, but it would be a mistake to assume that the universities were all quiescent tools of the government. Although the government exercised various degrees of official oversight of all universities and government and university personnel often enjoyed close family, personal, and old school ties with one another, numerous political confrontations occurred between state and academe during the prewar period. These usually arose as a result of the real or imagined espousal by professors of philosophies, such as communism, socialism, or liberalism, deemed hostile to the nationalist ideology of the times. Although by no means unbent by political pressures, the best universities sought to develop strong traditions of intellectual and administrative autonomy during this period, in spite of, or because of, governmental pressures. Important as the universities were in the production of key members of the governmental and economic elite, they were never, as institutions, the fully captive instruments of state power.

The tensions between elite and mass, public and private, and state centric and autonomous higher education became even more stark under the United States Occupation, and continued through the 1950s and the early 1960s.

During the Occupation, as the Americans sought to recast the nation's society and politics, higher education was naturally one of the many areas targeted for overhaul. The early political commitment to "democratization" and support for the political left resonated well with the general leftist orientation on campus. There was open guilt among Japanese intellectuals for their past failure to adequately speak out against the rise of the military, the growth of authoritarianism, and Japan's overseas wars. Combined with general academic proclivities, these sentiments made many on campus supportive of the political left and hostile to any actions by the Japanese government that hinted of authoritarianism or of threats to university autonomy.

Most of the early American activities in Japanese higher education served to reverse the polarities of prewar trends. The Americans sought to replace elitist higher education with more widely available and "democratic" forms. The multiple tracks beyond primary school were ended and a 6–3–3–4 system of education, following the American pattern, was introduced. The four-year liberal arts college was the capstone. In addition, the number of universities increased dramatically from 48 in 1944 to 226 in 1952. Student enrollments in universities shot up from 84,000 to over 500,000 during the same period. Junior colleges added 205 more institutions and 50,000 more students. Clearly, the roots of mass higher education were spreading.

Private higher education was a particular beneficiary of American policy. By the end of the Occupation, slightly more than one-half of the universities and over 80 percent of the junior colleges were private. At the same time, Article 89 of the new constitution forbade public expenditures for, among other things, "educational . . . enterprises not under the control of public authority." The government consistently interpreted this provision to mean that no public monies could be allocated for the private segment of Japanese higher education.

The changes wrought by the Occupation should not be underestimated, but many features of the prewar system remained intact. In particular, government officials and business leaders retained strong beliefs that higher education should be developed to serve the national interest as defined by the conservative coalition. As the economic policies of the 1950s and 1960s began to unfold, elements of higher education were redirected to serve the ends of high growth. Moreover, despite the many efforts of the Americans to create a less hierarchical structure among Japanese institutions of higher education, the former imperial universities remained the acknowledged summit of the system in faculty and student prestige, access to funding, and the employment opportunities of their graduates. Meanwhile, very much as in the prewar system, a much larger number of less lustrous public and private institutions competed feverishly and ineffectively for whatever prestige they could acquire, all without benefit of aid from the national treasury.

Agenda

In certain public policy areas, most notably economic management, the Japanese government was quick to establish a public, explicit, and coherent agenda of policy goals and to attempt to develop the instruments needed to reach these goals. In higher education in contrast, no explicit and active policy agenda emerged until the late 1960s. Perhaps the earliest date one can mention is 1960, when the government took specific steps to increase the scientific and technical relevance of various higher educational institutions. But truly serious governmental attention to higher educational reform did not materialize until the entire system had been severely wrenched out of shape by the chaotic student protests of 1968–69. Only after these events occurred was there a truly active political agenda directed toward change.

Nevertheless, a noteworthy "hidden agenda" shaped the higher educational system during the two decades or so prior to the outburst of the tumultuous protests of 1968–69. Most of the items on this agenda involved not so much intervention for change as nonintervention in support of continuity. One of the key goals was to allow for expansion into a truly mass higher educational system. But doing so was also designed to involve as little additional governmental expense as possible. This orientation was congruent with that of economic management. On the one hand, large numbers of children born immediately after the war began to enter junior high and high school during the late 1950s and early 1960s, and given the important role that a university degree had long played in the career chances of the bulk of the Japanese populace, there was an ever-widening demand for more higher educational opportunities. On the other hand, the government was seeking to allocate its scarce resources for industrial reorganization and was reluctant to begin pouring large sums into an area such as higher education where tangible economic payoffs would be slight. Yet, unable to ignore the political import of a more open higher educational system, the government sought to alleviate these competing pressures by allowing for expansion within the private sector; places were created rapidly, but at minimal government expense.

More concrete and focused demands on the government emerged from Japan's various business federations during the late 1950s and throughout the 1960s. In accord with the economic management policies noted in Chapter 2, Japan's economy was shifted away, at the end of the war, from its ponderous reliance on primary industry and light manufacturing toward an increased reliance on heavy industry and technologically and capital-intensive manufacturing. Japan's business sector perceived an increased need for well-educated white collar workers as well as workers skilled in science, engineering, and technology. Meeting the former need was relatively compatible with meeting the demands of parents for more places for their offspring. The business and industrial world found it necessary to make few explicit demands on government in that regard.

Much greater pressure was exerted by the various business federations in regard to increasing specialization within higher education and ensuring the development of more scientists, engineers, and middle-level technicians. A series of business federation reports, starting in 1952 and peaking in number during the late 1950s, called for increased scientific and engineering education, particularly within the former imperial universities, for the reestablishment of five-year technical schools that would combine the three years of high school with two years of technical training to produce middle-level technicians, for more occupationally relevant training within four-year schools, and for an overall increase in the number of scientists and engineers produced by the higher educational system (see Readings 5-1 and 5-2).

Business' demands did not fall on deaf ears. In 1957, the government announced a plan to increase by 8,000 the number of freshmen enrolled in science and engineering departments over the next five years. Then, in February 1959, the government established the Science and Technology Council as an organ of the Prime Minister's Office to coordinate the actions of various government agencies and to provide for comprehensive development of the government's policies in science and technology. One and one–half years later, the council issued an extensive plan, outlining a variety of government activities aimed at meeting the nation's alleged manpower shortage in science, medicine, and engineering. From 1960 until 1970, the government committed itself fully to this aspect of higher educational transformation as a major target tightly enmeshed with overall economic-management policies. Indeed, the Economic Advisory Council of the Economic Planning Agency declared in 1960 that "the most important thing in long-term planning for economic growth involves a numerical guarantee of and an increase in the quality of our scientists and technicians" (Pempel, 1978a, p. 178).

Finally, as another goal of higher educational policy during the two and one–half decades after World War II, the conservative camp, particularly its LDP parliamentarians, was concerned with ensuring that university campuses not become bastions of political radicalism and antigovernment activity. This aim was rarely clearly articulated as a goal per se. It also tended to ebb and flow in proportion to student protest activity. Yet it was clearly identifiable as early as 1951, and reappeared continually thereafter. Student protests and government efforts to curb them proved to be the higher educational issue which dominated the newspaper headlines and gained the most political attention during the period 1950–70.

On most of Japan's high quality campuses, significant numbers of individual faculty members and well-organized student groups began, during the immediate postwar years, to advocate drastic changes in the national political regime. Usually, they supported some variant of socialist or communist political systems. Until the 1968–69 protests, most such groups were closely aligned with the opposition parties, but as was true in social welfare, these opposition parties had only a limited and largely ritualized agenda concerning higher education. Rather, the campus was essentially a friendly base camp from which to launch verbal and physical attacks on the government. In turn, progovernment forces sought periodically to retaliate by curtailing protests directly and by threatening to restructure higher educational administration so as to minimize the potential for such activities. As a result, during the 1950s and 1960s there was a climate of mutual opposition and confrontation between state and university that mirrored the broader social and political bipolarities dominating Japanese politics.

In 1952, 1960, and 1968–69, gigantic campus protests developed in conjunction with broader challenges to the conservative political regime. Throughout these protests, there was consistent public debate over the "proper" political place of the university and the student. The earlier two sets of protests were met by government demands that university officials take responsibility to curb protest activities and by the threat if they failed to do so, the government would restructure higher educational administration so as to minimize the university's capacity to serve as a safe haven for anti-governmental activities by students or faculty members. In January, 1960, for example, the minister of education called on university presidents to take "all appropriate actions," including the expulsion of "those who are exerting a significantly bad influence over the general student body" (Pempel, 1978a, p. 102). In conjunction with the massive protests of May and June, 1960, an examination of the entire system of university administration was begun by the Ministry of Education. In May, 1962, Prime Minister Ikeda suggested that education was being used as "a stepping stone to revolution" and called for a reassessment of the system of university administration (see Reading 5-3). Yet, students protests withered before any actual restructuring of the universities took place, so that by the time concrete legislative proposals were made they appeared less necessary than they had a year or two earlier, and they were allowed to die in the legislature.

Such was not the case with the protests of 1968–69. Although by worldwide standards, the earlier protests had been enormous and politically significant, they were pale predecessors of the protests of 1968–69, which truly forced a comprehensive reconsideration of Japanese higher education. Like their counterparts in New York, Boston, Paris, Frankfort, Naples, and elsewhere, Japanese students occupied university buildings and took to the streets with a force unprecedented in modern history. Moreover, many of the protest groups, parallelling the environmentally related citizens' groups to be discussed in the next chapter, rejected ties to the established opposition parties. This left them freer to raise higher educational issues in isolation from broader (or narrower) party agendas. As one result, their following among non-partisan or anti-party students expanded rapidly.

During 1968, 116 universities were the scene of protest activities deemed "significant" by the police; the following year saw incidents at 40–75 universities per month. In 1968, the police were involved in 31 campus actions involving more than 10,000 police and resulting in 425 arrests; in 1969, the figures were 938 campus actions, 243,000 police, and over 3,500 arrests. Possibly more telling than such general figures was the fact that some institutions including Tokyo University, were closed for more than a year, forcing cancellation of classes, entrance examinations, and graduations. These protests, representing a major challenge to the national political regime and transmitted via television into homes throughout the country, produced a climate of reexamination of Japanese higher education and a growing awareness of deeply rooted flaws in the system. The result was a comprehensive reexamination of most major aspects of the country's higher educational system.

The first item on the government's agenda was to end the protests. The business federations, most conservative politicians, and even large numbers of professional educators, who typically were reluctant to support government intervention on campus, all demanded stringent measures to curtail the occupation of buildings and to resume instruction.

In the process of looking for ways to end the protests, a number of governmental and campus organizations were compelled to look more deeply at the university and the role it played in the society. Numerous criticisms emerged: structures were too rigid and hierarchical; individual faculties (*gakubu*) had more autonomy and power than the university as a whole; the entrance examination system was anti-educational in its results; universities, particularly in the private sector, were under-financed; there was not enough internationalism or universality in Japanese universities; faculty members were underpaid, overworked, and hostile or authoritarian in interactions with students; students, once admitted to universities,

rarely had to work hard to pass; higher education was overly restricted to the recent high school graduate and it was almost impossible for an individual to return to school in mid-career. These
and other criticisms mounted steadily.

To its credit, the government turned official attention to many of
these items even after the protests subsided in late 1969 and 1970.
Most significantly, the Central Council for Education, an advisory
organ to the Ministry of Education, issued a comprehensive report
entitled "Basic Guidelines for the Reform of Education" in June
1971 (see Reading 5-4). The guidelines became the basis for a
number of definite reform efforts during the subsequent decade.
The most important of these involved increased government funding for private universities, diversification of higher educational
structures, and limits on the university expansion that had gone
unchecked for about twenty years. These goals for the 1970s were
particularly compatible with the shifting emphasis in policies related to economic management, social welfare, and environment,
namely an increased commitment by the government to public
expenditures for the improvement of social overhead, a goal which
had been virtually ignored during the 1950s and most of the 1960s.

Process

The government directed comparatively little attention to the
area of higher education during the 1950s and most of the 1960s.
Even the Ministry of Education remained comparatively unin-
volved, mainly because of its focus on primary and secondary
education and the political problems it faced there with the mili-
tantly antagonistic Japan Teachers' Union (Thurston, 1974). The
recurrent concern, as noted earlier, was to curb student protests
and to prevent the universities from becoming base camps of radicalism. The primary policy-instrument utilized in this sporadic battle was the recurring threat of government intervention in internal
university administration. Following the protests of 1952 and 1960,
the government introduced legislation that would curb student
influence on campuses across the country and that would make the
university administration more directly responsive to Ministry of
Education oversight. Neither of these pieces of legislation passed,
however, because student protest waned before the legislation was
called up for argument in the Diet and because university adminis-

trators and their associations lobbied effectively against the proposals. Whether the threats had served their purpose or whether the protests died of their own accord was, however, irrelevant to government officials. The protests had ended; that in itself was satisfactory.

Probably more revealing of governmental instruments of effecting policy in higher education during this period is the manner in which the government dealt, not with protest, but with the more persistent, long-term problems of enrollment expansion and the changing occupational structure. Meeting the official agenda in regard to both problems involved measures that were much less overt than were taken to cope with protests. Instead, it necessitated a complex of bureaucratic steps that had profound influence on the shape of the system of Japanese higher education. In brief, the government followed policies that blended bureaucratic direction with nonintervention to create a system characterized by extremes of both elitism and popularism. To bolster the facilities and the prestige of the best of the country's national schools and to enable these schools to handle much of the increase in scientific and engineering education, government policy relied on a high degree of bureaucratic direction and financial inducement. At the same time, responsibility for providing mass higher education and absorbing the increased demands for university diplomas fell largely to the private sector. There, government intervention and supervision was minimal, and the economics of running a higher educational institution for profit dictated overall expansion, with a much higher proportion of students graduating with degrees in the humanities, social sciences, and commerce.

Enrollment-expansion was undoubtedly the most significant and long-ranging of the changes that occurred in Japanese higher education during the postwar period. As noted earlier, the United States Occupation had provided a stimulus for the development of mass higher education. This trend continued with virtually no abatement until 1975 when, as one of several policy changes to be examined below, the government finally intervened to check the expansion. Statistics tell but a part of the story. Between the end of the Occupation and 1979, the number of four-year universities went from 226 to 443; the number of junior colleges rose from 228 to 518; the total student body jumped from 450,000 to nearly 2 million; the percentage of the cohort of eighteen to twenty-two year olds attending higher educational institutions jumped from 7 percent to 37 percent; (when post secondary vocational schooling is included the latter figure is closer to 50 percent).

What is most striking about this increase is that it took place with exceptionally small increases in the number of public institutions and with very little increase in governmental funding. Virtually the entire expansion was privatized. Between 1962 and 1968, the peak years for expansion, an average of fifteen new universities per year were chartered; whereas in 1952 just over one–half of the universities, enrolling 57 percent of the students, were under private control, by 1979 these figures were up to 71 percent and about 80 percent.

Although the private sector obviously was anxious to claim the responsibility for expanding the number of institutions and the places in higher education, the government was more than a passive bystander in a laissez-faire process. The Ministry of Education, which had the ultimate responsibility for examining university-charter applications and also that for ensuring minimal standards of educational quality, virtually abdicated both responsibilities, particularly during the early and mid-1960s. From 1962 to 1968, nearly 80 percent of all charter applications were approved, most with only perfunctory scrutiny of the quality of the institution to be established. Furthermore, standards of existing and newly established private universities were also virtually exempt from examination by government officials. Expansion within private universities became exceptionally easy and profitable. Meanwhile, large numbers of institutions fell far below minimum legal standards. Library facilities, classroom space, numbers of part-time faculty, teacher-faculty ratios, and the like all showed the evidence of rapid expansion with minimal quality control.

Although the government, by being lenient, clearly aided expansion it provided very little in the way of financial inducement to assist this expansion. During the period in question, the government contributed no more than 4 percent of the expenses of the private universities, a figure lower than that of any other industrialized country. It is plain that government policy involved averting official eyes from problems of quality to allow the private market to meet rising demands for quantity.

In the more elite of the national universities and in the areas of science and technology the government was more active, though by no means did it produce any comprehensive assessment of higher education or its role in the society. Rather its actions involved primarily bureaucratic responses to powerful interest-group pressures. This was particularly true in meeting demands that business considered essential to the success of national economic-management policies. In response to the clear and frequently articulated demands of the peak business associations, and particularly in conjunction with the national economic policy aimed at doubling the national income in ten years (see Chapter 2), the government introduced a series of programs aimed at increasing the technical and scientific components of higher education, at improving facilities in these areas, and at vastly increasing the actual numbers of graduates in these fields. In response to reports by the Science and Technology Council and plans from the Economic Planning Agency, during 1960–61 the government committed itself to increasing the number of enrollees in departments of science and engineering by 16,000 per year starting in 1961, a quota which was subsequently raised to 20,000 per year. Through coordinated increases in funding opportunities and administrative oversight, the government induced more than a doubling of the number of science and engineering faculties and a 260% increase in the number of graduates in these fields during the period 1962–70.

Government funds, while designed to aid in the fields of science and technology and contributing very little to the ever-increasing private segment of the higher educational system, were by no means equally distributed among the national universities. The Ministry of Education exercised a high level of discretion in its particular budgetary allocations. Much of this discretion was used to favor the former imperial universities. Between 1948 and the mid-1960s, for example, Tokyo University's share of the ministry's budget for higher education rose from 8 percent to 15 percent. By the beginning of the 1970s, expenditures per student at Tokyo and Kyoto universities were about ten times those in the private universities.

Higher educational policy instruments during the two decades or so following World War II involved a mixture of bureaucratic cajoling, regulatory leniency, and occasional outbursts of bluster and threat, but they shifted noticeably after the demonstrations and protests of 1968–69. As had been the response to earlier protests, the government first threatened legislation designed to overhaul relations between the state and the university. Unlike the earlier periods, however, in 1969 it delivered, with a temporary five-year bill permitting the Minister of Education to close an institution of higher education that had experienced nine months of continuous protests or any that experienced a second wave of protests within a single year (see Reading 5-5). Then in 1974, when the five-year term of the bill was to expire, even though the ministry had not found it necessary to invoke the law's provisions during that entire period, the government considered a variety of measures to allow the law to continue in force or to be expanded in scope (see Readings 5-6, 5-7 and 5-8). Eventually, the government demonstrated its powers by the simple expedient of declaring that since the law had not been explicitly repealed after its five year term, its provisions continued to be legally binding.

The 1969 bill and its continuation in 1974 marked a substantial increase in government's active reshaping of higher education. Following principally the recommendations of the Central Council for Education, the government took a number of subsequent steps that further expanded its role in the system. One of the more noteworthy was a law to permit government funding of up to one–half of the operating expenses of the private institutions (see Reading 5-9). In conjunction with aid came several bureaucratic regulations to curtail the ease with which private schools were established and expanded. A five-year ban on new institutions, departments, and student-quota expansions was introduced in 1976, and similar restraints were being planned for the period 1981–86. Meanwhile, several new types of institutions were created, including vocational colleges which would meet the Central Council's call for institutions designed to be immediately relevant to post-educational employment. In addition, several experimental institutions were created. One of these was Tsukuba University which adopted a modular, nondepartmental internal organization. Between 1973 and 1978, twelve national medical universities were established. Two universities of science and technology at Nagaoka and Toyohashi were added in 1976. In 1978, two universities of education were created at Hyōgō and Jōetsu, and in 1979 the government established a University of Library Science. A University of the Air, which will offer courses and award degrees mostly through television, has been planned and the research-oriented United Nations University was also established. Less glamorous, but nonetheless significant, activities emerged else-where. Many universities formerly considered a notch or two below the former Imperial Universities were allowed and often encour-aged to develop new research institutions, to experiment with cross-disciplinary appointments or open-enrollment courses, to establish vocationally oriented master's programs, to relocate outside of urban centers, and the like. If unqualified expansion, private initia-tive, structural rigidity, and minimal governmental oversight char-acterized Japanese higher education until the late 1960s, Japan entered the 1980s with much greater degrees of flexibility, but also with more governmental direction and assistance.

Consequences

In terms of meeting governmental goals, higher educational poli-cies must be counted a sparkling success even during the period of passivity of the 1950s and 1960s. In that time, enrollment expanded at a rate unmatched anywhere in the industrialized world. More and more universities and university places were created to provide education to ever-larger numbers of students. By the beginning of the 1980s, 37–38 percent of the 18–22-year-age-cohort in Japan was attending a university or a junior college. In metropolitan centers the figure was over 50 percent. In addition, there was a significant increase in the output of scientists and engineers. In 1960, just over 18 percent of the total student enrollment was in science and en-gineering; by 1980 this was nearly 30 percent. In the national universities, the figures rose even more dramatically. Finally, the relative ease with which the government passed and then continued the "temporary" university control bill, plus ten years of relative campus quiescence, suggested that the government was willing and able to curtail clear and unmistakable threats to regime legitimacy.

An additional plaudit of sorts can be accorded because these successes came at low cost to the government. The public portion of expenditures for higher education decreased from 67 percent to 51 percent between 1950 and 1968. As a percent of total public ex-penditures, public funding for higher education dropped sharply as well. Such figures represented, typically, the lowest public con-tributions to higher education in the OECD countries. In this respect, the successful expansion of higher education involved no need to compromise economic management policies designed to minimize governmental expense.

Even after 1971, when the government developed its program to make public funds available to offset up to 50 percent of the operating expenses of private institutions, the total proportion of government expenditure for higher education rose only very little. And while it may be a bit premature for evaluation, many of the other changes in government policy begun in the mid- to late-1970s seem to have injected increased flexibility into the entire system.

From such macrolevel perspectives, Japanese higher educational policies at the beginning of the 1980s appear to have created a system that compared to that in most other countries is egalitarian, occupationally relevant, flexible, and cheap.

Though successful in terms of reaching government goals, the system that has evolved has had much more ambiguous social consequences. One of the foremost concerns the issue of quality, which has been addressed in earlier sections. At this point, it is sufficient simply to recall that much of the higher education provided during the period of maximum expansion took place under conditions not terribly conducive to deep learning. Even after the reforms, most private Japanese universities were characterized by overcrowding, dingy dormitories, postage stamp–sized campuses, and harried professors.

An additional problem to consider is that of the socioeconomic biases within the system. As was noted in Chapter 3, most of the permanent work force are hired directly after graduation, and they are paid salary-differentials based on educational level and on the prestige of the institution and faculty from which they have graduated. Moreover, these members of the permanent work force tend to remain for the bulk of their working lives with the firm they have joined after graduation, making the achievement of a degree, particularly from a high-prestige institution, a worthwhile, long-term investment. At a minimum, such a degree provides an occupational and income base below which it is difficult to fall. While graduation from the most prestigious national universities may provide a channel of upward mobility for the talented lower-class youth, graduation from even the less prestigious private universities ensure that there is little corresponding downward social mobility in the upper or middle classes.

Just as the low level of nationally available social welfare benefits has pressed home the importance of a hefty savings account to offset the hazards of ill health, unemployment, and retirement, so too the important career-role provided by a university degree plus the limited number of low-cost national university positions available have inspired many families to save more. And as was noted in chapters 2 and 4, Japan's high savings-rate aided in generating the investment capital that was utilized to hasten the country's phenomenal economic growth during the 1950s and 1960s.

However, because tuition and fees make up the bulk of the operating expenses of the private universities, and because scholarship programs were virtually nonexistent, it was impossible financially for large numbers of potential students from lower-income families to take advantage of the expanding higher educational opportunities. In many private institutions, notoriously high "contributions to the building fund" frequently made the difference between an applicant's success or failure. Full professors occasionally were able to control one, two, or more places in each freshman class, and not a few penurious or unscrupulous (or both) professors sold these positions to the highest bidders. Admissions to medical schools were even more dubious or corrupt. Thus, nearly 60 percent of the student body in private universities were from the top quintile of the nation's income earners. They were eleven times more numerous than those from the lowest quintile.

The national universities did have tuitions of only about one-eighth that of private universities in the early 1970s, making them financially more available to lower class students. But this had jumped sharply by the end of the decade. Entrance to these schools, particularly the most prestigious national schools, was based almost exclusively on the passage of rigid annual examinations. Although such fairness worked in one sense in favor in the bright but poor or socially unconnected student, the human toll exacted by the effort to pass such exams has been extremely high. The newspapers are full of morose stories of suicides by unsuccessful exam-takers or their parents, after virtually every exam period.

Furthermore, in that a well-to-do family can better afford to provide additional study time, a quiet study area, extra after-hours schooling and private tutors than can less affluent families, there is an element of social-class bias even in the national universities.

Although there is relatively equal representation from each of the three middle quintiles of income earners in the national universities, students from the top quintile of income earners are three and one–half times more numerous than are students from the bottom quintile. With nearly 80 percent of the student body attending private institutions, the entire system has thus been one with clear-cut favoritism toward the upper classes (see Reading 5-10).

Just how this bias differs from that in other countries is difficult to say. One must certainly balance it off against the comparatively high precentage of the total high school graduating class that now finds it possible, regardless of high costs, to continue on to some form of higher educational institution. It is also too early to assess the potential effect of the government's assistance on the socioeconomic biases in the private schools.

The program has been phased in slowly, with most monies going to aid engineering and science, and it ran into various budgetary stumbling blocks during the economic stagnation of the late 1970s. But still it possesses the potential, either as promise or threat, for following the course taken by the University Grants Committee in Britain, which also started slowly and with small funding but eventually came to control virtually all of the higher educational funding in the country. At the same time, this program is not all positive. One possible problem, like that discussed in the previous chapter on social welfare, concerns the potential for geometrically expanding costs in an era of economic slowdown. In addition, with aid has come the potential for increased control by government agencies. Increased financing contains the potential for even greater control. In this sense, while it may prove a boon to the private sector, such aid may ultimately work to undermine the university's potential for remaining a place somewhat apart from political control so that it can serve as the most important social institution capable of "speaking truth to power."

Readings

5-1. EMPLOYERS' DEMANDS FOR REFORM
OF THE EDUCATIONAL SYSTEM*

The following is an outline of demands made by the Japan Federation of Employers' Associations for greater responsiveness by the educational system to business needs. It illustrates the general direction of demands made by industry in the subsequent decade.

The Japan Federation of Employers' Associations, from its unique position in the industrial world that will be entered by new graduates believes that the present educational system stands rather aloof from the demands of the industrial world and fails to meet adequately the needs of the nation's business community. Therefore, the federation has established a Special Committee on Education. As a result of the committee's third investigation of the present educational system we offer the following demands to the appropriate authorities in the Ministry of Education and the various national, local public and private universities:
1. We must quickly rectify the overemphasis on the humanities within the universities. . . .
2. We must avoid national standardization in universities. . . .
3. We must plan for the enrichment of specialized education. . . .
4. We must train key managerial personnel and employees. . . .
5. We must reform and strengthen university administration. . . .
6. We must correct the abusive overemphasis on educational background. . . .

5-2. INDUSTRY'S CALL FOR COLLABORATION
WITH EDUCATION†

The following newspaper analysis of the position of the Japan Committee for Economic Development shows the combining of the concern for curtailing student protests with that for increasing the

---

*Yamamoto Tokushige, ed., *Daigaku Mondai Shiryō Yōran* (Tokyo: Bunkyū Shōrin, 1969), pp. 477–78.
†*Asahi Shimbun*, July 10, 1960.

responsiveness of higher education to industrial needs. Repeated throughout is the phrase "collaboration between industry and education" (sangaku kyōdō).

"On the JCED's Collaboration Between Industry and Education"

With an eye toward the modernization of management and technology, noticeable progress has been made in the business world's efforts to get both industrial and educational circles to cooperate in the interests of "collaboration between industry and education." However, in view of the student-movement demonstrations against the recent Diet, there has been a strengthening of opinion within the JCED that the financial world must make cooperative moves toward students through steps for the "collaboration between industry and education" so as to draw students into the capitalist camp. . . .

However, business contends that to bring the industrial world and the schools closer, the schools must become aware of realities in the industrial world, and on that basis they must become institutions serving the purposes and demands of the industrial world rather than simply making use of the scholastic experiences of the world of education to develop simple abstract theories. . . .

To these ends the JCED has been operating from the following premises in its calls for "collaboration between industry and education:

1. Japanese democracy is gravely threatened by the protests which have been going on since May 19. The financial world in particular cannot remain indifferent to the student movement which has become the driving force behind the demonstrations at the Diet.
2. For the development of a healthy democracy a commonsensical middle class must be trained to serve as a stable force in society. It is expected that students in particular will be educated to form the core of such a middle class.
3. Nevertheless the recent student movement is fraught with danger in that it is moving in anti-democratic directions.
4. In order to bring students into the camp of democracy and capitalism, the financial world must make cooperative moves toward students. For these purposes, it will be most effective to rely on the movement for "collaboration between industry and education."

5-3. PRIME MINISTER IKEDA'S CRITICISM OF STUDENT PROTESTS*

The following is a speech given by Prime Minister Ikeda before an LDP meeting prior to the lower house elections of 1962. In addition to praising the importance of education in Japan's overall development, he voices strong criticism of the radical activities of student protesters, suggesting that education is being used as a tool of revolution. The speech received widespread publicity and generated severe criticism from the political left.

The issue is education. How can we aspire to promote the development of our people if not by the propagation and strengthening of our educational resources? And how is world peace and the advance of human welfare to be brought about if not, once again, by educational and technological progress? Surely the primary objective of mankind must be to liberate its members from the restraining shackles of nature. Overcoming nature's limitations via mechanical and technological progress is none other than the path to the cultural advancement of the human race. Not only has scholarly and technical progress in the last few centuries brought us to our present advanced stage of development, but most recently the advent of man-made satellites has seen human evolution reach not just to the outer limits of our globe but beyond to the exploration of space itself. Human civilization has brought itself to the threshold of the space age.

I believe that education represents the sole means for bringing about not only national development but also peace and human happiness throughout the world. Our forebears were aware of this truth and our predecessors have devoted particular efforts in the field of Japanese education since the debut of our modern era in 1868. My friends, can we ever fail to remember how, when defeat robbed us of our territorial sovereignty and destroyed our material well-being, it was the high level of Japanese education and science bequeathed to us by our forebears that enabled the Japanese nation to reach its present development?

The phenomenon is not unique to Japan. And yet, notwithstand-

*Nomura Hyōji et al. (eds.) *Daigaku Seisaku: Daigaku Mondai* (Tokyo: Rōdō Junpōsha, 1969) pp. 540–42.

ing the remarkable investments of resources in education by England in the nineteenth and twentieth centuries, and more recently by the United States and the Soviet Union, Japan is fortunate in being the pacesetter in terms of educational diffusion. A current issue for Japan's educational system is the rapidly increasing number of high schools; this is related to the fact that Japan is number one or two in the world in terms of its rate of admission to secondary education of those who have completed the compulsory-education program. University admission rates are second to the United States but superior to England, Germany, France, and Italy. This gives some idea of the progress being achieved in Japanese education, although only from a quantitative perspective. What is the situation in terms of quality? Here, unfortunately, the facts of the matter will not allow me to boast as I would like. We are just going to have to apply ever-increased efforts in the coming years to this matter of quality in education, from the earliest years of grade school up to the university level. Leaving the Japan Teachers Union aside for the moment, and taking a look at the current situation in Japan, is there not a hint that our education is being used as a tool of revolution?

Even as uninformed a person as myself cannot help but be aware of this use of education for revolutionary purposes, and it is my strong conviction that, together with the people, we shall have to devise adequate measures for dealing with this issue in the future. To affirm one's rights to no end while forgetting one's duties is to mistake the meaning of liberalism and to espouse a creed of egoism; and who can assert with confidence that we are not in danger of losing a sense of respect for the individual and the universe, as well as sacrificing love of family and country, of losing sight of our homeland. The sages of old were wont to say that national degeneration is never due to enemies from without, but is a result of the loss of moral vitality among the people. It is the moral vitality of the people that raises up the nation and provides the best means for truly realizing a democratic state. It is in this sense that we must further expand and reinforce government programs in the area of compulsory education, and, in order to greatly strengthen the links between the younger generations, who make up the foundation of the country, and the state, I have conceived of the free textbook system.

Needless to say, if we are to build a truly strong Japan, we must build up our human resources. Japan may be narrow in terms of its land mass and deprived in natural resources, but fortunately the Japanese are endowed with the highest quality raw human material. By taking our highly endowed Japanese and greatly developing their strengths by means of education, we can demonstrate the capacities of our talented Japanese and their potential not only for their own country but on behalf of the people of the world, and thus contribute to the peace of Japan and the world.

Since the formation of my Cabinet, I have been involved in developing budgetary measures designed to promote compulsory education and scientific technology. In addition to pursuing these programs, we are making efforts to improve the quality of our teachers from the university to the grade-school levels, for they are involved in the most basic aspects of the human civilizing process. Moreover, and of course, with all due respect to academic freedom, I have given instructions to Education Minister Araki to undertake a reexamination of our system of university administration as it functions at the present time. This gives an idea of my thinking on education problems as we face the future.

To repeat, in order to become a truly fine country, a nation worthy of the world's trust, the entire Japanese people must love their homeland, and appreciate their national culture and history; they must acquire a high level of good sense and technical skill. What is required is a human evolution which inspires the confidence of the peoples of the world. This involves not only the construction of a new nation; it is, I believe, the only way in which we can contribute to world peace.

5-4. GOVERNMENT PROPOSALS FOR CHANGES IN THE EDUCATIONAL SYSTEM*

Following the protests of 1968–69, the Central Council for Education, an advisory organ to the Ministry of Education, produced an extensive report calling for comprehensive changes in the nation's educational system. These formed the core of various alterations during the 1970s. Below are excerpts from the part of the report that

*Japan, Ministry of Education, *Educational Standards in Japan, 1970* (Tokyo: Ministry of Education, 1970), pp. 185–91.

deals with higher education. Note the emphasis on diversifying the structures of higher education, on improving quality, and on increasing government financial aid.

The Basic Guidelines for the Reform of Higher Education
The Diversification of Higher Education

In order to diversity Japanese higher education in the future, institutions for higher education must be categorized according to students' qualifications and the number of years required for the completion of an average course of studies. At the same time it is desirable to provide different types of curricula in accordance with the aims and nature of the education. It is also necessary to establish a system where students can easily transfer at will, from one category of institution or one type of curriculum to another.

1) Category 1 (Provisionally to be called "University") This category would include institutions of higher education providing three or four years of education for graduates from upper secondary schools.

The following types of curricula are to be offered by institutions within this category:

(A) Comprehensive curriculum, providing professional knowledge and skills for those careers which are not particularly specialized.

(B) Academic curriculum, developed in accordance with the academic system of each discipline, systematically providing basic academic knowledge and skills.

(C) Occupational curriculum, providing the theoretical and technical training required for particular professional occupations so as to provide students with the qualifications or abilities for those occupations.

(2) Category II (Provisionally to be called "Junior College") Institutions within this category will offer shorter curricula, two years of education, to graduates from upper secondary schools. The following types of curricula are to be offered within this category:

(A) Comprehensive curriculum, aimed at giving students whose future careers will not be too specialized, the necessary cultural background to be good citizens in society.

(B) Occupational curriculum, providing knowledge and skills required by particular professional occupations to provide students with the qualifications and abilities for these occupations.

(3) Category III (Provisionally to be called "Technical College") Institutions in this category are to provide higher education over five concurrent years for those who have finished lower secondary education, enabling students to acquire the qualifications or abilities necessary for particular professional occupations or for other specific purposes.

(4) Category IV (Provisionally to be called "Graduate School") Institutions in this category are to provide an advanced academic education of two or three years' duration in specific fields, either for those who have graduated from institutions within Category I or for those who are recognized to have ability equivalent to or higher than the former. They are also to provide reeducation at this advanced level for people in general.

(5) Category V (Provisionally to be called "Research Center") Institutions in this category are to provide opportunities for research and training and research guidance for those who want to pursue an advanced level of academic research worthy of a doctor's degree.

2. Directions of Curriculum Reform

Curricula in institutions for higher education in Categories I and II (universities and junior colleges) should be developed along lines allowing for the provision of comprehensive or more specialized forms of education. The goals of general education pursued by existing universities would be more effectively approximated if the following improvements are made:

(1) General education has, in the past, sought to give students overall knowledge of various disciplines, an understanding of scientific methods, a grasp of problems in the context of cultural development, and a correct understanding of humanity and values. All these aims should be included in and pursued integrally with every revised program of study.

(2) Whatever fundamentals are required in specialized education

should be integrated into the specialized-education programs of the respective institutions.

(3) Foreign-language training should aim at giving students a knowledge of foreign languages for practical international use. As the occasion demands, language training centers set up on campuses may be assigned this responsibility and the results tested. (The education of those majoring in foreign languages or foreign literature will be considered on a different basis).

(4) Health and physical education should be improved by giving adequate guidance in .extracurricular athletic activities and by supervising the health of all students more thoroughly.

3. Improving Teaching Methods

It is desirable to effect an improvement in the teaching methods used in institutions of higher education in accordance with their teaching patterns, i.e.:

(1) In the teaching of systematic theories, the quality and efficiency level of lectures can be raised by widely utilizing broadcasting VTR (video-tape recorders) and other technological devices.

(2) Seminars, experiments, and practice sessions of small groups should be developed further in order to help students understand perfectly and to obtain the ability to apply what they have learned in lectures.

(3) As regards athletic and cultural activities on the campus, specialists should be appointed in designated training centers thus allowing students to enjoy student life thoroughly by giving them guidance and assistance.

4. The Necessity of Making Higher Education Open to the General Public and of Establishing a System of Certification

To allow all people in our rapidly changing society to receive education at any time and whenever necessary, higher education should be made available not only to students in specific age groups or with particular educational qualifications but also to the public at large. This means that it should be made easy for all institutions of higher education to accept those requiring re-education and also that educational opportunity should be expanded by using methods other than those of the traditional credit system of school education. It should also be made possible for those acquiring a certain number of approved credits from various categories of institutions to be granted higher-education certificates.

As regards existing bachelor's, master's and doctor's degrees, it is necessary to consider the elimination or the simplification of the existing classifications within each degree.

5. *The Organizational Separation of Teaching and Research*

In order to achieve a balance between the teaching and research activities of the faculty in institutions of higher education, the structure of the teaching body should be reformed into one carrying out education for students. At the same time, all teachers should be provided with an environment conducive to research, in accordance with the aims and characteristics of the institutions. For this purpose, in institutions of Categories IV and V (graduate schools and research centers), it is desirable to separate the teaching and research organizations and to develop each of them in a rational fashion. It is necessary to clarify teachers' responsibilities for each area, and thus to establish co-operation between teaching and research organizations having independent aims and objectives.

6. *Institutions of Category V (Provisionally to Be Called "Research Centers")*

The "Research Center" is a teaching and administrative organization giving research training to those wanting to engage in advanced academic research programs leading to a doctor's degree. As a rule, it will have a faculty with some full-time teachers of its own. Therefore, if it is to be established in affiliation with other institutions, institutions of Category IV (graduate schools) or research institutes where an appropriate research and training organization now exists should be chosen. Of those admitted to engage in research, those chosen as assistants for the teaching and research activities of the center or other institutions should be given appropriate remuneration. In relation to the establishment of these research centers, it will be necessary to examine the research institutes now attached to institutions of higher education, research institutes designed to be used jointly, and other academic research institutes.

7. Size of Institutions of Higher Education and Rationalization of Administrative and Managerial Organization

Institutions of higher education should avoid becoming too large simply as a means of meeting managerial needs or to become self-sufficient research institutions. They should be of such a size as to allow optimal coherent functioning as an educational institution. For the benefit of research, exchanges between institutions of higher education and research institutes should be encouraged by developing close relationships and cooperation between them.

The administration and management of institutions of higher education should avoid allowing internal organizations to exert sectional pressures. Integrated and efficient teaching and research should be protected from various external and internal influences. Also necessary is a structure in which administrative operation can take place without interference in the institutions' initiative and self-government. Regarding matters affecting the entire campus, such as administrative, financial, and personnel problems and student affairs, more emphasis should be given to the planning, coordinating, and evaluative activities of the central administrative organ, as headed by the president and vice-president. It is also necessary to secure the appropriate participation of learned persons outside the institutions and on relevant problems student opinion should be heard in order to further improve administration and management.

8. Improving the Employment of Teachers

Institutions of higher education should secure an adequate number of teaching staff well-qualified for the purpose and nature of the institution and suitable for a position in either teaching or research. At the same time, institutions of higher education should improve their administration regarding teaching staff. They should, that is, prevent that stagnation in teaching and research which results from insularity; they should obtain the participation of experts from outside the institution in the selection and evaluation of the performance of the teaching staff; they should limit the time that one teacher can remain in one particular position; they should also limit the number of teachers graduating from any one university.

At the same time, teachers' salaries and other conditions of employment must be extensively improved in order for institutions of higher education to attract a highly qualified staff and to make it easier to exchange personnel with circles outside the institution. The improvement in the salary level should also include devices to encourage teachers to make greater efforts for education.

9. *The Direction to Be Taken for the Reform of Establishment Procedures for National and Public Universities*

Among institutions of higher education, national and public universities in particular are, within the present system, considered to have the character of administrative governmental agencies in the broad sense and at the same time need special arrangements for their governance. They, therefore, are in a position where it is easy to have conflicts with the controlling authorities of the national or local government that has established the institution. Furthermore, because of the way in which they were founded, such universities have a tendency to rely on institutional stability and to lose their sense of autonomy and responsibility for university governance. Therefore the following two ways of reform can be envisaged to clarify their relationship with the founders and to allow them to govern themselves with real autonomy and responsibility. In doing so it is hoped that each university will be reformed in accordance with the university's purpose and character.

(1) The present form of establishment should be abandoned and universities should be incorporated in a new form allowing them to manage themselves autonomously with a certain amount of public funds and yet with some responsible public character.

(2) The universities must improve their administration, establish responsible management, and clarify their relationship with their founders.

10. *Improving Governmental Financing of Higher Education, the System of the Costs Borne by the Beneficiaries and the Scholarships System*

To develop higher education further, and to maintain and raise the quality of higher education, it would be desirable for the government to give qualified private institutions for higher education a subsidy amounting to a certain proportion of their expenditure reasonably estimated and fixed in terms of the institutions' objectives and the nature of their activities. In doing so, the government should have a long-range educational plan, and the institutions should be permitted to use the subsidy flexibly and effectively. The application of this formula to the provision of financial resources for national and public institutions of higher education should also be considered. In this case, however, it should be noticed that the sum including tuition fees borne by the beneficiaries should be made more appropriate, so that any great differences in the finances available will not result from differences between founders or from differences between areas of specialization.

When the government's measures for dealing with the above problems are discussed, a thorough examination should also be made of the national scholarship system, with the intention of furthering equality of educational opportunity and of encouraging talented individuals to enter those areas where they are most needed.

Furthermore, taking into account the social role of institutions of higher education it would be desirable for not only the government but also the society in general to give a considerable degree of financial support to them.

11. A National Plan for Co-ordination of Higher Education Improvements

National financial aid is indispensable to better establishment and governance of institutions of higher education in the future. Therefore, in order to utilize its resources to the fullest, the government must develop a long-range plan for the size of higher education as a whole, classifying the types of higher education in relation to the various purposes and characteristics of institutions, proportioning the enrollments in each specialized field and ensuring a fair, regional distribution of institutions. It is, therefore, necessary to develop such a plan now for the nation as a whole, to establish a new public framework responsible for its realization, and to reform and enrich higher education in general.

12. Improving Students' Environment

In order to make education in the institutions of higher education fruitful in the best sense of the word, in addition to the above-mentioned reforms an enriched student life should be secured by improving extra-curricular activities and students' environment.

We must help students to develop their characters to the fullest extent. In character formation the "dormitory" has been found to be very important, and it is important for institutions of higher education to improve the dormitories further. Since both now and at a larger stage some institutions may be unable to provide "dormitories," other ways must be found to offer the educational advantages of a "group-life" that the domitories have offered. In addition, some other methods must be found by which the great numbers of students who are studying may be given the chance to have personal communication with others, and the environment must be improved to provide them with adequate food and accommodations. If the institutions of higher education cannot accomplish this alone, then the government must consider some appropriate measures.

13. *Improving the Selection Procedure for Students*

Because the student selection system affects all education in Japan, we must try, from now on, to improve that system. The aim should be that in the selection of students for higher education, the records of those who, at the secondary level, studied the planned curriculum conscientiously should be fairly evaluated and that each student should be able to gain admittance into a university suited to his individual abilities without special preparation for entrance exams. The improvement of the selection procedure must be based on the following principles:

(1) School records, fairly showing what students have accomplished in senior high school, should be used as one element in selection.

(2) A common test with a broad range should be developed and used as a means to adjust the different standards of evaluation among high schools.

(3) When a university wants, it may initiate a test to examine certain abilities needed for a specific field or require essays and/or personal interviews. The results of all these should be used in making a comprehensive judgment.

5-5. THE UNIVERSITY CONTROL LAW*

The following are excerpts from the so-called University Control Law, passed in 1969 in an effort to curtail the student demonstrations that had rocked the country for two years. Note, in particular, the concentration of power in the hands of the Ministry of Education and the university president. Note, too, the cutback in student and faculty funding after extensive protests. Finally, note the ambiguity in Supplementary Provision Number 5.

(Purpose)

Article 1: In view of the university's mission and social responsibility and in view of recent conditions within universities, this law seeks to establish emergency administrative measures to be taken so as to assist the independent afforts of universities to restore order where disruptions have occurred and in this way to work for a return to the normal operation of education and research within the universities.

(Definitions)

Article 2: The words "university strife" [funso] in this law shall mean conditions in which the operation of education and research are interfered with because of the occupation or barricading of facilities under university . . . supervision, class boycotts or other abnormal acts by students (including research students).

(Duties of the University President and Others)

Article 3: The university president, faculty, and other staff members shall be mindful of the normal functioning and improvement of their university. If disputes break out, all members of the university shall cooperate and make every effort toward the quick establishment of a compromise settlement.

As the person chiefly responsible for his institution, the president of any university in which a dispute occurs shall demonstrate leadership and unite the staff of the whole institution in the search for a settlement of the dispute, in determining the policies and measures

*Japan, Mombushō, "Daigaku no Unei ni kan suru Rinji Sochihō" (Law No. 70, promulgated August 7, 1969).

relating to that settlement, and in working to implement them. In accordance with the essential purposes of the university he shall adopt appropriate measures to supervise and preserve the facilities, equipment and other property of the university.

The president and other officials of a strife-torn university shall endeavour to hear in a reasonable manner those desires and opinions of students which are appropriately presented and they shall, in the measures they take, consider ways to reflect those hopes and opinions which are recognized as contributing to a compromise settlement of the university's turmoil and to the improvement of its administration.

(Reporting University Disturbances)
Article 4: When disturbances occur at their university, presidents of national universities shall report immediately to the Minister of Education on the essential points at issue and the general nature of the disturbance.

(Advice from the Minister of Education)
Article 5: The Minister of Education may consult the Special Council on University Problems [see article 13 below] and give to the president of a strife-torn National University the necessary advice on measures to adopt in dealing with the unrest and in improving the administration of the university. . . .

The advice referred to in the previous paragraph shall be of such a nature as to assist the university's own efforts to find a solution to its problems and to improve its administration.

The president and other officials of a disrupted university who have received the advice mentioned in Paragraph 1 shall respect that advice and shall endeavor to implement measures in conjunction with it.

(Special Administrative Bodies)
Article 6: [Paragraphs 1 and 2 provide extensive detail on the various administrative agencies the university president may confer with or create in dealing with demonstrations.]

The university president shall consult the Minister of Education before establishing the bodies mentioned. . . . Based on the president's recommendation, the Minister of Education shall establish the bodies mentioned . . . and appoint their members. . . .

(Cessation and Suspension of Education)

Article 7: The president of a strife-torn university may, if he deems it necessary to reach a settlement of the dispute, suspend for up to six months all or part of the educational and research activities of a faculty, an institute or other departments or organizations (Referred to hereafter as "Faculties and other departments") in which a dispute has arisen. If conditions warrant, the period may be extended for three months.

The Minister of Education may, after hearing the opinion of the university president and consulting with the Special Council on University Problems, suspend education and research functions in any faculty or other department of the university in question, in cases where more than nine months have elapsed following the outbreak of a disturbance in a university's faculties or other departments, or where a dispute breaks out within a year after a previous dispute has been settled and then continues for more than six months, and where the settlement of a dispute is considered difficult. He shall direct the president of the university to take the necessary measures in such cases.

When it is recognized that the dispute has been settled, the Minister of Education must, after hearing the views of the university president, lift the measures imposed. . . .

(The Effects of Suspension of Education)

Article 8: When suspension, as noted in the previous Article, Paragraph 2, is imposed on a faculty or any other part of a strife-torn university, the following shall apply until the suspension is lifted:

(1) Staff members of the faculty or other part of the university in question (except those listed below) shall be suspended from their duties in spite of the provisions of Articles 89 and 91 of the National Civil Servants Law (Law No. 120, 1947).

(2) Persons suspended by the previous provision shall be paid seventy percent of their salary, family allowance, adjustment allowance, temporary allowance, and bonus. . . .

(7) Faculty vacancies in the affected faculties and other departments shall not be filled.

(8) The period during which suspension . . . is imposed, shall not be included in the period of residence required of students of that faculty or other departments as defined by law.

(9) Students of the affected faculties or other departments shall be exempt from paying tuition for the period of the previous article.

(10) The Japan Scholarship Foundation shall not lend school expenses to students of the affected faculties or other departments. . . .

*(Mediation of Disputes Between
Faculties and Other Departments)*

Article 10: When it is recognized that a dispute over university administration exists between faculties or other departments of a disrupted university, and that this is a serious obstacle to the settlement of the discord at the university in question, the president of the university may, with the concurrence of the deans of the faculties or other departments concerned, request the Minister of Education to mediate and to help settle the dispute between the parties involved.

When the Minister of Education receives such a request, he shall refer it to mediation by the Special Council on University Problems.

The aforementioned mediation shall be undertaken by a mediator appointed by the Chairman of the Special Council on University Problems from among the members of the Council or from among special members thereof.

(Consultation on the Admission of New Students and Other Matters at a Strife-torn University)

Article 11: When it is recognized that the normal operation of education and graduation of students is likely to be difficult at a strife-torn university, the president of the university in question shall consult with the Minister of Education concerning the admission or graduation of students.

(Application [of this law] to Public and Private Universities)

Article 12: The provisions of Articles 4 to 11 inclusive shall apply *mutatis mutandis* to local public universities and private universities. . . . [Appropriate changes in wording to accomplish this era provided.]

(Special Council on University Problems)

Article 13: A Special Council on University Problems shall be established in the Ministry of Education.

The Special Council on University Problems (referred to hereafter as "the Council") shall investigate and deliberate on matters which come within its purview under the provisions of this law, and shall perform the tasks of mediation provided for in Article 10.

The Council shall make recommendations to the Minister of Education on important matters with respect to the settlement of university disputes and reform of university administration.

The Council shall be composed of up to 15 members appointed by the Minister of Education, with the approval of the Cabinet. . . .

Supplementary Provisions

(Effective Date)

1. This Law shall take effect 10 days from the day of its promulgation.

(Rescinding this Law)

5. This Law shall be abrogated within five years of its implementation.

(Revision of the Ministry of Education Establishment Law)

Minister of Finance, Fukuda Takeo
Minister of Education, Sakata Michita
Minister of Local Autonomy, Noda Takeo

5-6. CONTINUATION OF
THE UNIVERSITY CONTROL LAW*

The University Control Law was a provisional law due to last five years. When the five years were up in 1974, there was a raging debate over whether it should be continued, modified, or allowed to expire. The following editorial explores the purposes of enacting the law and the extent to which it served these ends.

The Provisional Law on the Management of Universities, enacted in August 1969, during the numerous student disputes, is due to expire this coming August 16, according to a supplementary

*"Our Hope Regarding the Provisional Law on the Management of Universities," editorial, *Chūgoku Shimbun*, May 17, 1974.

clause which states "this law is to be abrogated within five years of its implementation." One of the prime questions in the current session of the Diet has been whether to let the law expire, to extend its term, or to enact a new law. The Liberal Democratic Party has decided to avoid taking any step in the current Diet session and to reexamine the problem in the provisional session following the House of Councillors election.

The reason for this is that, in contrast to Minister of Education Okuno, who wishes to enact a new law, many in the LDP would prefer a mere extension of the existing law. Many also believe there is not sufficient time to take the more positive step of enacting a new law. People who insist on the enactment of a new law emphasize the necessity of having "a law which thoroughly rectifies the management and administration of universities". Those who are satisfied with an extension of the existing law believe, in contrast, that "the enactment of a new law would provide nothing more than a superficial remedy short of a complete solution while moves for a new law would just provoke the opposition parties and university-related people."

Further discussion will follow over which policy should be chosen with regard to the Provisional Law on the Management of Universities: abrogation, extension of the term of validity, partial revision, or enactment of a new law. It is important to deepen public understanding of the problems of the universities by clarifying, in the course of such discussion, the background of the student disputes of five years ago, the kind of problems that were raised, the ways in which universities have coped with these problems, and present conditions in the universities.

The student disputes which peaked five years ago were not caused merely by failures in university management. Behind the disputes lay criticisms of public policy and the social system, discontent toward the university system's inability to satisfy student demands, and criticism that the universities lacked the creative power to alleviate such discontent. The disputes were also attributable to the policy of overemphasizing economic growth, to the belittling of education and research, to a social system which overemphasizes school backgrounds, to increases in the number of students attending universities only receive a diploma without any further sense of purpose, to families which place too much emphasis upon the admissions of their children into universities, and to the methods of education in the secondary schools and high schools which, yielding to such expectations, place unnecessarily large weight upon education designed to prepare students for these entrance examinations.

Although the aggravation of the disputes was due largely to the occupation and barricading of university buildings by an uncompromising group of students, it should not be forgotten that many other factors were involved. Most important was the strong criticism by young people of public policy and of the social system plus the latent view that universities had to be reformed. These lay behind the rapid, nation-wide spread of these disputes, behind the mobilization of student concern, behind the establishment of reform committees in many universities, and behind the increasing public concern about the problem.

The Provisional Law on the Management of Universities sought explicitly to assist those universities undergoing student disputes in finding their own solutions. To this end it gave the Minister of Education the authority to make recommendations and to close or abolish schools; and it obliged the various deans to present reports on the dispute, including any special measures for its settlement, for the improvement of university management, and on procedures related to suspension of education during the dispute. This law was adopted forcefully in a plenary session of the House of Councillors without sufficient deliberation and was enforced despite protests by many universities. Therefore, it is important to examine whether this law has been useful in solving disputes.

At Hiroshima University, education and research functions had been interrupted by students' occupation and barricading of the facilities for 170 days. Measures to recover the functions of the university were being explored in August 1969 when the Provisional Law on the Management of Universities was enacted. However, even before the enactment of the Provisional Law, the university had been making its own voluntary efforts by attending meetings for "collective bargaining" and by establishing a reform committee. Pending were questions of how to deal with uncompromising students and whether to bring the riot police onto the campus if no other solution could be reached through negotiation. The real problem was, therefore, not merely the success or failure of the management and administration of the university. The university brought in the riot police just after the Provisional Law was put into enforcement. However, judging from the progress of events up until that time, this decision was unrelated to the enactment of the law. Viewed nationally, a great majority of the disputes were solved through the mobilization of the riot police.

Thus, the Provisional Law on the Management of Universities, since its enforcement, has not played an important role in the solution of university conflicts. Regardless of the law, the number of student disputes declined rapidly from 64 in 1969 to 7 in 1970.

In the past five years, it has become clear that what is needed is not to strengthen the management and administration of universities but to encourage the universities themselves to make voluntary reforms and to accept public assistance in this effort. This is why, with regard to the Provisional Law on the Management of Universities, we emphasize the necessity of sufficient discussion so as to deepen public understanding toward the universities.

5-7. CONTINUED ENFORCEMENT OF THE UNIVERSITY CONTROL LAW*

The following newspaper item provides a description of the process whereby the LDP government continued to enforce the University Control Law.

The Provisional Law on the Management of Universities is to expire this coming August. Having examined the measures to be taken in the current session of the Diet concerning this matter, the Subcommittee on Culture and Education (Chairman, Nishioka Takeo) and the Investigation Committee on Cultural and Educational Institutions (Chairman Sakata Michita) of the Liberal Democratic Party confirmed, yesterday, their joint position that the revision of the law will aim only at extending the terms of its validity with no enactment of a new law.

The period of extension will be three years during which time the LDP plans to conduct a serious examination of a "New University Management Law." This would provide radical reforms in the

---

*"Hesitation of the LDP to Enact a New University Control Law," *Yomiuri Shimbun,* March 7, 1974.

management and administration of universities. The LDP plans to introduce such a bill into a Diet session at the end of the extension period. (1977).

However, since Prime Minister Tanaka, as well as Minister of Education, Okuno, still hold that the existing law cannot defend academic freedom and that a new law is therefore necessary, the LDP plans to adjust its position with that of the Cabinet and to make its final decision around the 20th.

The reason the Subcommittee on Culture and Education and the Investigation Committee on Cultural and Educational Institutions gave up enacting a new law in the current Diet session was given as follows by Chairman Nishioka: "Preparation for a radical reform of the management and administration of universities has been insufficient; the necessary conditions such as understanding by those in the universities and public agreement to the measure do not yet exist. We cannot expect to create an ideal situation in universities by enforcing a policy upon them without sufficient dialogue with those in the universities. This matter should not become the focal point of 'political confrontation' in the current Diet session."

As for moves toward the enactment of a new law when the existing law expires (August 16), the Minister of Education stated at a press conference after a Diet meeting at the end of January that "Mere abrogation is out of the question. A new law is necessary to provide the power to reform the universities as places of education based upon the principle of university autonomy. A new law will be enacted." The Prime Minister also has suggested repeatedly that it is necessary to enact a new law by publicly stating: "As long as universities are arenas for political struggle and students cannot receive any education, as a political leader I cannot evade my responsibility to alleviate such conditions. The enactment of a more severe law is indispensable to cope with the continued killings going on during internal conflicts among students."

Even within the Subcommittee on Culture and Education and the Investigation Committee on Cultural and Educational Institutions, the opinion was strong that the present university conditions should not be left untouched and that a mere extension or a partial revision of the existing law cannot cope with the present situation. In the end, however, it was felt that enactment of a law replacing the

Provisional Law without sufficient preparation would be rather damaging to the LDP's final purpose, namely the enactment of a New University Management Law.

In a joint meeting of the two committees, four points of view were considered: (1) Enactment of a New University Management Law, (2) Partial revision of the existing law to provide up-to-date measures for conflict solution, (3) Extending the existing law with no revisions except a change in the stipulation on the abrogation of the law from "within five years" to "within eight years" or "for the time being", (4) Letting it expire. In the end it was decided that the best course of action was to keep the existing law as a deterrent against disputes and at the same time to start preparing a New University Management Law.

With regard to the expiration of the Provisional Law, the opposition parties are against any measure other than abrogation. Therefore, even if the tactics shift from a new enactment to a mere extension, we are unlikely to see any "weakening of the conflictual character of the issue" as the LDP expects.

In the meanwhile, the LDP's intention to seek a point of contention in education is still lingering with the House of Councilors election in sight; instead of a frontal clash over the University Management Law, there are increasingly active moves in the LDP to legalize restrictions over the political activities of teachers.

5-8. DIFFERING VIEWPOINTS ON EXTENSION OF THE UNIVERSITY CONTROL BILL*

The following newspaper item discusses the problem of continuing the enforcement of the University Control Law of 1969.

The Ministry of Education has been examining the "Provisional Law on the Management of Universities," which expired last August, with a view to taking some legal measure such as extension or abrogation in the next regular session of the Diet. Minister of Education Nagai told the Cabinet meeting of the 21st that the Ministry is ready to submit to the Diet a bill tentatively entitled "On

---

*"The Problem of Extending the Provisional Law on the Management of Universities—Bill to be Introduced into the Current Diet Session," *Asahi Shimbun*, Jan. 22, 1975.

Measures Related to the Provisional Law on the Management of Universities."

The Provisional Law on the Management of Universities was enacted in 1969 to cope with student disputes. It expired last August in accordance with Supplementary Clause 5 which stated, "the law is to be abrogated within five years." Contrary to the interpretation that such abrogation means the legal termination of the law, then Minister of Education Okuno took the point of view that the law continues to be legally valid so long as procedures for its abrogation are not activated. His view was also endorsed in a Cabinet meeting.

However, there still lingers in the Cabinet and in the Liberal Democratic Party a view that this supplementary clause is but a "directory provision" [i.e. a non-compulsory instruction to the Judiciary or to the Executive]. Therefore many feel that some further legal measure is politically indispensable, and the Ministry has started again to study the possibility of submitting a Bill. The Ministry of Education wishes to reach, if possible, a conclusion endorsing the extension of the law with the consent of the Subcommittee on Culture and Education of the LDP. Considering the nature of the law, however, it is certain to arouse resistance from the opposition parties. The final decision on extension or abrogation will be based upon political judgments by the leaders of the Cabinet and the LDP.

5-9. THE PRIVATE SCHOOL PROMOTION AND ASSISTANCE LAW*

The following reading is from the law established to provide financial aid to privately endowed universities. Note not only the flexibility given to government agencies but also the accompanying powers over the schools.

Purposes

Article 1.

In view of the important role played by private schools in school education, this law, by prescribing measures whereby the national

---

*Japan, Ministry of Education, Private-School Promotion and Assistance Law (Law No. 61 of 1975), mimeo.

government and local public institutions will assist private schools, aims at maintaining and improving the educational conditions in the private schools, alleviating the financial burdens of education there, and increasing the soundness of private school administration, thereby contributing to the sound development of private schools. . . .

Subsidies to Defray the Operating Expenses of Private Universities and Private Specialized High Schools

Article 4.

1. The national government may grant subsidies to school juridical persons' which run universities or specialized high schools, covering up to one-half of the school's operating expenses for education and research.

2. The scope, the method of estimation and other necessary matters on operating expenses eligible for subsidization according to the stipulation in the previous clause will be determined by a government ordinance.

Reduction of Subsidies

Article 5.

In cases where a school juridical person, or a university or specialized high school run by a school juridical person falls into one of the following categories, the subsidies offered to the school juridical person in accord with the stipulations of Clause 1 of the previous Article may be curtailed.

(1) In cases where laws, or instructions of the authorized government offices based upon laws or the act of endowment are violated.

(2) In cases where the number of students exceeds the number prescribed in the school rule.

(3) In cases where the number of students does not reach the number prescribed in the school rule.

---

*"School juridical person" (*gakuhōjin*) is a legal term referring to the corporation or board formed to establish and administer a private school. It gains the status of a "legal person" upon government recognition.

(4) In cases where the financial conditions are not sound, e.g. where repayment of depts is not properly made.

(5) In cases where other educational conditions and management and administration are improper. . . .

Increase of Subsidies

Article 7.

In cases where it is deemed especially necessary for the promotion of scholarship in private universities or for the promotion of education in specialized fields or courses in private universities or in private specialized high schools, the national government may increase the amount of subsidization provided to the school juridical person in accordance with the stipulations in Clause 1 of Article 4.

Partial Revision of the Private School Law

Supplementary Clause 3. Article 59 (of the Private School Law) is revised as follows:

Aid—Article 59. The national government or local insitutions when they recognize it as necessary for the promotion of education, may give necessary aid to school juridical persons for private-school education in accordance with separately enacted legal measures. . . .The following clause is added to the Supplementary Clause 12, 13. The Minister of Education, except when, in consultation with the Council for the Establishment of Universities and the Private University Council, it is recognized as especially necessary will until March 31, 1981, neither grant permission for the establishment of new private universities, or departments or divisions of private universities nor will he allow for changes in school rules designed to increase the number of students.

5-10. THE COSTS OF A UNIVERSITY EDUCATION*

Every year the government surveys the costs of higher education. The news story below provides a description of the major findings of the 1978 survey.

*"Dear Mom, Please Send Me $5,000," Yomiuri Shimbun, Oct. 24, 1979.

In just two years tuition and living expenses for university students have increased by 20 percent, reports the Ministry of Education's 1978 "Survey of Student Living Conditions." The survey,
concluded October 23, 1979, places average annual expenses, including room and board, for full-time day students at private universities in Tokyo at $5,800. As parental stipends—now reported at
$4,910—creep upward, we enter the era of $5,000 allowances. Total
expenses for students at private universities in Tokyo who live at
home were estimated at $3,800, approximately $2,000 less than
what boarding students need, which may help explain the growing
popularity of local universities.

This "white paper on student living conditions" is compiled every
other year. Since 1976 average annual expenses (including tuition
and living expenses) of university students attending day classes
have risen by 21.3 percent to reach $4,500. which is more than twice
the approximately $2,000 reported for 1972. Similarly, university
students in night courses are paying out $4,750 (21.1% increase);
day students at junior colleges, $4,125 (19.5% increase); and night
students at junior colleges, $4,050 (12.6% increase). In all cases the
increase far exceeds the 12.2 percent rise in consumer prices for the
same period.

Not surprisingly, expenses for students living in lodgings are
greater. While students attending day courses at public universities,
and living at home pay an average of $3,650 a year (22.4% higher
than 1976), those in lodgings are paying an all-time high of $5,330.
Somewhat higher rates for room, board and utilities are to be
expected, but they are augmented by the "needs" of recent life-
styles among students in lodgings, which include televisions, re-
frigerators, washing machines, and even air-conditioners.

The difference in expenses for students living at home and those
living in lodgings depends on the cost differences between private
and national universities and according to locality of residence.
Expenses for national university students living at home average
$2,580, and for private university students, $3,880. For those in
lodgings and enrolled at national institutions expenses are $3,320,
but for those at private universities they jump to $5,700. Further, in
Tokyo, where over 30 percent of Japan's university students are
congregated, expenses for those at private schools are $5,800,
which is higher than the national average.

On what is this money spent? Annual living expenses (room and board, utilities, entertainment, and miscellaneous extras) are about the same for day students at national universities ($2,550), and private university students ($2,525). However, there is a vast difference in tuition and matriculation fees. Compared to the $450 national university students pay in fees, private university students pay $1,650. Also, private university students spend $625 for entertainment and miscellaneous extras, or nearly $100 more than national university students.

The net average amount contributed by family to students in day courses at national, prefectural or city, and private universities is $3,525 per year, a substantial increase over the $2,900 reported for 1976. But as a percentage of total living expenses, the amount contributed by parents has remained stable, increasing only 0.2 percent, from 78.1 percent to 78.3 percent. The parental allowance for students at private universities and living in lodgings is an outstandingly high amount of $4,720 on the average, and in Tokyo this reaches as much as $4,910.

6 Environmental Protection: Turning Adversity to Advantage

Environmental concerns are relatively recent additions to the agenda of public policy in Japan, as in most other industrialized countries. That governmental attention did not develop earlier was not, however, due to the sudden materialization of a new set of problems. Air, water, noise, waste, and other kinds of pollution have plagued Japan for decades, if not for a century or more. That official attention to these problems came when it did is a function of at least two different aspects of the politics of public policy in Japan.

The first involves economic and management policies. As noted in Chapter 2, economic reorganization and high growth were the dominant political priorities during the two decades following World War II. Other concerns either received lower priorities or were explicitly ignored or suppressed in the interests of bringing about "the economc miracle." Environmental protection, like improvements in social welfare or in higher education, was simply one other item that, while perhaps desirable in the abstract, was either not affordable or was seen as detrimental to the government policies of economic management. Consequently, a combination of inattention plus suppression by key political forces kept environmental questions in the category of "non-issue" for most of the 1950s and 1960s.

As environmental problems in Japan became more acute and as the predominant political forces were, at best, sphinx-like in the attention they gave to them, a number of new political power-centers emerged. It was these new forces, rather than the established centers of power, that ultimately forced the government to devote substantial attention and resources to the problem of pollu-

tion and environmental protection. Just as higher educational problems had festered until lanced by the heavily nonpartisan student
protests on 1968–69, environmental concerns bubbled beneath the
surface of Japanese politics until, as a result of pressures from
citizen groups, local governments, and the courts, they burst
through to command the attention of the media, the general public,
and the national government. And despite the fact that their
strengths had crystalized around the specific problems of the environment, many of these new political forces, having forced their
way into positions of influence, have since come to utilize that
influence in regard to other questions. Whether or not they have the
potential to form the core of a new political coalition is one of the
more exciting questions on the agenda of Japanese politics for the
1980s.

There is a third element of the politics of environmental protection which demands consideration as well. The government and
major business circles in Japan were reluctant to consider environmental questions until forced out of this recalcitrance by upstart
political forces, yet when they did begin to tackle the problems,
they were tackled with much greater vigor than might have been
expected, given earlier elite hesitation. Either as a reluctant response to political inevitability or as a creative effort to turn adversity to advantage, the Japanese government took numerous important steps to cope with the country's environmental problems. And
in doing so, it had by 1980 reduced much of the political momentum
that had been generated by antipollution forces a decade earlier.
This poses a possible alternative to any scenario which portrays the
1980s as a decade in which the political regime that has dominated
Japan for thirty years is toppled by a new political coalition catalyzed by the failure of the government to deal satisfactorily with
environmental and related problems. It is very possible that the
government in part by its effective activism on environmental problems during the 1970s has managed to give itself a new lease on life
for the 1980s.

Context

Geographically, Japan is an enviromentalist's nightmare. The
country's total land mass is small, and only about 16 percent of the
mountainous archipelago is arable. As a result, since its earliest

history Japan's population has been concentrated on the central plains and in coastal areas suitable for farming. In itself a problem, this compression is compounded by the nation's high urbanization. Before the Meiji Restoration, for example, the city that is now Tokyo was larger than London. The present population of about 115 million is one-half that of the United States but is crowded into an area about the size of California. Ten cities have populations of over a million. Tokyo, the capital, has a population of about 9 million, while Osaka, Yokohama, and Nagoya all have 2 million or more inhabitants. These four cities, plus three more of a million-plus residents, all lie along a narrow stretch by the Pacific Ocean that is about two hundred miles long. Quite obviously, such density contributes greatly to environmental problems. Any doubts on this subject should be banished by imagining the impact in any major city if every one of the citizens concentrated there dropped simply one gum wrapper or cigarette butt in the nearest park or waterway.

The demographic aspect of Japan's environmental problems was exacerbated by the pattern of its industrial development. Fundamentally, the international pressure to industrialize both in the early Meiji period and after World War II meant that economic development was given clear precedence over environmental protection. Quite surely, other countries, even earlier industrializers, shared the general bias for profit over environmental amenities. But in Japan the preference seemed overly strong for economics. As just one example, one can cite Fuji City. When the Fuji Paper Manufacturing Company appeared in 1889 and quickly began befouling the local waters, local farmers initially succeeded in gaining financial compensation from the plant's owners and agreement to farmers' rights to dam up local waters for rice cultivation at key times of the year. By 1909, however, as industrialization proceeded, these agreements were shifted drastically away from the interests of agriculture, and the development of the paper and pulp industries in the area proceeded with virtually no attention to environmental or agricultural concerns for the cleanliness or availability of water. Before long, the city began a descent into environmental decay from which it has only recently begun to recover (Okamoto, 1972, pp. 7–8).

During the war, any opposition to industrial expansion and development was tantamount to treason. And then when the war was over and the government sought to redevelop Japan's industrial base, a series of specific decisions further exacerbated industrial pollution. As was noted in Chapter 2, the focus of the government's economic management policies at that time was to develop heavy industry and chemicals. Between 1960 and 1970 alone, there was a fifty-fold increase in plastics production, for example. In addition, the government explicitly decided to concentrate industries along the coastal areas so as to take advantage of natural harbors and to minimize internal transportation costs (see Reading 6–1). Thus, the country's historical concentration along the Pacific Belt between Tokyo and Osaka was intensified by the economic and industrial plans of the 1950s and 1960s. By the mid-1970s, the area defined by fifty-kilometer circles around the centers of Tokyo, Osaka, and Nagoya contained only about 1 percent of the total land-area of the country, but contained about one-third of the population and accounted for approximately three-fourths of the nation's industrial production. In Gross Domestic Product (GDP) per square kilometer of inhabitable land, Japan ranks twenty times higher than the United States, six times higher than Britain and twice as high as the Netherlands (OECD, 1977: p.83).

As development proceeded during the decades after the war, new highways and high-speed rail lines cut through the countryside; coastal beaches were converted into tightly concentrated industrial parks (*kombinato*); waterways became convenient sluices for washing away industrial waste products; parks and countryside were replaced by paper mills and petrochemical plants. Given the comparatively high availability and low cost of oil, the government also decided in 1960 to shift Japan's energy supply from coal and hydroelectric power to this more available but heavily polluting form of energy. Through all of these shifts, business and government were primarily concerned with economic efficiency.

Comparatively speaking, Japan's growth during the period 1960–70 was the most extensive in the industrial world, but at the same time this growth contained the seeds of tremendous environmental disruption. As the table presented in Reading 6-2 makes clear, Japan's rate of growth of GNP, industrial productivity, energy consumption, and automobile usage far outstripped that of any other OECD country. Such rapid growth created environmental problems. One government study of the Tokyo metropolitan area between 1960 and 1970 showed a doubling of the mass emission of carbon monoxide, a tripling of the emission of hydrocarbons, and a six-fold jump in nitrogen oxides. Increased use of plastics, convenience foods, and the like added to the mountains of human-generated wastes. Perhaps the most striking symbol of this problem was found on the famous Mt. Fuji, which the Japanese regularly climb as a leisure activity. Every spring, hundreds of tons of orange peels, soda and sake bottles, paper wrappings, and chopsticks had to be shovelled off the once-pristine mountain paths.

In addition to the usual types of pollution—air, water, noise, and waste—that pervaded urban Japan, several specific diseases developed between the late 1950s and the end of the 1960s that were far more serious in their immediate consequences for human health. Three were particularly notorious. Minamata disease, which destroys the brain and nervous system, was first recognized in 1956 in the city of Minamata; in 1965, it broke out along the Agano River in Niigata and, in 1973, along the Sea of Ariaka. Itai-itai disease, (literally the "ouch-ouch disease") caused by cadmium in rice, was first noticed in 1955 in Toyama Prefecture. Yokkaichi asthma, a lung ailment, was the result of complex smoke and soot emissions in the city of Yokkaichi.

In all of these cases, the disease was traceable to the emission of specific industrial waste products from identifiable factories. Unlike the more general pollution problems that emerged largely as unwanted byproducts of careless or malinformed decisions regarding economic expansion, specific industrially generated diseases involved more than simple ignorance of human consequences. In these, industry and government suppressed scientific studies that established connections between particular industrial wastes and diseases or death.

Nor were the normal opponents of the dominant coalition particularly active in pressing for alternatives, either to general or to specific problems. The organized opposition, particularly those parties with close links to organized labor, similarly collaborated in the silence. Although academic Marxists, the JSP and JCP might easily have been able to find the theoretical basis on which to side with the victims of industrial pollution, most in fact did not. Instead they concentrated their opposition to the government around its alleged reliance on "monopoly capital" and "U.S. imperialism."

Meanwhile, most enterprise unions were worried primarily about the threats to jobs generated by concern for the environment. They found it much easier to side with polluting employers than to take principled but materially damaging stands favoring pollution victims. In several instances, union members resorted to strong-arm methods to defeat those who opposed the waste disposal practices of their industrial plants.

By the mid-1960s, therefore, Japan was experiencing a general breakdown in the character of its environment. The economic miracle became a noisy, smelly, overcrowded, unhealthy testament to human greed. Few established centers of political power were motivated to press for alternatives. It was in this context that Japanese politics saw the germination of what came to be called the antipollution or environmental movement, a combination centered around citizens' groups, local governments, the court system, and the media. Ultimately, it was this aggregation that provoked national action to curb the environmental deterioration.

Agenda

Two different but related aspects of the environmentally relevant political agenda stand out. First of all, one must note the tremendous difficulties that those concerned with environmental issues faced in even getting a place for them on the official agenda of the national government. As noted above, neither within the dominant coalition nor within the established political opposition was any strong voice raised against the problems of pollution until the late 1960s. By then opponents of pollution had organized and been politicking outside the existing parameters of Japanese politics. So-called citizens' movements, organized pressure groups united by place of residence and/or common suffering from some specific pollutant, were the key elements in this antiestablishmentarian movement. The media, the courts, and local governments were often important channels through which these groups could exert their political influence. It was these unconventional channels of political influence that eventually stimulated the national government to tackle more seriously the problems of the environment.

The second aspect to note, and one that clearly is related to the first, is the lack of consensus on goals and the blurring of many traditional lines of political division that accompanied the environmental problems. Although most important issues in postwar Japanese politics were characterized by a division between the conservative coalition on one side and the opposition camp on the other, in the case of environmental problems the lines of cleavage were far less clear. More significant were the divisions within both the conservative and the progressive camps. These were multiplied by divisions between central and local government, between newly formed citizens' groups and established power centers, and between legislative and party forces on one hand and judicial forces on the other. As a consequence, the major actors had fewer clearcut and predictable preferences than they did for economic policies, or labor-relations policies, or even higher educational or social welfare policies.

Politicizing of the environmental problem arose initially as a result of specific, industrially related pollution problems, rather than from pressure for improved environment in general, such as motivates the Sierra Club in the United States, for example, or the so-called Green Party in West Germany. For the victims of pollution, the major concern was cessation of the immediate cause, whether it was excessive smoke or sludge emissions or specific items such as mercury or cadmium. Of lesser concern initially but of increased importance as the scope of the environmental problems expanded was some measure of compensation for those who suffered injury or disease as a result of such environmental pollution. Although the specifics differ from case to case and region to region, most citizen efforts were uniform in revealing the resistance faced by environmentalists and pollution victims when they sought redress. They also show the irregularity of the lines of political cleavage on environmental issues, and demonstrate the importance of new political channels for dealing with the problems.

The Minamata case is perhaps the most famous and most useful for purposes of illustrating these points. It was in Minamata in 1956 that the first major victims of a major pollution-related disease were officially recognized by medical experts. Although the cause of the disease was initially unknown, it gradually became clear that methyl mercury, formed as a byproduct in the manufacture of acetaldehyde and vinyl chloride at the Chisso Petrochemical Corporation, was at fault. Establishing this causal link technically was not easy. As bloated fish floated belly up in Minamata Bay, as cats and dogs leaped violently about, convulsed, and died, as birds dropped inexplicably from the sky, and as the number of human cripples mounted into the hundreds and as dozens of deaths took place, it became increasingly clear to victims and supporters that Chisso's dumping of this methyl mercury into the closed harbor of Minamata was the first link in the causal chain. As the mercury deposits built up in the waters, the sea life became contaminated, and once sufficient quantities of contaminated fish had been ingested, brain disease and destruction of the nervous system took place. Moreover, the disease could affect children born to victims. The end result was the creation of large numbers of human vegetables in the small city of Minamata.

The initial reaction of many families was to place the blame on themselves and to hide the victims. But as the scope of the problem became clearer, many of the local citizens began to organize to obtain redress from Chisso. This proved to be exceptionally difficult. Local fishermen, victims of the disease and unable to sell polluted catches, protested vigorously. Local merchants and non-victims resisted protests. More importantly, Chisso dominated the local economy, providing 45 percent of the city's tax revenue and accounting for approximately 70 percent of the city's total economy (Thurston, 1974, p. 32). It also dominated the city's politics, with left-of-center assemblymen coming largely from the Chisso union and conservatives coming from its active or retired managerial staff. With local employment, politics, and revenue so heavily dependent on Chisso, the fishermen and victims found few immediate allies in their demand for redress.

In fact, the opposite occurred. Even though tests at Kumamoto University and its own laboratories indicated that Chisso's waste products were the cause of the disease, the company did all it could to prevent any disruption of production. Falsifying and suppressing test results, hiring thugs to break up residents' protest meetings, and denying any legal responsibility were the cornerstones of Chisso's policy. Although the Chisso plant's union eventually split over the issue, initial labor reaction was also to side with the company, with union members frequently providing additional muscle to break up protests.

At the national level, there was not much more dispositon to help. The economic ministries, the LDP, and the business federations sought to continue the high levels of economic growth that had been targeted in successive economic plans. MITI in particular viewed itself as the official ally of industry. Only within the Ministry of Health and Welfare and to some extent within the Ministry of Home Affairs was there even the remotest official inclination to tackle the emerging problems of pollution and the environment. The former ministry, explicitly charged with the protection of the nation's health, had conducted a survey on general pollution problems and their medical implications as early at 1953. Between 1958 and 1962, it had pressed successfully for legislation to control factory effluents, water quality, sewerage, and smoke and soot. The Home Affairs Ministry, concerned with increasing the scope of local government responsibility, often encouraged local government agencies to enact their own programs to deal with local pollution problems. But neither agency was much of a match for the combined power of the major business federations, the LDP, and the economic ministries, particularly MITI, all of who were far less concerned with what seemed to many to be, at worst, slightly adverse side effects of the basically beneficial policy of high economic growth. There was great reluctance on the part of these groups to allow environmental concerns to interfere with economic policies. The predominant governmental bias was hostile to environmentalists or pollution victims (McKean, 1976).

In 1959, the Ministry of Health and Welfare conducted a study which concluded that methyl mercury from Chisso was the probable cause of Minamata disease. Yet MITI was able to have the study group dissolved and reestablished under the Economic Planning Agency where concern for health could be more effectively counterbalanced by concern for the economic impact of any link between industry and pollution. As late as 1968, MITI was still effective in resisting any national government conclusion that industrially released methyl mercury was directly responsible for Minamata disease (either in Minamata or in Niigata, where the disease had broken out in 1965). Thus, toward the end of the 1960s, unions were closely linked with their polluting firms in opposition to any demands for environmental action likely to interfere with production and profits. Few local governments were willing to act against industries deemed vital to the economic well-being of the

community. The national government contained only two ministries even minimally interested in pressing for increased attention to
the problems of pollution and its victims. At the national level both
opposition parties and union federations were also lax, with the
possible exception of Dōmei and the DSP, which proposed environmental legislation from around 1965 on.

Facing a wall of seeming indifference and impotence, environmentalists and pollution victims organized themselves into citizens'
movements *(jūmin undō)* that sought to operate outside conventional party, bureaucratic, and legislative channels. As noted, most
members of these citizens' movements were otherwise apolitical
individuals concerned with the single issue of pollution. In most
instances, their protests were geographically based; their targets
were the local governments and, eventually in several key cases, the
courts. In their cause, they gained considerable help from media
publicity. Ultimately, the growing acuteness of the environmental
situation, plus the combined actions of these forces—citizens'
movements, courts, local governments, and the media—made it
impossible for the national government to ignore the problems any
longer. Yet when the government first began to act, at the end of the
1960s, it was with little unity of purpose. Individual ministries
pressed the interests of their natural consituencies so that the only
coherence involved coping with pollution without seriously disrupt-
ing high economic development and industrial freedom. Not until
the so-called pollution Diet of 1970 can one speak meaningfully of a
governmental agenda aimed at vigorously attacking the environmental problems of the country. Even then meeting the issue involved a balancing act between environmental and economic demands, and the government was never fully unified in its approach
to environmental policy.

Yet what is also striking is that despite the internal conservative
dissensus on the scope of the attack to be made on pollution, once
the issue was seriously taken up, it was handled with a force, clarity
and effectiveness that belied earlier expectations that, as the ally of
big business, the government would resist all efforts for a meaningful commitment to environmental protection. Quite the contrary,
when the government finally acted, it did so with vigor and turned
potential adversity into advantage.

Process

National executive and legislative action on the country's environmental problems was stimulated by the combined pressures of the media, local government, citizens' movements, and court decisions. Environmental policy clearly reflects a process in which pressure was built from the bottom up, rather than exerted from the top down, in direct contrast to economic policy, for example.

As was noted above, in many of the more polluted areas of Japan, groups of residents joined together on a largely autonomous, nonpartisan basis. Hitherto unpolitical and motivated primarily by the extremity of the environmental conditions they faced in their neighborhoods, they sought a reversal in the apparent disinterest that established political groups showed toward these conditions. By the early 1970s, there were an estimated 1,500 to 3,000 such groups, usually with memberships of 500 or fewer (*Asahi Shimbun*, May 21, 1973).The targets of their wrath varied, but most normally they included the industrial source(s) of the pollution whenever it was clearly identifiable; local branches of national political parties; village, town, and prefectural assemblies; and the courts. In some larger urban areas, certain of the citizens' groups sought to exercise their influence through the electoral process, supporting or opposing candidates on the basis of stands taken on environmental matters. The preponderant tactics, however, were nonelectoral, and consisted of monitoring the output of pollutants, lobbying individual officials, massive petition and telegram campaigns, sit-ins, marches, street demonstrations, product boycotts, and the like. Confrontation, rather than passivity before power, was the dominant motif.

In some instances, such as that in Kawasaki City as early as 1961 and many others during the late 1960s and early 1970s, these groups won a number of local-level victories. Industrial plants began to sign agreements promising to alter polluting practices; local rural assemblies adopted resolutions which restricted agricultural land-sales to industries; sympathetic university research teams were enlisted to study pollution outputs and establish causation; other assemblies adopted local or regional anti-pollution regulations in advance of, and at times in defiance of, the wishes of higher levels of government; smog-warning systems were established, with local schools being forced to close and residents warned to remain inside when certain air pollution levels were reached; local governments offered low-cost loans to small firms to enable them to purchase antipollution equipment.

The highpoint of local initiative was the passage of the Tokyo Metropolitan Environmental Pollution Control Ordinance in 1969 and its strengthening in October 1970 (see Reading 6–3). This ordinance, passed under a leftist administration headed by the popular ex-academic, Minobe Tatsukichi, went much further than any existing legislation, local or national. It declared that citizens had a right to a clean and safe environment and provided for comprehensive environmental coverage and criminal penalties for polluters. Given the concentration of industry in Tokyo, the potential impact of this ordinance was definitely national, and the central government fought a losing battle to have its provisions voided.

As action proceeded at the local level, parallel developments were occurring in the courts. Although the Japanese courts have traditionally been dismissed by most analysts as of little relevance to national policymaking, they were critical in the environmental area. Four cases proved especially vital in influencing environmental policy. Two of these related to Minamata disease, one to Itai-itai disease, and one to Yokkaichi asthma. The suits were all instituted between 1967 and 1969 and were not resolved until 1971–73. In all cases, the courts held in favor of the plaintiffs, the victims of pollution, and against the defendant industries. The courts also admonished the executive branch with varying degrees of severity to consider its own role in having aggravated the nation's environmental problems. Collectively, the cases had at least two important consequences. First, the court decisions established important legal principles concerning industry's responsibility for the disposal of waste products. Second, as the trials proceeded amid national media attention to the most sordid details of the pollution-caused diseases and government and industry negligence, public pressure accumulated for national government legislation to block further pollution of the environment.

One of the major problems faced by pollution victims was that of establishing scientific causality between specific industrial discharges and the pollution-related diseases. In the Itai-itai disease case, the court held against the Mitsui Mining and Smelting Company, deciding that establishing scientific causality was not necessary to establish legal causality, thus removing the burden of proof from the defendants. Ironically, when Mitsui appealed the case its appeal was rejected, and the appeals court awarded compensation that was double the original demand.

In the Minamata disease cases, the court held that general negligence, rather than specific intent on the part of the polluter, is sufficient ground to require payment of compensaton. Chisso, along with Shōwa Denkō in Niigata were held to have been guilty of varying degrees of carelessness or neglect, and enormous compensation judgments were rendered.

In the Yokkaichi asthma case, the court held that even though the amount of smoke and soot emitted by a single factory may be relatively small, when the combined amount from several associated factories is great each firm can be held individually responsible for the damage caused by the collective emissions. The court also found the defendants guilty of not having done sufficient examination of the possible impact of their collective activities before they began production. It held that negligence can exist in siting firms too closely together without an adequate assessment of environmental impact and in the failure of a company to provide the best technology available to prevent environmental damage (see Reading 6–4).

In all these cases, the courts rejected industry's claims that absence of specific intent or compliance with existing regulations in the nation's civil code eliminated company guilt. They also rejected any implication that solutions to pollution problems must be counterbalanced by considerations of economic investment, profits or growth. With this view, they undercut the fundamental principles upon which earlier inaction had been based. As the courts made it progressively easier and more worthwhile for pollution victims to bring court suits, business' attitudes toward the environmental impacts of their production processes changed significantly, and planning to prevent pollution problems began to be built into company thinking.

As the cases unfolded, they began to strengthen the hand of those in and out of government who called for major legislation to check pollution. The first significant success came in 1967 when, after several years of intra-agency bickering and legislative delay, the passed the so-called Basic Law for Environmental Pollution Control. The law, while going further than anything to date, proved a major disappointment in many respects. Most importantly, it included what came to be known as the "harmony clause" (Article 1, Par. 2), which stated, "Preservation of the living environment shall be carried out in harmony with the healthy development of the economy." The law also failed to specify standards for the emission of various pollutants, nor did it provide any mechanism for the relief of pollution victims. Most analysts saw the bill as an unreasonable capitulation to the pressures of the economic ministries and the business federations. On the other hand, it was the first national measure in which the government recognized its duty to protect citizens from environmental harm (McKean, 1976).

Passage of the Basic Law did little to mitigate pressure for further antipollution measures. It was clear that the 1967 law was inadequate to cope with the problem, while the combined effect of the court cases, citizens' movements, and local government bodies was to shift the initiative on what was fast becoming the most serious problem facing the country away from the central government. As the mass media continued its drumbeat for action and as the LDP continued to lose seats in what were once considered invulnerable areas, the government once again seized the initiative in the pollution Diet of 1970. During a special session, fourteen major pieces of environmental legislation were passed at the government's behest. The Basic Law was revised and strengthened, and all references to the need to harmonize environmental protection with economic expansion were removed (see Reading 6–5). Criminal penalties were instituted for certain violations of the civil code. Increased powers to regulate air and water pollution within their jurisdictions were delegated to the local governments. Mechanisms for identifying, certifying, and compensating pollution victims were created. Finally, in the next regular session of the Diet, a new and independent government agency (the Environment Agency) was established with the specific power to consolidate the administration of environmental protection. Many environmentalists remain unsatisfied with what they considered the limited nature of the protection provided or with what they feared were dangerously wide loopholes; but the fact remained that, at least on paper, Japan had enacted some of the world's strictest environmental protection measures. What remained unclear was the extent to which the legislation itself represented a clear-cut governmental commitment to curb existing pollution problems and to reverse the deterioration of the environment.

For much of the decade following the pollution Diet, there was an ebb and flow in bureaucratic power, pitting the Environment Agency against the economic ministries, and support for environmental protection against support for economic development. Prior to the economic depression of 1975, the environmental side did very well. The Environment Agency successfully pushed for strict rules regarding ambient air and water quality standards; these regulations were left to local governments to improve upon and enforce. As early as October 1972, some 3,200 businesses had entered into pollution control agreements with local governments. Various legislation pushed through by the Environment Agency aimed to broaden the scope of environmental protection and to strengthen the ambient and emission levels for various toxic wastes. In June 1972, for example, a Law for the Protection of the Natural Environment was passed; the next year saw passage of a law designed to compensate pollution victims. In June 1974, a law was passed to establish a plan for national land use. At the same time, the Air Pollution Control Law was revised to establish a system of total emission control, the first of its kind in the world. In April 1976, Japan became the first country to enforce auto-emission standards. Various other regulations were passed or tightened, and additional legislation continued to be passed throughout the decade. Environmentally related court cases also continued to build in number throughout the decade.

What is striking about this period is that environmental concerns were transformed from a problem to an opportunity. It has become something of a cliché to note that when governments throughout the world began to enact legislation designed to curb pollution, American industry responded by hiring more lawyers while Japanese firms hired more engineers. When they were first published, the government's standards for nitrogen oxide emissions were considered technically unmeetable; yet it took only several years for new technologies to be developed to make them possible. Advances made by Japanese automobile firms in pollution control devices undercut arguments in Detroit that asserted the technical infeasibility of proposed United States auto-emission standards.

The government, through various loan programs, encouraged industrial investment in pollution control technology. Before long, manufacturing such devices was becoming highly profitable in its own right, and Japan was exporting pollution control devices. Within the country, antipollution equipment is turning out to be one of the most substantial new profitmaking industries. During the period 1970–75, the manufacture and purchase of antipollution equipment expanded steadily, partly because regulations governing pollution were tightened but also because the government set investment in pollution-prevention equipment apart from its tight-money policies so as to bolster spending in this area. Moreover, in the private sector there was fierce competition among many small and relatively specialized firms for shares of the growing environmental protecton market, a competition which led to rapid innovation and attractive marketing arrangements. In fiscal year 1975, Japanese industry set aside nearly 20 percent of its equipment-investment budget for pollution control equipment. For the five years 1970–75, corporate expenditures for pollution control rose at an average of 40 percent annually (OECD, 1977).

Many intriguing efforts to control pollution have been made, including funding by MITI for a prototype of an electric automobile, an industrial treatment cooperative in Gyoda City that handles a variety of wastes from its 150 members, numerous recycling projects, an emission tax on automobile production, victim-compensation programs, and cleanups of contaminated riverbeds and seabeds, funded primarily by polluters. Tsukuba University, created during the educational reforms of the early 1970s (see Chapter 5), is the site of a National Institute for Environmental Protection. Environmental protection has become a central goal and was included in the two national economic plans adopted during the 1970s (see reading 6–6). Such apparent successes led many countries to request pollution control advice from Japan (see Reading 6–9).

Still, the shift in environmental policy in Japan is not exactly analogous to the reformation of the Prodigal Son or the conversion of St. Paul. Investment levels in pollution equipment fell off significantly with the economic recession of 1975. Although total governmental expenditures for environmental improvement increased greatly during the 1970s, large portions went to agencies such as MITI or the Construction Ministry, both closely tied to industry, while the budget of the Environment Agency expanded much more slowly than that of most other agencies. While many standards of emission control have been met and improved upon, certain others have been relaxed because of industrial pressure.

Most disappointing to the Environment Agency has been its inability to secure passage of environmental impact legislation (see Reading 6–7). By 1980, the Agency had submitted roughly the same bill five times without success. The bill would require environmental impact statements on major new projects by government or private industry before they begin construction, and obviously such legislation would provide the agency with tremendous powers it currently lacks. That it has been opposed by the business community and the economic ministries is not surprising; that it has not passed may suggest that the messianic commitment to ending environmental pollution that prevailed from 1970 to about 1975 may be waning because of competing demands, particularly those for a greater focus on the economy in the face of a world recession. As the OECD Environmental Committee put it in a 1977 report (p. 83) "...Japan has won many pollution-abatement battles, but has not yet won the war for environmental quality" (see Reading 6–8). The process of winning that war, which may have begun most seriously with the 1970 pollution Diet, will be going on for a long time. And it is clear that all elements of government and industry are not equally committed to fighting pollution.

Consequences

The fundamental outlines of the Japanese government's environmental policy were in place by the beginning of the 1980s, and it is possible to delineate the general ecological consequences of that policy. Yet because many environmental problems remain and because there are ongoing political debates about how to cope with them it is more difficult to see clearly the policy's political consequences.

From a technical standpoint, the policies have been successfully implemented. A large proportion of the goals set regarding air, water, and noise pollution had either been met or were rapidly being met in the early 1980s. The result has been substantial improvements in Japan's air quality, with sharp reductions in sulfur dioxide, carbon monoxide, photochemical smog, and dust fall. Although improvements in the nitrogen oxide content of the air has been slower, at least the rise that occurred until 1973 has been curbed. Water quality has also been improved, particularly by reducing the presence of harmful substances such as cadmium, alkyl mercury, cyanide, and hexavalent chromium. These no longer constitute a serious health hazard. There has also been a flattening out of the earlier growth curves of organic pollution, and most of Japan's waterways are clear by international standards. There have also been significant improvements in curbing noise and offensive odors. More vivid evidence of the measures against pollution is the fact that whereas during the late 1960s Mt. Fuji could be seen from downtown Tokyo only three or four days out of the year, and its visibility was an event marked by gawking from elevated train lines, alterations in the topics of office conversation, and newspaper headlines, by 1980 its majestic presence was so common as to be met by uniform boredom. Swans could once more survive in the moat around the Imperial Palace; fishing sites were popular again; and the sales of earplugs declined sharply.

Although improvements have been made in many areas, more remains to be done. Public complaints about noise and industrial odors remain frequent; the once-beautiful Seto Inland Sea is less clear than other semi-enclosed bodies of water in Japan; high-speed rail lines and increased air traffic cause constant noise, annoying those living near their routes; ground subsidence is a significant problem in Saitama, the suburbs of Yokohama and Osaka, and on the Nobi and Shiraishi plains.

A great deal of need remains for tightening existing standards to cope with these and other similiar problems. The Environment Agency has various long-term plans to move toward applying increasingly strict standards to most pollution problems, and it actively promoted legislation to enforce such standards throughout the 1970s. In a comparable vein, much can be accomplished in ameliorating the effects of decades of unchecked pollution. Pollution victims of known diseases are still to be certified and aided; there are surely also countless victims of as yet undiagnosed congenital diseases related to environmental pollution who will need help; dredging harbors and rivers for accumulated wastes is only beginning.

Finally, as problems of the past are solved, satisfaction with the environment is unlikely to be attained. As the more overt symptoms of a polluted environment are removed, the demands for environmental amenities are sure to increase. What was once seen as tolerable or inevitable will appear ever more odious; the environment will be expected to provide conditions for a higher quality of life. Quieter trains and planes; better smelling factories; more well-stocked fishing grounds; more suitably sited factories, garbage disposal plants, and airports; clean and nonthreatening energy sources; increased park and recreation areas—these will be among the most audible demands for an improved environment. Environmental policy will almost certainly be an area of expanded demand, just as social welfare and, to some extent, higher education are likely to be, all perhaps as surrogates for greater economic well-being.

This perspective makes it even more important to examine carefully the sociopolitical implications of Japan's environmental policies. These have not fully sorted themselves out as yet, but certain consequences seem relatively clear. What is critical is to determine which consequences are permanent and will project themselves into the future, and which are epiphenomenal, reflecting short-term remedies for the specific and acute pollution problems of the 1965–75 period.

Local governments and the court system have undoubtedly been underevaluated in terms of their capacity to influence policymaking. They were surely important in environmental matters and probably cannot be ignored either by national officials in the executive and legislative branches or by analysts of Japanese politics. It was the local governments in areas such as Tokyo, Kawasaki, Yokohama, Fuji City, and Mishima that provided much of the initiative in the national battle against pollution. It is the local governments today that have the principal responsibilities for setting and enforcing ambient emission standards, often through plant-by-plant negotiations and agreements to establish specific emission allowances for each potential pollutant facility in their areas. In many instances, these standards are more stringent than the national ones.

The courts have also proved to be a major force for change, as their role in the important pollution cases in 1971–73 attest. Here too, elements of continuity appear; major court cases were pending in 1980, for example, involving noise pollution from the so-called bullet train and from Osaka Airport. In addition, according to figures from the General Secretariat of the Supreme Court, the number of pollution-related suits in litigation rose from 168 in 1970 to 368 at the end of 1977. (Japan Environment Agency, 1978: p. 26). Japanese citizens and citizens' groups appear to be increasingly willing to bring environmental complaints before the courts, which in turn seem increasingly willing to act on them.

The creation of the Environment Agency, which has made persistent efforts to tighten regulations on environmental quality since then, is also significant, for it provides environmentalists with an official ally whose orientation is contrary to that of the economic ministries, even though it has yet to establish itself as a power in bureaucratic infighting.

Just what role these relatively ignored structures of Japanese politics will play in the future depends heavily on the possible long-term continuity of two other consequences of environmental politics: the rise of the citizens' movements and the apparent decline in the significance of partisan cleavages. Like issues such as abortion in West Germany and the United States or immigration in England, the Japanese environmental problem was one that political parties were incapable of dealing with in established ways. Hence, the issue slipped from their grasp and was taken up by new organizations devoted to its resolution in ways that precluded partisan approaches. One consequence, in sum, was that the fixed ideological spectrum of Japanese party politics that had been altered by the increased strength of small "middle" parties during the 1960s was further changed by the environmental issue, its patisans refusing to line up in their former "logical" way.

A second consequence involves the citizens' movements themselves. In 1973, there were an estimated 3,000 such movements, largely related to problems of environment quality. During the decade of the 1970s the phenomenon of the citizens' movements expanded in various directions, as they began tackling problems such as prices, the quality of consumer goods, education reform, increased local government, women's rights, and other issues related to the quality of life. Mass movements and periods of citizen activism have ebbed and flowed in Japanese political history, just as they have elsewhere in the world. At the same time, citizens' movements , which grew out of the environmental issue may well prove to be the forerunners of increased citizen activism, particularly in the form of single-issue campaigns, which have come to challenge the capacity of political parties to monopolize the articulation of political issues in other advanced industrial societies. If this would be the case, the transformation in postwar Japanese politics would be profound.

Readings

6-1. PLAN FOR THE REDISTRIBUTION OF INDUSTRIES*

Japan's phenomenal economic growth in the 1960s took place under the direction of the 1960 Plan to Double the National Income in Ten Years (see Reading 2–3). Excerpts below from the plan show its focus on taking advantage of natural industrial concentration and available harbors. Though the plan also called for dispersion of industries, high concentration pesisted, mostly because of the autonomy given to industries, and exacerbated Japan's pollution problem.

Proper Redistribution of Industries

The importance of redistributing industrial facilities is expected to increase with the implementation of this plan. The main role in this plan is to be played by industries. Assuming that industrial production will show a 3.3-fold increase during the 1960–70 period, there is a grave problem of how to secure land, water, roads, and harbors needed for such a production increase.

The problem of where to locate such industrial facilities cetainly has much to do with future economic development.

Main factors in considering industrial location facilities will be: (1) Respect of economic rationality in enterprises, (2) correction of income and interarea differentials and (3) prevention of the emergence of excessively large cities. . . .

Primarily, it is up to the enterprise to decide where to locate its plants. In this plan, too, freedom for enterprises to select their sites

---

*Japan, Economic Planning Agency, *New Long-Range Economic Plan of Japan (1961–1970)—Doubling National Income Plan* (Tokyo: The Japan Times, 1961).

on the basis of economic rationality is respected in principle. Yet, if such enterprises are left entirely free to make the choice, that will add to the trend of cities becoming excessively large in scale and augment the interarea income differentials, causing the national economy to be operated inefficiently.

This points to the need of giving full consideration in industrial redistribution to the correction of the income gap and prevention of excessive growth of city scale.

But if excessive emphasis is placed on this matter, the result will tend to be an inefficient and unsystematic decentralization of industries which is harmful to economic growth. Therefore, industrial facilities should not be decentralized at random. The decentralization itself must be carried out systematically. This is an important rule that must be followed by government investments designed to relocate industrial facilities and disperse social overhead capital. . . .

The details of the picture of industrial location during the planned period on the basis of the above considerations are:

(1) The belt-shaped areas linking the existing big-four industrial zones (Keihin, Chūkyō, Hanshin, and North Kyūshū) have far better locational conditions than other parts of the country, because they are close to large consumption-centers and favored by employment-related facilities, related and subcontracting industries, and affluence of land and water supply. Hence, social capital can be operated so efficiently in these areas that they are expected to play a vital role in the plan in regard to locating of industrial facilities. In order to cope with the trend of growing size of production units and enterprises turning into combinates, it is suggested that a medium-sized new industrial zone should be created in the middle of the belt-shaped region linking these four industrial zones.

(2) In this belt-shaped region, industrial concentration in the congested sections of the four industrial areas should be prohibited or restricted in principle. Instead, additional investments will be made in such facilities as water supply for industrial purposes, road traffic, housing, and sewage. This step is designed to increase productivity and remove bottlenecks to production by way of redevelopment. . . .

Coastal shipping tends to see marked fluctuations in its cargo handling under the influence of economic activities. But it is expected to perform an extremely important role during the planned period because land transportatin is likely to level off and because of possible increases in railway fares. Along with rationalization of the fare structure and improvement of port facilities, this calls for qualitative improvement in coastwise vessels and attainment of a higher transportation efficiency.

What is urgent in connection with harbor facilities is to improve and expand facilities at key harbors where huge quantities of cargoes are handled. The growth of foreign trade and the present acute lack of facilities in these harbors are major reasons why such expansion work is urgently needed.

6-2. GROWTH OF THE JAPANESE ECONOMY

The following comparative table shows the massive changes in the Japanese economy. All are closely associated with increased environmental pollution.

GROWTH RATES, JAPAN AND SELECTED OECD COUNTRIES, 1960–70
(percent per year)

Country	GNP	Industrial Production	Energy Consumption	Stock of Automobiles in Use
Japan	10.8	14.8	11.6	25.3
U.S.A.	4.2	4.8	4.5	3.7
U.K.	2.7	2.8	2.3	6.6
France	5.6	5.9	5.3	8.2
Italy	5.5	7.0	8.9	24.1
Sweden	4.6	6.1	5.0	6.4
Netherlands	5.3	7.3	8.4	15.7
OECD	5.0	5.9	3.0	6.2

Source: OECD, *Environmental Policies in Japan* (Paris: O.E.C.D., 1977), p. 9.

6-3. THE TOKYO POLLUTION CONTROL ORDINANCE*

In 1969, the Tokyo municipal government, under a leftist administration, enacted an environmental pollution control ordinance. This ordinance was more severe than existing national legislation and sparked a controversy over the right of local government to go so far beyond the national government. Penal provisions for polluters were

*Tokyo Municipal News 19, no. 8 (Nov., Dec. 1969): pp. 13–20.

especially nettlesome to the national government and industry. The controversy was resolved in favor of Tokyo, and this ordinance stimulated subsequent national legislation, especially that enacted by the 1970 pollution Diet.

Preamble

Men have founded civilization by exploiting natural resources under a law of nature and tried to put it [sic] to good use, enjoying natural endowments. Civilization has worked havoc upon nature, on the other hand, and brought about environmental pollution, such as air pollution, water contamination, noise, vibration, and offensive smells.

Environmental pollution has its sources in the industries and cities which man has created and it is evidently a social calamity. It stands out in cities, the manifestation of complex civilization, especially in a mammoth city like Tokyo. It infringes on the right to maintain the minimum standards of wholesome and cultured living which the Constitution of Japan guarantees to all the nation. Pollution is furthermore increasing in intensity and prevalence.

Thereupon, we Tokyo citizens make a declaration of the following principles to strictly prevent and to exterminate all environmental pollution that will disturb the wholesome, safe and comfortable life of the people in this big city, and, to carry out the principles, enact this Ordinance.

Principle 1.

All the citizens shall maintain the right to a wholesome, safe and comfortable life, undisturbed by environmental pollution without due reason.

Principle 2.

All citizens shall respect the rights of others to a wholesome, safe and comfortable living, and shall not spoil nature and the life-environment by creating any environmental pollution that will infringe on such rights.

Principle 3.

The Metropolis of Tokyo, the autonomous body of Tokyo citizens, shall bear the maximum responsibility to assure citizens of the right to a wholesome, safe and comfortable life, and, to carry out this responsibility, shall try in every possible way to prevent and exterminate environmental pollution.

This ordinance shall be interpreted and applied so as to fulfill the aims given in the above principles.

Article 2.

The Governor shall secure a good life-environment by striving to prevent environmental pollution through every possible measure and thereby shall ensure a healthy, safe and comfortable life for the residents of the Metropolis.

Article 5.

The Governor shall make public to the residents of the Metropolis the actual conditions of environmental pollution which have been brought to light as a result of the investigation and monitoring provided for in the preceding two Articles. The Governor shall make public, in such cases, the name of any person who causes serious environmental pollution in violation of the provisions of laws or ordinances.

Article 12.

An entrepreneur shall, in order to prevent environmental pollution ascribable to his business activity, take necessary measures on his own responsibility.

Article 13.

An entrepreneur, even in cases where he is not in violation of the provisions of this ordinance, shall not neglect to make every possible effort to prevent environmental pollution ascribable to his business activity, simply because he is not in violation of the provisions concerned.

Article 15.

An entrepreneur shall conduct monitoring at all times on the sources, causes and evolving conditions of environmental pollution under his own control, and shall make necessary notification to the Governor of the required information as provided by this ordinance.

Article 33.

Whenever the Governor affirms that a factory falls under certain conditions of pollution, he may order with a time limit a person who has established said factory to improve the preventative method for the evolution of soot, smoke, dust, poisonous gas, or offensive smells therefrom, or to improve the structure or layout of buildings or facilities, or to improve the position of an entrance for automobiles or the embodiment of their entry and exit or the process of operation.

Article 34.

In case a person who has been served the order as provided by the preceding Article does not obey same...the Governor may cancel the validation to the establishment of the factory or order the temporary suspension of the operation of the factory.

Article 35.

In case the Governor affirms that the soot, smoke, dust, poisonous gas, polluted water, noise, vibration or offensive smells from a factory which is being operated in breach of the order as provided in the preceding Article or other relevant official actions are causing serious damage to the health and life environment of human beings and that it is difficult to suspend the operation of the factory by any other means, he shall demand...that the supply of water for industrial or business use to said factory be suspended wholly or partially.

Article 58.

To the extent necessary for the enforcement of this Ordinance, the Govenor may have his staff members concerned enter into a factory, a designated workshop, or other relevant places to inspect books, machinery, equipment and other installations, or to give the instructions or guidance to the person concerned.

Article 61.

A peson falling under any of the following items shall be punished with penal servitude not exceeding one year or with the imposition of a fine not exceeding ten thousand yen.

6-4. THE YOKKAICHI ASTHMA CASE*

The courts were especially important in stimulating changes in Japan's environmental policies. One of the four most significant cases was the Yokkaichi Asthma Case. The collective emissions of several plants in the Yokkaichi industrial combine caused a severe throat and respiratory disease. In the decision against the combine, the court held that business has a responsibility to assess possible environmental impacts of siting decisions.

"It is understood that when there is the intention of establishing a new factory and commencing operations, the obligation exists to comprehensively carry out preliminary research and surveys regarding the character and volume of waste substances to be emitted, location of and distance between waste disposal facilities and inhabited areas, wind direction and velocity, etc., together with the obligation to give careful attention to location of the plant in such a way that no danger is incurred upon the bodies or lives of nearby residents." In the Yokkaichi Pollution Case, the above-stated obligations were not complied with, and so the accused enterprises were convicted of "negligence in siting."

6-5. DIET DEBATE ON THE PASSAGE OF
ANTIPOLLUTION LAWS†

Kyodo News Service cited Japan's pollution as the major domestic news story of 1970. The year climaxed with the passage in December of fourteen antipollution bills, including a revision of the Basic Law of 1967. While the bills substantially tightened existing controls, most opposition parliamentarians contended that they were not strict enough. The following reading summarizes portions of the Diet debate just prior to final passage. Note both the detail of the criticism and the formality and unyielding nature of the public exchanges. Note also that the public debate fell along straight party lines.

The opposition, in severely criticizing the Government's drafted air pollution-control bill in the Diet Monday argued it was ineffec-

*Environment Agency, *White Paper on the Environment, 1974* (Tokyo: EA, 1974), pp. 18–19.
†"Pollution Bills Said Ineffective by Opposition," *Japan Times*, Dec. 8, 1970.

tive and did not cover the electric power industry, which was responsible for most air pollution.

During the debate by the Industrial Hazards Special Committee of the House of Representatives, International Trade and Industry Minister Kiichi Miyazawa countered their attack by saying that his ministry had given priority to the smooth supply of electricity, and not to the electric power industry's interests.

He added the smooth supply of electricity was essential to a full life for the people.

The House of Representatives last week finished joint discussions of eight committees and started debating their views at Monday's committee meeting.

The debate lasted from 10:30 A.M. until the evening.

A Socialist, Haruyoshi Hosoya, asked Miyazawa why the bill stipulated that the electric power and gas industries should be exempt from its provisions.

Miyazawa explained that such an exemption has been made in order to protect the public interest and ensure that the people had sufficient electric power, in view of the difficulty in securing adequate amounts of low-sulfur-content heavy oil.

Ryutarō Hashimoto, Parliamentary Health and Welfare Vice-Minister, said that he believed that the bill, which gives prefectural governors authority to inspect industrial plants responsible for pollution, was adequate.

Hosoya said that about 70 percent of nitro-oxides—said to be the cause of photochemical oxidant and more than 99 percent of sulfur dioxide discharged in the atmosphere were attributable to industry, mainly electric power plants, so far as Tokyo was concerned.

He claimed that exceptions stipulated in the bill provided just the sort of loophole that would make the bill virtually ineffective in curbing air pollution.

In reply, Miyazawa said that he thought agreement could be reached between local governments and private enterprises which would impose more stringent controls on emission of poisonous substances than the pollution control law would.

Jurō Matsumoto, a Liberal-Democrat, proposed that the Government set up a pollution-consultation system to appoint pollution monitors who could deal more adequately with environmental problems.

Miyazawa said the Government was in favor of such a proposal and added that local chambers of commerce and industry had been creating pollution consulting centers at their head offices.

Miyazawa also said he considered it necessary for the Government to finance the training of the pollution consultants.

Matsumoto mentioned that the U.S. Council on Environmental Quality advised U.S. President Richard Nixon in July to introduce "an emission tax."

Matsumoto asked if the Government had any intention of imposing such a tax on enterprises releasing industrial waste into the atmosphere or water.

Home Affairs Minister Daisuke Akita replied that a study was in progress on the introduction of such a tax.

Yamanaka told the meeting that the Government was also studying a plan to issue so-called "pollution bonds" to raise funds for antipollution measures and industry would be persuaded to buy most of them.

Sadanori Yamanaka, director general of the Prime Minister's Office, and a cabinet minister in charge of pollution control, said that even if the bill was full of loopholes, as Hosoya alleged, the Government had determined to cope with air pollution by plugging all the loopholes it could find.

Asked exactly what attitude he is taking toward the proposed legislation on the "compensatory responsibility of industry irrespective of fault," Yamanaka said he would study whether the Government should work for the enactment of an independent law or attain the purpose through revision of existing laws.

Masaki Ino, a Socialist, demanded to know the Government's policy regarding the control of lead contents in auto exhaust.

Kiyoshi Sho, director general of the Pollution Control and Labor Safety Bureau, the Ministry of International Trade and Industry, said that MITI has set standards to be observed by 1973 and 1975. MITI would like to complete by 1972 the development of auto engines which will release such gas as meet the requirements, he added.

Ino asked how many automobile engines are designed to use high-octane gasoline. Yutaka Sumita, director of the Automobile Maintenance Division of the Transport Ministry, said about 11 percent of the engines on 16 million cars are thus equipped.

When Ino pressed for the replacement of such engines with ones using regular gasoline, based on the argument that the high-octane

gasoline has much lead content, Sumita only said that MITI will
have automobile makers design new cars not using high-octane
gasoline.

Transport Minister Tomisaburō Hashimoto said at the same
committee meeting that his ministry bans jumbo jets from arriving
or taking off at Tokyo International Airport except at specified
times of day so that residents around the airport will not suffer from
their noise.

6-6. THE EPA'S PLAN TO CONTROL POLLUTION*

*The Economic Planning Agency's Five-Year Plan for 1973–77
devoted substantial attention not only to economic planning, but to
planning for social improvements. The following excerpts from the
plan deal with the need to control pollution, including specific attention to waste treatment and industrial location. The Plan also calls for
the export of certain highly pollutant industries.*

Control of Industrial Pollution and Industrial Location

1. Thorough Elimination of Industrial Pollution

1) Preventing Industrial Pollution (5211).   Industry must observe
the anti-pollution standards strengthened in accordance with this
plan's environmental conservation goals and must implement the
necessary measures to prevent the generation of pollution-
accompanying industrial activity. At the same time, along with
strengthening environmental standards and implementing other
such steps, the Government is to institute all necessary measures to
achieve these environmental protection goals soon.

(1) With strengthening environmental standards, other necessary
policies to be taken by the Government include strengthening
desulfurization, promoting industrial relocation plans, and encouraging environmental consideration when plants are built.

(2) In order to meet stronger regulations and to ensure their
effectiveness, industry must make positive efforts to develop anti-
pollution techniques and to install antipollution equipment satisfying these regulations and standards. In order to advance private
industry's anti-pollution technological development and equipment

---

*Japan, Economic Planning Agency, *Basic Economic and Social Plan, 1973–1977*
(Tokyo: EPA, 1973), pp. 85–88.

installation, the Government, as well as providing information, offering guidance, and doing technical development work on its own as necessary, is to implement the appropriate fiscal and financial measures respecting the polluter-pays principle of the OECD. At the same time, means should be studied of allowing private industry to utilize state-owned patents and know-how at reasonable cost.

2) Policies Promoting Product Safety etc. (5212).   Regarding unsafe products, general waste, and other problems of safety and pollution caused by consumption, the Government is to conduct a thorough-going crack-down on unsafe products under the present laws and government ordinances and is to take a variety of other legal and administrative actions, including the aggressive application of Japanese Industrial Standards and Japanese Agricultural Standards, the passage of new laws relating to product safety, and new legislation aimed at ensuring the safety of PCB [polychlorinated biophenyles] and related products. Responding to the strong popular concern with safety, industry must act in full awareness of its social responsibility.

As waste treatment policies, new physical distribution techniques are to be utilized, packaging rationalized, industries for recycling waste plastic, papers and the like fostered, and recovery systems established for automobiles and other volume junk and for other waste, both industrial and non-industrial.

(2) Promoting Industrial Location in Harmony with Environmental Conditions and Local Society (5220).   Future industrial location must be directed toward contributing to regional development and increased welfare for local residents and workers, seeking harmony with primary industry and other industries of the area, preserving the natural environment, maintaining coordination with other policies for regional development, and considering the scarcity of land, water, and other social resources. Accordingly, the following measures are to be taken:

1) Promoting Industrial Relocation (5221).   (1) With all due consideration to preventing pollution and continuing to seek harmony with other regional development plans, the Government is to draw up and make public a long-term plan for industrial relocation.

(2) In keeping with its plan for industrial relocation and while giving overall consideration to the characteristics of various industrial locations, the availability of land, water, and labor, and the functional concentrations in each area, the Government is to take the following measures to promote industrial relocation in addition to those fiscal and financial advantages already noted (1131). In so doing, the national and local governments are to cooperate in implementing the necessary measures.

a) For the relocation of small and medium enterprises, financial and other measures, such as assistance in acquiring new plant sites, are to be instituted with full consideration to the characteristics of the business. Appropriate steps are especially to be taken to help subcontractors move easily to help those that do not move maintain stability in their business relations with clients.

b) In order to facilitate moving by laborers who take their families, such forceful policies are to be adopted as securing homes and schools at the new location, expanding health and welfare facilities, and providing an urban environment. At the same time, smooth re-employment for those laborers who can not make the move is to be promoted.

c) Study is also to be given to strengthening the various regulations and assistance measures to induce relocation, such as systems levying special charges on factories locating in Industrial Department Promotion Areas.

d) When industrial relocation involves a move to a former coal-mining area, agricultural area, or other area [to] which new industry is induced in a planned way, efforts are to be made to have the new plant's entry done in accord with the plans regarding plant induction.

2) Factory Environmental Improvement (5222). The Government is to take all necessary measures, including legal, so that industrial location is done in harmony with the living environment of the surrounding area and contributes to preventing pollution and ensuring safety.

(1) Standards are to be set for environmental improvement, such as the maximum percentage of the site which may be used for production facilities, the minimum percentage of the site used for

greenery and other environmentally effective ends, or regulating the layout of facilities within the site.

(2) Submission of environmental improvement plans is to be required when a plant builds anew or expands, and the necessary warnings or orders for improvement are to be issued in case of non-compliance or unsatisfactory plans.

(3) When an industrial complex is to be built, it is hoped that every effort will be made to prevent pollution, including in addition to complete advance studies of the total industrial pollution situation, efforts to improve anti-pollution systems, and the like.

(4) The achievement of industrial parks in all areas throughout the country is most strongly recommended.

3) Acceleration of the Overseas Location of Resource-processing Industries (5223).   Because the overseas location of resource-processing industries is thought desirable from the long-term perspective when the agreement of the host country is obtained, the following measures are to be taken:

(1) Surveys of basic conditions in appropriate overseas sites are to be strengthened.

(2) In accord with the host country's plans for industrialization, improvement of the basic social and economic infrastructure as it relates to private projects is to be undertaken as part of economic aid programs.

(3) Efforts are to be made to foster [the development of] people possessing both a broad international perspective and specialized knowledge in governmental agencies and elsewhere.

6-7. THE LDP'S REJECTION OF AN ENVIRONMENTAL ASSESSMENT LAW*

One of the major problems in environmental protection involves the assessment of potential impact in advance of industrial development. From the mid-1970s on, the Environment Agency unsuccessfully sought passage of an environmental assessment law. The bill was continually blocked by industrial supporters in the LDP.

*"LDP Puts Brake on Environmental Assessment Law Bill; Policy Board Sub-Committees Also Heading Toward Co-ordination of Opinions," *Asahi Shimbun*, Jan. 24, 1979.

The LDP decided on the 23rd that opinions will be co-ordinated between the Commerce and Industry and Environment Sub-Committees of the Policy Board in presenting to the Diet session the Environmental Assessment Law Bill which is aimed at "preventing the destruction of the environment." This decision is in accordance with the intention of the Commerce and Industry Sub-Committee, which is strongly opposed to the presentation of the bill during the current Diet session. Thus, a strong brake has been applied from within the ruling party on the Evironment Agency, which was scheduled to present the bill to the current Diet session.

At the Cabinet meeting on the morning of the 23rd, the bill was reported by Chief Cabinet-Secretary Tanaka as "one of the bills scheduled to be presented to the current Diet session." At his press conference after the cabinet meeting, Environment Agency Director-General Uemura stated: "I want to find a breakthrough for the presentation of the bill by working with various ministries and agencies, and then to move energetically."

However, at the Commerce and Industry Sub-Committee meeting held at the party headquarters that day, strong arguments against the presentation of the bill were brought forth: "In May of last year we reached the conclusion that 'the presentation of the bill to the Diet session was premature.' There has been no big change in the social and economic situation since then, and it cannot be said that the time is ripe." Others argued that: "Construction of power plants and roads is being delayed because of the severe restrictions set by the local governing bodies in response to the inhabitants' opposition movements. In the present situation, it is not necessary for the state to establish further restrictions." Sub-Committee Chairman Watanabe conveyed this mood to Policy Board Chairman Komoto, who acknowledged that if a stage for the presentation of the bill comes, the Chairmen and Vice-Chairmen of the Commerce and Industry and Environment Sub-Committees will co-ordinate their opinions.

6-8. THE OECD'S REVIEW OF ENVIRONMENTAL PROBLEMS*

In 1976–77 the Organization for Economic Cooperation and Development reviewed environmental policies in Japan. Although the

*OECD, *Environmental Policies in Japan* (Paris: OECD, 1977), pp. 87–88.

report was highly supportive of most policy efforts, its concluding comments noted the need to consider environmental problems in an extremely broad context.

The Japanese experience can also show that ambient concentration levels are but one dimension of environmental quality, and that pollution abatement should be only one aspect of environmental policies. In Japan, in the late sixties, environmental discontent focussed on pollution, and environmental policies concentrated on pollution abatement. The result was somewhat surprising: although these policies largely succeeded in abating pollution, they did not succeed in eliminating environmental discontent. The illness, so to speak, survived the elimination of its main cause. This would suggest that the real cause of environmental discontent was not—and is not—increasing pollution, but decreasing environmental quality. Environmental quality, or as it is often called "amentities", refers to quietness, beauty, privacy, social relations and other non-measured elements of the "quality of life". People were not so much suffering from high ambient concentration levels as from the gradual degradation of their living environment. The reasons why they complained about pollution, not amenities, are twofold. Pollution problems are fairly well-defined: pollution levels can be measured, pollution sources can be identified. Amenities, by contrast, are difficult to define and are a much vaguer concept. Also, pollution has an impact on health, whereas amenities "only" impinge on well-being. Politically, the abatement of pollution was, therefore, a much better battlefield than the provision of amenities. What could be called "apparent" social demand was for pollution abatement; but "real" social demand was for the provision of amenities. It is because environmental policies satisfied only this apparent social demand, and largely ignored the real social demand, that they did not eliminate environmental discontent.

The Japanese people and the Japanese authorities are now trying to develop broader-based environmental policies, dealing not only with pollution control but also with the preservation of their natural and cultural heritage and with the promotion of well-being in general.

This is indeed a new and difficult task. It will require new types of instruments and mechanisms. It is more difficult than pollution abatement, because the problems at hand are mainly of a social, not just technical nature. The setting of standards will certainly not be sufficient and technological innovations will not be of much help. What is required is careful global planning, which could be described as the use of mechanisms to prevent environmentally dangerous developments and to promote environmentally desirable developments. Mechanisms of the first type are more or less available, under the names of technology-assessment and impact-statement procedures, but are difficult to implement. Mechanisms of the second type are not quite ready as yet. This kind of planning has to take into account both the nature and the location of developments; it has to find out what to do, and where to do it. This is why land-use planning has an important role to play.

In this new type of environmental policies to be developed the key element is probably the organisation of public participation. The possible long-term, indirect costs of a given project are often difficult to imagine; the possible long-term, indirect benefits of another project are even more difficult to think of. This can only be done if a number of people—including the people involved—participate in the decision-making processes. This is difficult to organise, and will be done at great cost. But there are reasons to believe that Japan is well equipped to do it, and that it will in the years to come, improve environmental quality as efficiently as it reduced pollution levels.

6-9. JAPANESE ENVIRONMENTAL MISSIONS ABROAD*

In conjunction with Japan's perceived success in combating various forms of pollution, a number of countries have invited Japanese environmental experts to assess their problems and propose solutions.

Despite or because of Japan's reputation as one of the world's most polluted nations, there is increasing interest, especially among developing countries, in Japan's pollution control technology.

The Environment Agency and pollution control industry sources report a sharp rise in requests for missions of Japanese experts to be

*"Polluted Japan Teaches the World What Not to Do," *Nihon Keizai Shimbun*, June 3, 1980.

sent abroad and for researchers to visit Japan to study pollution control technology. In many countries, successful economic development has caused new environmental problems.

The *White Paper on the Environment* attributes the requests for assistance to the fact that Japan has "survived the crisis in industrial pollution," and is the one nation which has "accumulated" such extensive pollution control know-how.

In January, the Industrial Pollution Control Association of Japan sent four technical experts to India at that country's request, and the association recently sent two more experts to Chile. They conducted pollution control seminars and diagnosed pollution problems in local factories and other facilities.

The association is trying to find qualified personnel and funding to assist several pollution control projects, mostly in Southeast Asia. Research teams have also come to Japan. For example, the association has arranged for a 30-member team from Taiwan each year. At the request of Chinese officials, the association will host two missions this year.

Concerned about the pollution of Lake Ontario, the government of Ontario has requested the Japan Society of Industrial Machinery Manufacturers, an organization of pollution control equipment makers, to send a delegation of technical specialists. Although Ontario's stated objective is to acquire Japanese knowledge of water drainage disposal, there have been reports that an illness resembling Japan's Minamata disease has broken out around the shores of Lake Ontario. A technical mission is scheduled to go to Canada this year.

As indications of interest in Japan's experience, 12 persons from 10 countries participated in the Environment Agency's seminars on Environmental Administration held in March and April 1980, nearly twice the nations represented at the 1973 session. Participation in the Ministry of Health and Welfare's training program on waste disposal increased to eleven countries in 1979 from five or six in the past. Similar increases are expected in the future.

7 Administrative Reform: Scrap And Build

One of the major factors contributing to Japanese success in meeting various official policy-targets has been the national bureaucracy. Since the Meiji Restoration, the Japanese civil service has attracted some of the country's most talented individuals. A rigorous education, legal training, and highly competitive examinations have ensured the selection of Japan's "best and brightest." Early bureaucratic retirement followed by high-paying and high-prestige jobs in the private sector guaranteed mobility and opportunities for responsibility within the bureaucracy as well as successful second careers for retired officials.

The efficiency of the Japanese bureaucracy in the contemporary period is linked to many historical factors. But it is due as well to the administrative reform measures followed by the government. Through a series of innovative procedures, the government has streamlined the national bureaucracy and reduced or stabilized the numbers of personnel, commissions, agencies, and paperwork. In turn, this has forced much greater top-down clarification of goals by individual agencies. As a result, the Japanese government on the whole has been relatively selective in the targets to which it has allocated manpower, money, and talent.

In keeping down the size and cost of government, Japanese political leaders have utilized a procedure which has made creative use of the conflicts built into Japan's bureaucratic structures. As in economic policy, conflicts and priorities have been shifted to individual agencies with positive results for process and policy outcome.

Context

When the modern Japanese civil service was established in the years immediately following the Meiji Restoration, it was modelled quite closely on that of Germany, which in turn had been patterned on the organization of the Prussian military. In addition, the Chinese ideology of Confucianism played no small role in informing modernizing Japanese officials how to organize and behave. In both these traditions, politics was sharply demarcated from administration. Politics represented division and partisanship; bureaucratic organization represented unity and transcendent loyalty. The prime goal of the Japanese bureaucracy was to aid top-level officials in making national policy and to ensure its reliable implementation. Bureaucratic efficiency was central; policymaking autonomy, political initiative, implementational sabotage, or partisan decision making were all to be scrupulously avoided. In these respects, prewar Japanese officialdom resembled structurally, if not normatively, Max Weber's portrait of the ideal bureaucracy.

Such goals were particularly strong in the thinking of Yamagata Aritomo, a major military figure, one of Japan's foremost state builders and the man generally regarded as the father of the Japanese bureaucracy. Yamagata sought to keep government as "transcendent" of partisan politics as possible. The entire political system established by the Meiji Constitution was premised on the existence of a talented bureaucratic service prepared to serve state interests once they had been articulated in laws and decrees ratified by the Emperor. Indeed, under the prewar constitution, all members of the national bureaucracy were designated "servants of the emperor," not civil servants, as in Britain.

Reality was always removed from this ideal, but the concept received tangible practical support. The imperial university system, crowned by Tokyo Imperial, was the keystone in the production of well-educated and legally trained individuals to staff the civil service. Salaries, perquisites, and prestige, particularly of senior civil servants, were extremely high, and upon retirement many former civil servants were appointed to the House of Peers. Particularly important, in comparison with many other democracies, the national bureaucracy was never a haven for patronage appointees. Instead, a rigorous examination system governed entry into the civil service from 1869 on, and in 1899 Yamagata succeeded in imposing a series of government ordinances which effectively insulated most of the bureaucracy from the influence and patronage of political parties. The end result was a state bureaucracy which, in comparison to those in most other industrial countries at the time, was hierarchical, efficient, self-confident, and loyal, and commanded public respect.

From an American perspective, many features of this system were contributors to Japan's authoritarianism in later years, and several memoranda during the early months of the United States Occupation called for sweeping administrative reforms, including comprehensive decentralization, democratization of recruitment procedures, structural reorganization of various functions, and more democratic procedures (see Readings 7-1). Like many Europeans in the 1960s, Americans in the 1940s believed that democratic values could be easily transmitted through administrative systems.

In fact, very few such reforms were ever implemented. When the United States Personnel Advisory Mission was sent to Japan in November, 1946, fifteen months after the end of the war, it was chaired by a strong devotee of scientific management, Blaine Hoover, and staffed by members whose experience had been limited to personnel work and improvement of managerial efficiency. Presumptions of administrative rationality were compatible with existing Japanese notions of how best to "reform" the national bureaucracy. Pressures for increased administrative efficiency had become particularly acute in Japan, Europe, and the United States during World War II. With countries on a wartime footing, with national expenditures running high, and with a premium on smooth government operations, many elements of the scientific administration drawn from the theories of Frederick Taylor were widely considered. Taylorism was implemented quicker and more comprehensively in the United States, but during the last years of the war the Japanese government considered a number of plans along similar lines. Defeat prevented most from being implemented, but the government was ideologically and administratively ripe for precisely the approach suggested by the United States Personnel Advisory Mission.

To assist the mission, the Japanese government created the Adminstrative Research Bureau, later called the Administrative Management Agency (AMA). This agency was charged with drafting plans for the reformation of the central administration, but its role was explicitly limited to that of ensuring rational and efficient administration.

With such a background, it was no surprise that the recommendations of the United States Personnel Advisory Mission were virtually all directed toward the improvement of managerial efficiency. They called for the creation of a nonpartisan National Personnel Authority, modelled after the United States Civil Service Commission, and for the introduction of "specialization and scientific management" so as to develop "an efficient system of personnel administration for the Japanese government." Its specific proposals were concentrated on the establishment of detailed standards for recruitment, training, position classification, compensation, employee evaluation, health, safety, welfare, recreation, employee relations, retirement, employment statistics, and the like. There was no consideration of structural change, expansion of the recruitment base of the civil service, decentralization, or new principles changing the relations among government, bureaucracy, and citizenry. The social and political content that had animated early American criticisms was forgotten. Virtually the only "political" provisions of the reform proposals were those making ineligible for examination or appointment any person who "advocated or belonged to an association or political party which advocated the overthrow by force of the Constitution of Japan . . ." and those which prohibited strikes by public employees (see also Chapter 3). This equation of "administrative reform" with "improved bureaucratic efficiency" continued to shape most public policy efforts even after the Occupation had ended. Within the national government, the newly created National Personnel Authority was charged with ensuring conformity with these goals of efficiency and neutrality through the National Public Service Law. It has continued to play this role in subsequent years (see Reading 7-2).

Prewar traditions and the American emphasis on scientific management combined to produce a Japanese bureaucracy structured for clarity of organization and responsibility. The primary units of government are the twelve ministries (*sho*), and the seven to ten agencies (*cho*) under the Prime Minister's Office. Each ministry or agency is divided into six to twelve functional bureaus (*kyoku*) or departments (*bu*) which in turn are subdivided into sections (*ka*). The Japanese government is relatively free from the many autonomous commissions, bureaus, and regulatory agencies that mark the American bureaucracy.

There is a particularly high premium placed in Japan on ministerial, agency, or bureau loyalty. Although beneficial to intraorganizational efficiency, this has the effect of developing rivalries among the various ministries, agencies, and bureaus. The story, perhaps apocryphal is often told of the prewar government official who was sent to another section within his agency to obtain routine information and was sent away with the comment that if his section considered the data so important, it should have collected it itself. And when new recruits enter MITI, they are allegedly told that they will all have to work twice as hard as usual if they are to outperform their rivals in the Ministry of Finance.

Such bureaucratic parochialism and competition means that agencies fight vigorously to protect their spheres of influence and budget shares. Few are willing voluntarily to declare their mission and their personnel expendible, no matter what the changes in national priorities may be. As in Europe and America, more often each agency tries to expand its individual sphere of control and to gain an ever-larger mouthful at the public trough.

While all organizations display elements of such loyalty, in Japan the competition is exacerbated by the fact that government careers tend to start and end in the same agency. Kubota's study (1969) showed that some 70 percent of all bureaucrats follow this pattern. In a few agencies, particularly high-prestige agencies like the Ministry of Finance or the Ministry of Foreign Affairs, the figure is over 90 percent. Obviously, such career patterns reinforce organizational tendencies toward bureaucratic protectionism.

In addition to scientific management, there was a second objective in administrative reforms during the United States Occupation, namely, reduction of the size and expenditures of the national government. Between 1931 and 1951, national government employees had jumped from 591,000 to 1.4 million while the number of prefectural and local government officials had skyrocketed from 90,000 to 1.3 million. After the war personnel costs soared just as economies in government were being demanded by the Americans and by Japanese conservatives. Moreover, public sector unions had gained a large membership among blue-collar and lower level white-collar government workers, and it was precisely these public sector unions which had become the main source of vigorous opposition to conservative continuity.

In 1949 and again in 1951, with American concurrence the Japanese government put forward plans for administrative rationalization. These called for the elimination of numerous government bureaus and personnel cuts of over 300,000 government employees. Most of these cuts were in the National Railways Corporation, the Ministry of Postal Services, and the Ministry of Telecommunications, the agencies employing the largest numbers of government officials and those which were the hotbeds of public sector union activity. To bypass various protective provisions of existing civil service regulations, the government imposed the cuts by setting a legal limit on the total number of government personnel that could be employed by each agency and ministry. Conservative dominance of the parliament made the passage of such limits relatively easy, but at the same time, as will be seen, reliance on such explicit legislation gave rise to major problems of administrative flexibility during the next fifteen years.

The basic principles of Japanese administrative reform, in sum, had become increased efficiency and constraint on the size of government. Post-Occupation practices remained fully congruent with these notions. Subsequent government efforts at administrative reform were virtually all in similar areas, and although implementation was rarely easy, the policy directions of administrative reform had been set.

Agenda

The cuts in government personnel begun during the Occupation and continued immediately thereafter were not insignificant in their impact. Nor were the rationalizations of government organization subsequently undertaken in 1954 and 1956. Yet the size and expenditures of the national government continued to expand as they did in nearly all other industrial countries. In Japan, this involved nearly 10,000 new posts per year, and between 1952 and 1963 government expenditures as a percentage of national income rose from 17 percent to 24 percent. Yet, whereas the expansions in countries such as France, Britain, Sweden, and the United States were largely attributable to those governments' taking on additional functions, particularly in the area of social welfare, in Japan, as was seen in Chapter 4, social welfare barely changed during this period. In fact, as will be recalled from Chapter 2 in economic policy, one of the primary fiscal goals of the government, particularly in the Ministry of Finance, was to avoid deficit financing and to keep down any growth in expensive government programs.

Much of the expansion that took place in the Japanese bureaucracy must be attributed to bureaucratic protectionism, sectionalism, and imperialism. Basic organizational predilections towards protecting personnel and power were aided by the fact that, as noted above, the government had set specific legislative limits on the number of personnel authorized for each of its many agencies. The result was that even minor changes in personnel needs, such as the addition of one more chauffeur to a ministry's roster, required a revision in the existing law. Furthermore, even cases involving no increase in the total number of ministry personnel, such as the reallocation of the authorized strength between a central ministry and its external agencies or local offices, required a similar revision of the law. Practically speaking, this meant that agencies could usually demonstrate additional needs for new personnel and gain legislative support for upward revisions in their authorizations, but that individually and collectively they could easily frustrate legislative efforts to *reduce* the number of their authorized personnel. The result was continued expansion in government size, despite official goals.

In their protectionist efforts, many agencies were aided by the unions representing public sector employees. Stung by the drastic cuts of 1949–52, the public sector unions were anxious to protect all existing jobs by whatever means seemed possible.

During the period 1952–60, the Administrative Management Agency issued a number of reports calling for improved management, rationalization, and efficiency in government, aimed at curtailing the rises in government expenditure and personnel. The partisan and particularized nature of many of the agency's proposals, however, impeded their implementation. The political left, in particular, was concerned that "administrative reform" would prove to be little more than a code phrase for additional personnel cuts. Most agencies targeted for reforms mustered extensive arguments and constituency pressures to demonstrate why they should not be singled out.

Finally, in November 1961, under the Ikeda cabinet, which was committed among other things to reducing confrontations with the opposition, the government established a Provisional Council on Administrative Reform. The Council was established with the explicit provision that its recommendations should transcend any simple demand for reductions in personnel. Established with the support of all parties except the JCP, the council was patterned after the Hoover Commission in the United States. It engaged some 138 members, specialists, investigators, and administrators for three years at a cost of ¥ 110 million. The council's report covered sixteen major areas of reform, including wide-ranging suggestions for coordination between the cabinet and the planning staff of various agencies; simplifications of procedures for obtaining government permits; regrouping of administrative organs and public corporations; rationalization of budgeting and accounting; and a full-fledged commitment to ongoing administrative reform. The latter was to involve a permanent body charged with administrative inspection and management and the publication of an annual white paper on administrative reform.

A series of bodies were established in subsequent years to provide the organizational framework needed to give permanent inpetus to administrative reform. The main thrust of the report, and of subsequent efforts was to improve managerial efficiency and to rationalize administrative functions. No explicit calls were made for cuts in personnel, so that potential hostility to the measures from opposition parties was largely defused. Most proposals were directed toward the entire central bureaucracy rather than toward individual agencies, with the result that particularistic agency opposition was also reduced. With most of the potential opposition eliminated and with all major actors committed in principle to "administrative reform," implementation fell to the cabinet, the Prime Minister's Office and the Administrative Management Agency. It was their agenda that dominated administrative reform efforts over the next decade and a half. All were agreed that operations should be steamlined and that costs should be cut.

The agenda that resonated constantly through governmental reform efforts stressed efficiency, procedural rationalization, cost cutting, and personnel reduction. Muted in all discussions of reform were such problems as improved service delivery to the citizenry, changes in the recruitment system for higher-level civil servants, corruption, or curbing the practice of *amakudari* whereby retiring civil servants "descend from heaven" to important posts in public corporations or private sector industries in fields related to their past positions. All these issues have been raised by the media or by the opposition parties, but for the most part they have occasioned few governmental responses. They remain largely symbolic items paraded occasionally before the public, but rarely are they the targets of systematic and sustained reform efforts.

Process

The government never completely abandoned the notion of cutting down government costs through reductions in the number of government employees. However, its approach to such reductions was much less heavy-handed in the 1960s than had been the layoffs and budgetary cuts of the early 1950s. The new strategy was subtly designed to reduce potential opposition from individual agencies anxious to preserve or expand their relative influence in the government, while at the same time allowing top government leaders to set and effect changing priorities.

The process whereby this was carried out was a forcing of each government agency to set its own priorities internally regarding functions and personnel use. Rather than being able to add on automatically new activities and personnel in response to changing social and economic conditions, agencies were forced to reexamine existing activities first. If something new were to be added, it would have to come at the expense of something no longer of central concern to the agency. Just as in the case of budget making, agencies were called upon to do much of their setting of priorities in-house, rather than to attempt to expand their activities at the expense of other agencies or by drawing on some presumed bottomless reservoir of resources. In this way, a great deal of the potential conflict of agency against agency was reduced to conflicts of an intraministerial nature. This level of conflict was infinitely easier to cope with.

At the same time, central government decision makers retained the power to set national priorities, transcending narrow ministerial or agency boundaries. Once such priorities were set, as will be seen subsequently, agencies were presented with a direct incentive to conform to them; doing so made it more likely that requests for additional functions or personnel would be granted.

The first moves in this direction came in 1964 as a follow-up to the proposals of the Provisional Council on Administrative Reform. On August 14 of that year, Prime Minister Ikeda announced a plan to leave a portion of all vacant posts unfilled. On September 4 of that year, the cabinet agreed, and the Administrative Management Agency was charged with implementing the plan (see Reading 7-3). The main directives were to freeze a certain portion of the positions vacant as of September 4 and to allow only partial refilling of vacancies created by employee termination. Any increases in personnel were to come from the unfrozen portion of the new vacancies. In 1966 and 1967, the recruitment freeze was expanded. By the end of 1967, some 15,000 vacant positions had accumulated. Although about half of these were filled to meet new needs, there was a net total of 7,500 positions left unfilled.

This relatively evenhanded restriction of expansion involved few if any actual layoffs. Yet there were cuts in the total number of authorized personnel. As in Britain in 1980, natural attrition rather than wholesale firings caused the reductions. This method tended to reduce union opposition. More importantly, since all government agencies were uniformly affected by the cuts, few could object.

Instead, all were forced to meet changing internal priorities through reorganization and reallocation of existing personnel rather than simply through new additions and expansion. Each government agency reserved certain vacancies, a part of which could be filled by necessary staff increases within the limits determined by existing laws governing agency organization. Yet since the number of authorized personnel was fixed by law for each agency and ministry, the pooling and reallocation of as many as 7,500 frozen vacancies across agency lines was extremely difficult.

Allocating new positions was tackled in late 1967 by the Cabinet Council for Provisional Administrative Reform, an agency created as a result of the 1964 reform proposals. To provide flexibility in meeting changing needs for governmental services while at the same time holding down the total number of government personnel, the legal limits on personnel strength for individual agencies were replaced by a single limit on the total number of government personnel. Allotments for individual agencies were established within that total by government decree. The system of leaving positions vacant was terminated, but the fixed personnel strength of each ministry and agency was permanently reduced by the number of its existing vacancies (see Reading 7-4). The general principle of increasing efficiency and holding down size was spelled out in the cabinet decision of October 20, 1967 aimed at effecting the plan: "In order to upgrade the efficiency levels of the public service and to diminish the taxpayers' burden, the filling of vacancies must be kept to the minimum through streamlining and simplifying existing administrative operations. In response to fluctuating demand for administrative services, positive efforts shall be made to transfer personnel to areas where the need is greatest, thereby effecting a planned reduction in the number of total fixed personnel."

Three related steps were taken to achieve the desired changes. The first, based on a cabinet decision in late December 1967, called for a cut of one bureau by each of the government's main agencies or ministries. The decision as to which bureau to cut was left to the agency itself. This impartiality, plus the even-handedness with which the cuts were made, reduced some bureaucratic opposition to the plan, while at the same time the number of central government bureaus dropped from 120 to 102 (yet see Reading 7-5 for a critical appraisal).

The second aspect of the policy was a systematic 5 percent reduction in the fixed number of personnel within each agency, to take place over a three-year period, 1969–71 (see Reading 7-6). These cuts were to be effected through retirement, deaths, and other kinds of natural attrition and followed by internal reorganization of the energy or ministry. The eliminated positions were to go into a collective pool from which all agencies could request supplements to their personnel. Individual agency requests were evaluated in comparison with one another, thereby allowing for sensitivity to national priorities. When additional personnel could not be acquired from the national pool, agencies were forced to determine their own priorities regarding personnel within fixed and declining limits. The result was the elimination of many sections or subsections which had outlived their original purposes and the transfer of the staff of such bodies to units deemed more essential.

Also targeted for cuts and reorganization were the various public corporations and advisory commissions under the control of the national government agencies. General procedures were established by the cabinet, with the assistance of the AMA, requiring each agency to reduce cases requiring government permits by 10 percent and cases requiring reports to government agencies by 20 percent. Grants-in-aid of under one million yen (approximately $50,000) to either municipalities or prefectures were to be eliminated, and internal administration and organization were to be simplified.

The third element in the plan involved a National Personnel Authorization Law. A single law was to take the place of the numerous and laws authorizing specific numbers of personnel for each agency ministry. Such a law was critical to the entire reform effort, yet was not passed with ease. Only after extensive parliamentary debate and two unsuccessful efforts by the government did the bill finally become law in May 1969 (see Reading 7-7). By fixing the total number of national government officials at a maximum of 506, 571 (the number authorized at the time of the law's passage), the government sought simultaneously to freeze the total number of personnel, to eliminate the problem of continual legal revision to meet changing needs of individual agencies, and to allow for more flexible and prompt shifts in the number of personnel authorized for any particular government agency.

The basic proposals of this 1968 plan were extended in the second (1972), third (1975), and fourth (1977) plans for reductions in the fixed number of personnel. In each plan, a specific percent of an agency's personnel was to be eliminated and put into a central pool. All new allocations of personnel would be made from this pool. The result was a continuous freezing in the total number of government personnel at just over half a million.

Further efforts along comparable lines were made by the Fukuda Cabinet in December 1977, following the world economic downturn of the of the mid–1970s (see Reading 7-8). This decision called for: a 5 percent cut in the number of divisions, offices, and titled officers within two years; a drastic reduction in the number of central government field offices; reorganizations among certain central offices; and cuts in the number of public corporations and advisory councils as well as revision of the basis on which members to them were selected. In addition, small grants-in-aid were to be eliminated, and there was to be a drastic rationalization of existing bureaucratic regulations, inspections, and certifications. Certain government functions were to be shifted to local governments, and cuts were to be made in the local branches of national agencies. Finally, the government recommitted itself to implementation of existing plans for elimination of another 28,000 personnel over a three-year period (1977–80).

By these methods, the cabinet and the Administrative Management Agency were able to confront effectively a problem that bedevils central governments in all industrial societies: how to shift priorities without incurring the wrath of their component agencies and without the gigantic expenses that result from simply adding new functions to old. The central government in Japan was able to utilize bureaucratic rivalries in a process that all could accept as fair. By forcing agencies to internalize the bulk of the conflict over administrative reallocations, the government, in all likelihood, also increased its overall efficiency.

Consequences

The most obvious and immediate consequence of administrative reform in Japan was the levelling off in the growth of national government. Between 1957 and 1967, when the major programs aimed at reduction were begun, the number of government personnel (*teiin kanri*), exclusive of military personnel which were not affected by the reforms, had jumped from 377,000 to 507,000. Employees in the five major government enterprises (the Post Office, National Forestry, and the printing, alcohol, and mint monopolies) rose from 288,000 to 373,000. The staffing of national government field offices had more than doubled, from 8,800 to 19,000. Twelve years later, in 1979, each of the figures had levelled off or were below these 1967 levels. Civilian government personnel stood at 504,000, those in the five enterprises had fallen by about 15,000, and staff in local offices were at 18,900.

There were also cuts in various public and semipublic organizations. The number of public corporations had soared from 33 in 1955 to 113 in 1967 but had dropped to 111 in 1979. The number of government bureaus which had risen from 77 to 120 between 1955 and 1967 dropped to 101 three years later before creeping back up to 114 in 1979. The number of official advisory councils which had risen from 194 to 277 between 1955 and 1967 plummeted to 210 in 1978. In short, a lid had been put on growth in national government. This represented a stark contrast to government growth elsewhere, especially in Sweden and Britain.

Curtailing absolute growth did not entail a freezing of all structures and expansions of the national government bureaucracy, however. Innovation and reallocation continued to occur. For example, the government established an Environment Agency in 1971, a Price Bureau, and a Natural Resources and Energy Agency in 1973, and a National Land Agency in 1974. There was an overall growth of about 18,000 in the number of government personnel assigned to national schools and hospitals, while in 1977 a new system of national medical colleges was created *de novo*. Initially staffed by 6,400 people, two years later it was employing over 11,000. But such expansions were paralleled by significant cuts in the number of authorized personnel in the Ministry of Agriculture, Forestry, and Fisheries, the Ministry of Construction, and the Prime Minister's Office, among others. Reallocation rather than expansion was the guideline.

Overall constraint in the size of the national government was, furthermore, balanced by expansion at lower levels of government. As was noted in Chapters 1 and 6, the late 1960s and early 1970s saw a sharp rise in citizens' movements and in the electoral success of progressive mayors in most major cities. Many local governments took on expanded activites in social welfare, environmental protection, education, transportation, health care, and the like. In the absence of any national government commitment to such goals and in an effort to demonstrate increased sensitivity to citizen demands, many local governments began diverse programs in these areas. To staff such programs meant to increase the number of local government personnel. Consequently, while the number of national government employees remained stable or declined following 1967, the number of local government officials grew steadily from 1.8 million in 1958, to 2.5 million in 1970, to over 3 million in 1977. In effect, local governments picked up much of the policy implementation left by the stability in the national government's size. From a slightly different perspective, it can be said that the policy of administrative reform encouraged the national government to siphon off less critical functions to local levels of government, while concentrating on items of extremely high national significance.

In spite of the growth in local government, however, Japan still has a much smaller proportion of government employees than any other major industrial state. Differences in administrative structure, institutional variation, and methods of calculation make accurate comparisons difficult, but one can say that government employees represent roughly from 6 percent to 9 percent of all public employment in the United States, Britain, West Germany, and France and between 14 percent and 30 percent of the working populations of these countries. In Japan, the figures are 4.5 percent and 9 percent, respectively. Clearly, government is still quite a bit smaller in Japan than elsewhere.

Although all in all government service might have appeared to many as a declining sector, national government service remained an extremely attractive option to Japan's potential elite. Typical salaries were comparable to those of major private firms; allowances and perquisites could become quite high; there were exceptionally good chances to gain responsible positions quickly; as in Britain, West Germany, and France, pensions for civil servants were at least 1.5 times higher than those for the general citizenry (see Chapter 5); and the possibility of lucrative post-retirement careers was extremely good. As a result, there was no shortage in applicants for higher civil service positions. Between 1970 and 1979 alone, the number of applicants tripled from 20,000 to 60,000, despite the fact that only 1,311 individuals would gain posts. Whereas in 1964 there were fewer than ten applicants per position, by 1979 the competition ratio had more than quadrupled to nearly forty-three applicants per position. While such figures in themselves say little about the quality of the individuals being hired, it seems likely that the cuts in the the civil service did little to impair it. In all probability, they even raised the quality level, as increased exclusiveness attracted more exceptional candidates.

Improvements in quality appear to have been felt at the local level as well. There, unsuccessful candidates for the national civil service found an expanding arena with increased responsibilities, and the consensus in Japan seems to be that there was a sharp rise in the quality of local government bureaucrats from the mid-1960s on.

A relatively small national government with high-quality personnel has also meant a government capable of setting, and responding to, clear priorities. Particularly impressive throughout all of the Japanese policy cases studied is the apparent ability of the government to develop a relatively coherent and consistent set of policy objectives and to then concentrate attention and energy on their achievement. This would have been far more difficult had each government agency been allowed to follow its own narrowly defined priorities and interests. By forcing cutbacks in all agencies, the government forced most to examine their internal priorities regularly. And by allocating new positions only as demands from one agency could be demonstrated to be stronger than those from another, the central government encouraged its agencies to be sensitive to overall national priorities and to develop programs designed to meet them. The organizational success of individual agencies in Japan has depended and still depends on their willingness and ability to adapt to changing national priorities.

Such a picture is necessarily somewhat idealized. No doubt, waste, graft, inefficiency, overlap, and incompetence remains in Japanese national government offices. Not all government programs fit tightly and conveniently into a well-ordered utility matrix. Many irrelevant units and programs remain. But compared to most other countries, the Japanese government has taken more concrete steps to minimize the debilitating features of modern bureaucracy which can remain hidden from view and erode governmental efficiency. Smaller size has meant greater control, concentration, and quite possibly, efficiency.

By curbing the natural tendency toward bureaucratic sprawl, administrative reform in Japan has also contributed greatly to the conservative coalition's goal of low-cost government. Since expenditures for personnel are often two-thirds of some governments' budgets, keeping down the total number of employees automatically holds down government costs. Unlike what tended to happen earlier in Britain, the United States, and France, the public sector in Japan has not been used as the employer of last resort since the Temporary Unemployment Relief Projects in 1949. Perhaps more significantly, fewer government officials has meant fewer sources of new program initiatives. Existing personnel are kept quite busy with limited opportunities to press for new programs.

Thus, among sixteen OECD countries Japan showed one of the lowest average annual increases in the percentage of national income allocated to government expenditures, and the lowest absolute level of total spending. In the three decades following World War II, government agencies spent from 30 percent to over 60 percent of national income in Denmark, Sweden, Norway, and the Netherlands, and around 40 percent in virtually all of the other

OECD countries. Japanese public expenditure, in contrast, was still below 30 percent, the lowest figure among all the OECD countries. Even relatively conservative countries, like Switzerland (31 percent), Australia (39 percent), and the United States (40 percent), spent more (Nutter, 1978, pp. 12, 58–73). Allowing local governments to institute various new programs also meant much more selective service delivery throughout the country. To phrase it differently, certain cities and regions expanded their governmental functions and provided benefits that were not available nationwide. But from a national perspective, such selectivity also kept down the total size and expenditures of government.

Finally, a low-cost government, particularly one which was not expanding its scope of activities into social welfare, was critical to the success of economic policies. Lower government costs also meant lower taxation rates for both industry and the individual citizen. Taxes represented only 19 percent of national income in Japan in 1977, compared to 28–29 percent in the United States and France, 37 percent in Britain, and 53 percent in Sweden (Zusetsu Rōjin Hakusho, 1980 p. 95). This law taxation encouraged high levels of reinvestment by firms and political support for the LDP. Possibly even more importantly, an expanding public sector might have attracted labor from low-productivity sectors, such as agriculture and declining industries to government service and kept it from seeking entry into the high productivity sector, private employment. The larger labor supply for the high-growth private sector in Japan helped that sector to expand more rapidly and cheaply, while increasing tremendously the country's overall productivity and economic success.

In many of these ways, therefore, administrative reform along the lines followed by the Japanese government after 1967 was one of the most critical links in ensuring the overall success of many of its other policies. In this way, Japan provides a striking contrast to virtually every other industrial democracy, in which administrative reform has consistently been the policy area most characterized by failure. Kept nonpartisan, these reforms exemplified the government's overall ability to set national priorities and to ensure their implementation. They also served in a behind-the-scenes way to support the government's economic policies, the most visible aspect of its conservative policy agenda.

Readings

7-1. AMERICAN RECOMMENDATIONS FOR CIVIL SERVICE REFORM*

The following memorandum by Lt. Milton Esman contained the first recommendations for a thorough reform of the prewar Japanese bureaucracy. Although the letter was widely cited in both the English and Japanese literature on bureaucratic reform, its proposals were largely ignored in subsequent reform efforts during the Occupation.

MEMORANDUM FOR CHIEF, GOVERNMENT SECTION.
Subject: Japanese Civil Service Reform

APO 500,
30 January 1946.

1. Of all the major bulwarks of feudal and totalitarian Japan only the bureaucracy remains unimpaired. The bureaucracy will definitely outlast the occupation and play a decisive role of moulding the future of Japan.

2. As yet, there are no signs of reform in the bureaucratic structure. All our evidence indicates that without constant pressure and guidance from this Headquarters the present bureaucracy is neither willing nor competent to reform the system.

3. Modern democratic government requires a democratic and efficient public service. Merely to reform obvious abuses—which has not yet been accomplished—will not provide the minimum level of efficiency necessary to democratic administration now that the police are no longer available to perform the operating function of government. The present Japan bureaucracy in incompetent to manage a modern democratic society.

4. Only relentless pressure from this Headquarters will induce the Japanese to make these essential and fundamental changes. They may even require guidance on the proper techniques to employ. Unless a thoroughgoing democratization and modernization of the civil service is carried out, it is difficult to see how the objectives of this occupation can be fully realized.

*Japan, Jinjiin, *Kokka Komuinhō Enkakushi—Shiryōhen ichi* (Tokyo: Jinjiin, 1969), p. 3.

5. In my opinion, civil service reform should continue as an active interest and a major priority of the Government Section.

(S) Milton J. Esman,
MILTON J. ESMAN,
First Lieutenant, T.C.

7-2. MORAL GOALS OF PUBLIC SERVANTS*

Following are excerpts from a book on the National Personnel System written by the former president of the National Personnel Authority, Satō Tatsuo. His comments reveal the highly moral goals assumed to be held by those in public service.

Objectives of the National Public Service Law

The efficiency of government depends on the ability, fairness, honesty, and dedication of national public service personnel. Therefore, the main purpose of any civil service system is to place the right man in the right position and let him demonstrate his abilities to the fullest. The NPS Law aims at the above-mentioned goal and provides the general and basic rules regarding appointment, salaries, working conditions, duties and status guarantees of civil servants.

Article 73 of the NPS Law states that the law seeks to establish the basic rules for national public service personnel (including adequate measures to protect the officer's welfare and interests). Furthermore, it provides a democratic way of selecting those officers who have demonstrated high abilities in their past official duties. This method of promotion seeks to guarantee that the nation will have officials who will conduct their duties democratically and efficiently.

The law also provides the specific rules for government officials called for in Article 73 of the Japanese Constitution. Thus it can be said that this law tries to establish a rational and reasonable administrative structure. . . .

---

*Satō Tatsuo, *Kokka Kōmuin Seidō* (Tokyo: Gakuyo, 1970), pp. 1–4.

A Servant of the Whole

The Japanese Constitution expressly stipulates that a person in public service is a servant of the whole and not a servant of any part. (Paragraph 2, Article XV). This means that people in public service should perform their duties as public servants so as to gain the trust of the people. This can only be done by serving the whole nation, and not serving only a certain party or faction, a certain power in society, or some other personal interest group. This is an important fundamental rule for all public service personnel and shows the difference between private and public employees. . . .

The principal goal of the modern public service personnel system is to assure the neutrality of officers towards political pressures. For this purpose, the system rejects the spoils system in favor of the merit system, awarding promotions according to ability. For personnel administrators all special connections with political parties or other special interest groups should be avoided so that new appointments will be based only on the ability of the applicant. This policy is assured by examining all applicants for all appointments in a common manner. Rules and regulations must be more restrictive for public service personnel than the rules governing private industry's labor relationships. . . .

7-3. GOVERNMENT FREEZE ON PUBLIC SERVICE VACANCIES*

A cabinet decision in 1964 to freeze a portion of the vacancies which developed normally was one of the first steps in the government's effort to reduce the government.

Any increase of the number of [government] personnel is, in principle, to be avoided in 1965. Any increase in the duties of officials should be coped with by raising administrative efficiency and by transferring personnel to appropriate positions. The restriction on filling vacancies is to be strengthened according to the instructions in the attached document.

---

*"On Strengthening the Policy to Keep Vacancies Unfilled," Cabinet decision, September 4, 1964, mimeo.

Instructions on Not Filling Vacancies

1. During the period between September 4, 1964 and March 31, 1966 ministries and agencies should employ no new personnel to fill vacancies.

2. However, where the failure to fill a vacancy would create extreme hardship in the exercise of impending duties or where peculiar circumstances exist, vacancies can be filled after consultation with the Director General of the Administrative Management Agency.

3. The employment of new personnel through the National Civil Service Examination and its equivalents is to be kept to a minimum. In cases of new employment, the procedure in the previous clause should be followed.

4. For the time being, at the end of every quarter each ministry or agency is to submit, by the twentieth of the following month, a report concerning its vacancies to the Director General of the Administrative Management Agency. The number of vacancies on September 4, 1964 should be reported to the Director General of the Administrative Management Agency by September 30, 1964.

5. Cooperation in similar measures will be requested of the Diet, the Courts and the Board of Audit.

6. Local public institutions will be requested to follow measures similar to those at the national level.

7. With these measures in force, the Cabinet decision of October 12, 1962 concerning the non-filling of vacancies is to be abolished.

7-4. CABINET AGREEMENT ON STEPS IN ADMINISTRATIVE REFORM*

The following is a cabinet agreement in principle concerning the main steps in the 1967 administrative reform effort.

1. Numerical restrictions on personnel should, in the future take the form of limiting the total number of government personnel by curtailing as many personnel as possible through simplifying admin-

---

*Japan, Administrative Management Agency, "Future Numerical Restrictions on Personnel and Measures for Keeping Vacancies Unfilled," Cabinet verbal agreement, Oct. 11, 1967, mimeo.

istrative work, and raising efficiency and by actively carrying out rational personnel transfers in accordance with the changing demands for administrative services.

2. Numerical limits on personnel according to the existing laws organizing each Ministry or Agency are to be discarded. Hereafter, only the total number of the personnel in all Ministries and Agencies will be fixed legally. More specific internal limits for each Ministry or Agency will be stipulated by Ordinances within the limits on the total number of government personnel.

3. Current measures for keeping vacancies unfilled are to be discarded when the above-mentioned measures are put into effect. The number of semi-permanent vacancies should be subtracted from the number of personnel assigned to each Ministry or Agency.

4. Concrete measures for clauses one through three are to be studied further.

7-5. CABINET DECISION TO REDUCE
THE NUMBER OF BUREAUS*

The following is an excerpt from an evaluation by a committee of the Administrative Management Agency of the Satō Cabinet's 1964 decision to cut one bureau from each ministry and agency.

As previously mentioned, it was Prime Minister Eisaku Satō who first gave instructions to reduce the size of each ministry and agency by removing one bureau from each. It was a highly commendable move in that it showed the eagerness of the cabinet to simplify the administrative approaches of the government. The Administrative Management and Inspection Committee, too, is eager to see the plan accomplished.

However, the specific details of the plan hardly make it ideal in terms of how an administrative reform ought to be carried out. The following are some of the problems inherent in the plan.

First, selection of the bureau that would be abolished was left up to the minister in charge of the ministry or agency, with no uniform standard applicable to the entire bureaucracy. Since no standards

---

*Japan, Gyōsei Kanri Iinkai, *Gyōsei Kaikaku no Genjō to Kadai (1967)* (Tokyo: Gyōsei Kanri Iinkai, 1968), pp. 56–57.

for reduction were given, the selection of the bureau to be abolished tended to be made to suit the convenience of a given ministry or agency.

Second, the plan called for mechanical elimination of one bureau from the ministries and extra-ministerial agencies of the Prime Minister's Office which are headed by cabinet ministers, with the exception of the Hokkaidō Development Agency, which was exempted from the plan since it has no internal bureaus. As a result, the plan did not necessarily contribute to an organizational reform of agencies and ministries to make them better able to respond to the changing demand for administrative services.

Third, there were quite a number of instances when a bureau was simply reduced in rank to a department. Such methods could hardly accomplish the original goal of substantially streamlining the administrative organization. Particularly in view of the fact that administrative reform is often discussed today as part of larger efforts to reduce administrative expenses in order to cope with the increasing rigidity of public finance, it is safe to conclude that simply abolishing one bureau in each ministry and agency is not an adequate measure.

As a program of administrative reform, the plan is quite problematical, but it is nevertheless valuable as an expression of the cabinet's enthusiasm for simplifying the administrative structure, and for the very fact that it was put into practice on the prime minister's initiative. The Administrative Management and Inspection Committee hopes that the plan represents a breakthrough for administrative reform. It also hopes that reform will be based on truly rational standards and aggressively promoted by the prime minister's strong leadership.

7-6. CABINET DECISION TO CURB PERSONNEL GROWTH*

The following is an excerpt from an evaluation by the Administrative Management Agency of the Satō Cabinet's 1967 decision to curb the growth in national government personnel. The government called for a specific percentage reduction by all agencies, with all new positions to be filled from a central pool created by the newly established vacancies.

*Ibid., pp. 57–62.

SECTION 9. Reduction of Fixed Personnel and Reform in the Method of Control

I. Changes in the Number of National Public Service Personnel

Needless to say, administrative reform should not aim simply at restraining or even reducing the scale of public administration. But, in order to lighten the financial burden borne by the people, it is necessary to check meaningless increases in the number of personnel and reduce it to the greatest extent possible, as well as trying to simplify and curb the growth of the administrative apparatus.

In a cursory glance at the administrative reforms carried out since 1945, there has been no substantial decrease in the number of national public servants, except the few instances of so-called administrative readjustment (i.e., personnel cuts) during the immediate postwar period. Figures for the past five years show that there has been a steady increase in the fixed number of government personnel. In 1963 the number was 1,128,650; in 1964 it was 1,142,945; in 1965 rose to 1,156,808; in 1966 to 1,116,189 and by 1967 the figure had increased to 1,179,061.

II. Leaving Vacancies Unfilled

In September 1964, the government adopted the following plan, as part of its efforts to restrain personnel increases, to be applied to all government agencies, except the operational divisions of the five government enterprises and the Self-Defense Forces: 1) filling of vacancies existing as of 4 September 1964 will not be permitted (freezing of vacancies); 2) fifty percent of the vacancies in administrative positions and ninety percent of those in non-administrative positions (research, teaching, medical or security) created on and after 5 September 1964 may be filled.

When a personnel increase is required for the coming fiscal year, a ministry or agency may unfreeze its vacancies. If that is not enough to meet the need, then revisions for an increase in fixed personnel may be made in pertinent law or governmental ordinance.

Through these measures, approximately 15,500 frozen vacancies were created from September 1964 through September 1967. During the period 7,500 of those positions were unfrozen to allow for increases, still leaving 8,000 vacancies at the end of September

1967. (See Section 2-IV for measures taken in examining the administrative structure and the fixed number of personnel in fiscal 1967.)

III. Problems in Control of Fixed Personnel

Looking at how the fixed personnel in national government offices is controlled, it is quite evident that in some sectors more people are needed because of the increased demand for administrative services, while in others the fixed number of personnel has not been reduced enough to keep pace with a decrease in demand. This shows that there is an urgent need for appropriate reallocation of personnel as well as a more streamlined, efficient administrative operation to cope with the increasing demand for administrative services.

Under the existing legal system, however, the fixed number of locally-hired officials of the central government and workers in the five government enterprises is determined by ordinance, but that of national civil servants in all categories is stipulated by law for each ministry and agency (National Administrative Organization Law, Article 19). The present system is intended to place both administrative organizations and the fixed number of personnel under the statutory control of the Diet, thereby trying to restrain personnel increases by the force of law. But this method has produced a number of problems. For example, if one more driver or chauffeur is required, then the law has to be revised; and the creation of posts, which is closely related to fixed personnel numbers, is a matter handled by government or ministerial ordinance, at least for those positions below section chief in central ministries and agencies, while the number of personnel is fixed by law. This causes an imbalance in the legal system.

Leaving vacancies unfilled was effective in restraining personnel expansion and improving administrative operations. But it also impeded personnel turnover, and increases were held down in certain areas, when necessary to meet increasing demand for administrative services. This led to imbalances in personnel allocation among ministries and agencies.

In order to effectively control the number of personnel in response to changes in demand it is necessary to reconsider the measure of leaving vacancies unfilled. Also the transfer of fixed personnel should not be confined within each ministry and agency, but carried out across ministerial lines so as to enable the government as a whole to make flexible and dynamic use of its personnel.

More specifically, the present system of fixing the personnel number of each ministry and agency by law must be replaced by a new system under which the total number of personnel in all ministries and agencies of the government will be set by law, and within that range personnel can be distributed throughout the bureaucracy by government ordinance.

IV. Cabinet Council and Cabinet Decisions

The following decisions were made by the Cabinet Council for Provisional Administrative Reform at its meeting of 6 October 1967.

1) The total number of fixed personnel will be held down by making administrative operations simpler and more efficient and through the rational reallocation of personnel.

2) The total number of personnel alone will be fixed by law and the number allocated to each ministry and agency determined by ordinance.

3) With the implementation of the above measures, the current method of leaving vacancies unfilled will be abolished and frozen vacancies will be subtracted from the number of fixed personnel.

The 20 October cabinet decision on "Salary-Scale Revision for Public Servants" declared that in carrying out these revisions the government would seek "simplification and greater efficiency in present administrative operation, so as to keep the filling of vacancies to a minimum." It went on to say that personnel transfer should be encouraged to respond to fluctuating needs in administrative operations. Through these methods, it was hoped, planned reductions in the total number of fixed personnel could be made. (4-[1])

Based on these guidelines the Administrative Management Agency made a thorough examination of specific measures that could be implemented. The examination led to decisions made on 14 December by the Cabinet Council for Provisional Administrative Reform and on 15 December by the cabinet regarding ways to reduce the number of fixed personnel and improve the methods of controlling it. The text of those decisions is as follows:

Methods of Controlling Fixed Personnel

In order to simplify administrative operations and make them more efficient and thereby lighten the taxpayers' burden, the following measures will be adopted to control the total number of fixed personnel:

1. A planned reduction will be made in the present number of National Government employees with the exception of Self-Defense Forces personnel, so that the total shall be decreased by five percent in three years. In cases where an increase in personnel is needed due to fluctuating demand for administrative services, they will be handled, as much as possible, through transfers of personnel from one area to another, so that the total number of fixed personnel will be reduced.

a. With regard to the approximately 540,000 National Government workers, not the Self-Defense Forces personnel and employees of the five government enterprises, the following measures will be undertaken:

i) In each of the three years beginning with fiscal 1963, ministries and agencies shall leave their vacancies unfilled and subtract that number from their authorized strength in the following year in order to achieve their respective goals set forth in the above-mentioned personnel reduction plan.

ii) The target for personnel reduction for each ministry and agency shall be determined by separate decisions.

iii) As part of efforts to implement this plan, the number of vacancies that exist in fixed personnel as of 30 September 1967 shall be subtracted from the number of fixed personnel for fiscal 1968.

iv) The currently enforced measure of leaving vacancies unfilled shall be discontinued at the end of fiscal 1967.

b. For the approximate 360,000 workers in the five government enterprises, measures equivalent to a-i and a-ii above will be adopted.

2. In order to carry out flexible and rational management of fixed personnel that the above measures will require, the present method of fixing personnel for each ministry and agency by its establishment law shall be revised, and only the total number of personnel for all

ministries and agencies shall be determined by legal statute. The number of fixed personnel assigned to each ministry and agency shall be determined by government ordinance. Bills pertaining to this decision will be submitted in the next ordinary session of the Diet. The total number of fixed personnel shall be determined by separate decision.

3. In order to carry out the stipulations of paragraph i of this decision as smoothly as possible, all agencies affected by it shall make every effort towards simplification and efficiency of operation through office mechanization and by reducing the work load relating to subsidies, authorizations and permissions. They will pay particular heed to the streamlining of internal management-operations such as accounting and personnel. Streamlining and rationalization of the administrative structure encompassing the central and regional offices shall be carried out as progress is made in implementing the above measures.

4. The three public corporations (Nippon Telegraph and Telephone Public Corporation, Japanese National Railways, Japan Monopoly Corporation), the national finance corporations and other national corporations will be dealt with in line with the stipulations of this decision as the situation demands.

5. Local government bodies shall also be required to institute measures in line with those taken by the national government. The national government shall assist in carrying this decision out by consolidating pertinent laws, ordinances and subsidies.

Reduction of the number of fixed personnel by five percent in three years as the decision calls for was considered feasible for the following reasons: 1) in areas where the measure to leave vacancies unfilled was applied, three percent of the total number of positions were frozen in three years, although part of that number was freed in response to the need for more personnel; 2) the rate of termination among national government personnel in recent years has gone above four percent annually. 3) A forced reduction in personnel must be avoided since it would mean dismissal of many workers; and 4) new employees must be brought into the work force to a certain extent.

If the decision is put into practice, an approximate 1.5 percent in frozen vacancies will be removed from the fixed personnel of about

540,000, excluding those in the Self-Defense Forces and the operational divisions of the five government enterprises. Another 3.5 percent will be trimmed between fiscal 1968 and the beginning of fiscal 1971. The average annual rate of decrease will be approximately 1.2 percent. For a total of 360,000 workers in the five government enterprises which have been exempted from the measure to freeze vacancies, a similar policy will be applied since it should be possible to reduce the numbers of fixed personnel in those areas through improvement of efficiency, particularly through automation. Thus the total number of national government employees to be reduced will be about 45,000 or 5 percent of the total of 900,000, which does not include the Self-Defense Forces personnel. This does not mean, however, that there will be a net reduction of 45,000, for although personnel transfers will be carried out in response to changes in demand for administrative services, there will be certain times when personnel increases are unavoidable.

In the new plan, each ministry and agency will leave vacancies unfilled until their respective personnel reduction goals are reached. These vacancies will then be reduced from the table of organization in the following fiscal year. The difference between this and the old method of not filling vacancies is that with the latter measure vacancies were frozen in an accidental and mechanical fashion. Sometimes one in every two vacancies was frozen, for example, while at other times only one in ten was so designated. It tended to obstruct the normal turnover of personnel and make a systematic transfer of personnel difficult. The new plan requires each ministry and agency to set the number of personnel that will be decreased and to attain this goal in a systematic way. This will correct deficiencies in the old measure of simply not filling vacancies as they appear, and with it we can expect a decline in the number of personnel in areas where administrative demand has decreased.

V. Future Prospects

The bill for the National Civil Service Personnel Authorization Law will be submitted to the 58th session of the Diet. This change to a new system of fixing the total number of personnel by law for all parts of the bureaucracy, rather than for each ministry and agency, is a fundamental reform in the method of personnel management. It is hoped that the system will accomplish the objectives for which it is created, but the following points must be taken into account in implementing it:

1) In order to make planned reduction of the number of personnel each ministry and agency will have to set a specific target. Judging from the results of the measure to freeze vacancies and from the need for personnel transfer, it is advisable to differentiate the rate of reduction according to type of job and category of position.

2) The method of leaving vacancies unfilled produced a great variation in the percentage of vacancies in each ministry and agency. In determining the target of personnel reduction for each ministry and agency, adjustments will have to be made to ensure the fairness of the plan.

3) As stated earlier, the core of this reform lies in fixing the total number of government personnel by law, and deciding the authorized strength of each ministry and agency by cabinet ordinance. This measure is designed to allow the government to carry out personnel transfers across ministerial lines and make a dynamic control of the fixed personnel within the framework of the legal maximum in response to the changing demand for administrative services. Its success or failure depends on how actively intra-ministry personnel transfers will be implemented. Under the old system the number of fixed personnel in each ministry and agency was determined by statute, making personnel management too rigid and inflexible. The current reform should help eliminate these obstacles, but if any ministry or agency is opposed to reductions in its personnel, the cabinet will find it very difficult to effectively transfer personnel from one ministry to another. To make this reform truly effective the cabinet will have to do away very determinedly with bureaucratic sectionalism and actively enforce personnel transfers in line with the demand for administrative services.

7-7. ENACTMENT OF THE NATIONAL PERSONNEL AUTHORIZATION LAW*

The following is a summary of the committee of the Administrative Management Agency's views on the National Personnel Authorization Law. It outlines the key problems and goals of reform as seen through official eyes.

I. Deliberations on the Bill for the National Personnel Authorization Law and Opinions of the Administrative Management and Inspection Committee

The bill for the National Personnel Authorization Law was shelved in the 58th session of the Diet. In the 60th extraordinary session, the government reintroduced the bill, but no deliberations were made and the bill was dropped again.

The government submitted the bill for a third time at the 61st ordinary session of the Diet which convened on 27 December 1968, and recessed on 5 August 1969. The deadlock in deliberations continued. As far as the government was concerned, the number of fixed personnel for fiscal 1969 had already been decided on the assumption that the bill would pass. The cabinet ordinance for a temporary personnel increase issued after the 58th Diet session was also to become ineffective at the end of March 1969. For these reasons, the government had to have the bill passed by that time. The newspapers and other media strongly supported the bill, in hopes that administrative reform, then at a standstill, might be pushed forward.

The [Administrative Management and Inspection] Committee gathered opinions from all members with the exception of the chairman, and published on 26 February 1967 a statement entitled "On the National Personnel Authorization Law." In this statement the committee strongly urged the government to make every effort for the passage of the bill. A full text of the statement is as follows:

Administrative reform has been a national aspiration for a number of years. Public opinion is critical of the present administration where many sections which have grown less important still retain manpower they no longer need, while many others ought

*Excerpted from Gyōsei Kanri Iinkai, *Gyōsei kaikaku no genjō to kadai 3 (1968–69)*, Dec. (Tokyo: Gyōsei Kanri Iinkai, 1969), pp. 38–42.

to be reinforced to meet the people's needs and demands of the national economy.

It is of course important that we strengthen the administrative system to make it responsive to the new demands for services arising from social and economic changes. In order to reinforce the system while restraining increases in the number of fixed personnel, it is necessary to thoroughly review the existing administrative organizations and operations and reduce and even abolish offices wherever possible. It is also necessary to carry out a flexible transfer of personnel to areas where needs are greater.

Strong sectionalism on the part of the ministries and agencies has led to persistence of the status quo in organization and personnel strength. State administration has thus tended to expand in a chaotic fashion, rather than being reduced and streamlined. Under the present circumstances it is impossible to implement a flexible and dynamic policy of personnel transfer. The Provisional Commission for Administrative Investigation, in its "Opinion on Government Personnel Reform," states: "In order to ensure a more dynamic and efficient allocation of personnel, a system of personnel transfer must be established as quickly as possible. Without such a system, it will be next to impossible to have an efficient and systematic program of manpower allocation."

The bill for the National Personnel Authorization Law, designed to fix the total number of government personnel by statute and to determine the distribution of personnel in each agency and ministry by cabinet ordinance, is considered one of the most important keystones in administrative reform. This law will help make administration simpler and more efficient and will provide an important institutional basis for smooth transfer of personnel in response to the changing demand for administrative services.

In implementing the provisions of the proposed law, full care must be taken not to jeopardize the status guarantees given to civil service personnel. The government must take it explicit that it will not make undue transfers of personnel, nor will it resort to dismissals for the sake of personnel reduction. Government must seek the early passage of the bill, thereby establishing a base for comprehensive and effective administrative reforms that the people have been demanding.

II. Points Brought Up in Diet Deliberations

Following this statement, both houses of the diet eventually began deliberation on the bill. During the deliberations heated debate focussed on how fixed personnel had actually been controlled and how the law would be enforced after its enactment, as well as the content of the bill itself. Major points brought up in the interpellations were: 1) appropriateness of the cabinet ordinance issued after the 58th Diet session to increase personnel; 2) the connection between the law for personnel authorization, the plan to reduce personnel by five percent in three years and the three-year plan for administrative reform; 3) the relationship between deliberative rights of the Diet and the distribution of fixed personnel to ministries and agencies by government ordinance; 4) the possibilities that personnel reductions might entail dismissals and that unjustifiable personnel transfers might be carried out; and 5) the problem of temporary personnel now working on a full-time basis who fall outside the framework of fixed personnel as defined in the National Personnel Authorization Law. The government responses regarding the three problems of Diet deliberation right, personnel cuts and undue transfers, and temporary personnel were:

1) Even after the law is enacted, the number of fixed personnel in agencies and ministries will still be subject to Diet deliberations on the budget. This is the standard practice in Great Britain, the United States, France, and West Germany. In no country is the number of fixed personnel determined by separate law. Of course, revisions of the law will be necessary if the number of fixed personnel has to go above the maximum limits provided by the law. It is not correct to say, therefore, that this reform limits or ignores the Diet right of deliberation on the number of fixed government personnel.

2) In the supplementary resolution made by both houses of the Diet in enacting the law for the establishment of the Provisional Commission for Administrative Investigation, it was stated that there should be no change made in the status of civil servants nor should their numbers be reduced through dismissals. It goes without saying that the government must respect this resolution.

After debate on the problems, the bill for the National Personnel Authorization Law was adopted by majority vote on 16 May 1969. Through parliamentary revision of supplementary rules, the law took effect retroactive to 1 April of that year. A joint proposal for a supplementary resolution was made at the House of Councilors' Cabinet Committee by all parties with the exception of the Japan Communist Party. The resolution, as it was adopted, reads as follows:

Supplementary Resolution on the National Personnel Authorization Law

In implementing the provisions of this law the government should give particular attention to the following points:

a) As the Government pledged during the process of deliberation, the number of government employees should not be reduced by terminating any worker, nor should a worker be transferred to a post counter to his wishes.

b) In determining the number of personnel in any administrative organization, an effort should be made to secure enough manpower to meet the demands for administrative services so that employees are not overly burdened with work.

c) An examination should be made immediately of the conditions for temporary personnel and efforts should be made to rationally improve their status, including conversion of status to fixed personnel.

d) The government should fully implement the recommendations submitted by the National Personnel Authority.

Since the National Personnel Authorization Law is based on the idea that personnel transfer should be encouraged in order to respond to changes in demands for administrative services, it should be possible to avoid any unnecessary dismissals of personnel to the extent that this system functions smoothly. Even if a serious situation does arise, there would have to be Diet deliberations on the budget and revision of related substantive laws and laws establishing ministries and agencies. These procedures would prevent the government from arbitrarily carrying out unjustifiable personnel transfers or reducing personnel through dismissals.

3) During the period from fiscal 1958 to fiscal 1962, the government shifted a total of 117,000 temporary full-time employees over to fixed personnel status. During that period a cabinet

decision was made on 26 February 1961 under the heading, "Preventing the Practice of Employing Temporary Personnel Full Time." It stipulated: a) that for those temporary workers who would predictably go on a daily employment basis, their term of appointment must be confined within the same fiscal year that the appointment was made; and b) that measures be taken to keep them from working beyond their designated term of employment. By means of the 19 January 1962 cabinet decision, "Measures Pursuant to Conversion of Temporary Personnel to Fixed Status for fiscal 1962," the government announced that the practice of transferring temporary workers into fixed status would be discontinued at the end of fiscal 1962. Since it has been pointed out, however, that there are still temporary personnel working full time in the civil service, the government will conduct a survey of the situation.

III. Significance of the Enactment of the Authorization Law

The National Personnel Authorization Law has provided the government with a means by which to overcome the barriers across the ministries and agencies, and to place the entire administrative apparatus under a unified system of personnel management. Fixed personnel can now be controlled more flexibly and with greater facility depending on fluctuations in the demand for administrative services. The law offers a powerful tool by which the most important part of the plan, rational distribution of fixed personnel, can be effected. However, it is just a tool and the actual rational distribution of fixed personnel will have to be made by the government by the correct use of this law. As changes in demand for administrative services occur they must be dealt with by revisions in government ordinances designed to handle the distribution of fixed personnel in agencies and ministries. To that end the government will have to have a more accurate understanding of the fluctuations in administrative demands than it has had up to this time. The government has to be able to make valid, realistic judgments of the situation in each part of the bureaucracy, which areas must be augmented and which reduced. Since the purpose of the law is to relocate personnel in a more flexible manner, the government must be aware that its responsibilities for dynamic personnel management are even greater now than ever before.

In line with the tenor of the law that an upper limit on the number of fixed government personnel should be determined, the government needs a precise understanding of the situation of temporary personnel. While holding down increases in the overall numbers of government workers, the government should also endeavor to allocate fixed personnel according to fluctuations in the demand for administrative services. The government must handle the problem of temporary personnel along this basic guideline.

7-8. CABINET DECISION TO
       PROMOTE REFORM EFFORTS*

Following ten years of cutbacks in the size of government, the cabinet in 1977 decided to continue and extend earlier efforts. Included were restrictions on members of public corporations and general cuts in required paperwork.

In view of the severe conditions inside and outside the country, for the present the following measures will be taken so as to rationalize administration and raise efficiency.

Instructions

1. Administrative Organizations

(1) Reforms of Central Ministries, Agencies, Bureaus, and Departments. A flexible and positive policy for administrative management is strongly needed because of recent changes in the international environment and in domestic socioeconomic structures. In view of this situation, the Ministry of Construction and the National Land Board are, for the time being, to be supervised by one Minister; a minister without portfolio will be used for the active promotion of foreign economic policy. A further study will be made on the reorganization of the central administrative system involving ministries, agencies, bureaus and departments.

(2) Reduction in the Number of Sections, Offices, and Divisions in the Central Ministries and Agencies. In accordance with the following plan the two-year reduction in the number of sections, offices

*Japan, Gyōsei Kanri Iinkai, *Gyōsei Kaikaku no Suii ni tsuite* (Tokyo: Gyōsei Kanri Iinkai, n.d.).

and divisions in the central ministries and agencies (including commission secretariats) will be carried out starting in 1978.

Details for enforcement will be discussed, if necessary, between the head of the ministry or agency concerned and the Director General of the Administrative Management Agency.

Name of Administrative Offices	Number to Be Eliminated
Cabinet Secretariat	1
Cabinet Legislation Bureau	0
National Defense Council Secretariat	0
Prime Minister's Central Office	2
Fair Trade Commission	0
National Public Safety Commission	1
Environmental Pollution Coordinating Committee	0
Imperial Household Agency	0
Administrative Managment Agency	1
Hokkaidō Development Board	0
Defense Agency	2
Economic Planning Agency	1
Science and Technology Agency	1
Environment Agency	0
Okinawa Development Board	0
National Land Board	1
Ministry of Justice	3
Ministry of Foreign Affairs	3
Ministry of Finance	4
Ministry of Education	2
Ministry of Public Welfare	3
Ministry of Agriculture and Forestry	5
Ministry of International Trade and Industry	7
Ministry of Transport	6
Ministry of Posts and Telecommunications	3
Ministry of Labor	2
Ministry of Construction	2
Ministry of Home Affairs	1
Total	51

2. Numerical Restrictions

(1) Numerical Restrictions on National Civil Servants With regard to numerical restrictions on national civil servants, personnel reductions should be firmly carried out in accordance with the existing reduction plan; new demands for administrative services which are really needed should be coped with as much as possible through personnel transfers. Any increases in personnel must be strictly restricted. This fact must be considered in the formation of the 1978 Budget.

(2) Retirement Age for National Civil Servants A system fixing a set retirement age for national civil servants will be introduced. Concrete preparation for this system and a revision of the relevant institutions will be carried out.

3. Special Juridical Persons

(1) Reduction and Rationalization of Special Juridical Persons

(2)Selection of Directors in Special Juridical Persons In the selection of directors of special juridical persons such as Public Funding Agencies and Public Corporations, the following matters should be taken into consideration so that the most suitable persons can be chosen from among well-informed people in various fields.

(a) The Employment of persons from the private sector should be positively promoted in accordance with the nature of the duties of each juridical person.

(b) In cases involving selections from among former civil servants the most suitable persons should be chosen. There should be no attempt to limit the selection to officials from closely related ministries or agencies; rather there should be a selection from among people in all ministries and agencies.

(c) The transfer of personnel from one special juridical person to another should in principle be avoided.

(d) Employment of older persons should be avoided so as not to impede the introduction of new vitality.

The age limit on directors is, in principle, to be 65 years of age. However, under special circumstances, this need not apply to the president, the chairman of the board of directors or equivalent officials (hereafter referred to as "president/chairman") or to the vice-president, the vice-chairman of the board of directors or equivalent officials (hereafter referred to as "vice-president/vice-chairman). In such cases, 70 years of age is to be the limit.

(e) Any long-time retentions of a directorship should be avoided. Six years should be more or less the limit for remaining as director. Although under special circumstances this need not apply to the president/chairman and the vice-president and vice-chairman even then eight years should, in principle, be the maximum term.

In the selection of full-term directors (including part-time presidents), the Chief Cabinet Secretary should be consulted in advance. In selecting the president/chairman, in addition to consultation with the Chief Cabinet Secretary, verbal agreement of the Cabinet is also necessary. However, this need not apply to cases exempted by the Chief Secretary in view of special circumstances, such as specific methods of appointment for different special juridical persons.

These rules are to be applied to those persons who become directors after April 1, 1978.

The Cabinet Verbal Agreement of May 14, 1965, "On the Selection of Directors of Public Corporations and Public Funding Agencies" and the Cabinet Verbal Agreement of February 7, 1967, "On Personnel Administration in Public Corporations and Public Enterprises," are to be abolished.

(3) Salaries and Retirement Allowances for the Directors of Special Juridical Persons

(a) In 1977, increases in the salaries of directors of special juridical persons should generally be proportional to those in the private sector and those of civil servants.

(b) After 1978, the retirement allowance for the directors of special juridical persons is to be reduced from 45 percent to 36 percent of his monthly salary for every month in service.

(4) Numerical Restrictions and the Salary Problem for Employees in Special Juridical Persons

(a) With regard to the numerical restriction of employees in special juridical persons, reduction measures similar to those in the reduction plan for national civil servants should be carried out. At the same time, the employment of new personnel should

be restricted as much as possible. This matter should be considered in the formation of the 1978 Budget.
(b) With regard to the salaries of employees of special juridical
persons, proper measures should be studied and then gradually
enforced, using the salary system for civil servants as a reference.

4. Advisory Councils

(1) Abolition or Consolidation of Advisory Councils Inactive
councils and councils whose necessity has dimished considerably
shall be abolished.

Councils with similar objectives or terms of reference shall be
consolidated.

As a result of these measures, the number of councils shall be
reduced by 15% from 246 to 210.

(2) Reform of the Composition of Members of Advisory Councils
  a. Government officials shall be excluded from council mem-
     bership unless their inclusion is regarded as vital for the pur-
     pose of the council in question.
  b. The system of having advisory councils chaired by a minister
     or another government official shall be abolished if the coun-
     cil's reports or recommendations can be dealt with mostly
     within the ministry or agency concerned.

(3) Reduction of the Number of Members of Advisory Councils In
advisory councils with more than 20 members, 30% of the membership in excess of 20 shall be reduced.

With this and the exclusion of government officials, in all there
should be a reduction of about 1,000 members.

5. Subsidies and Grants-in-Aid

*(1) Abolition and Rationalization of Subsidies and Grants-in-
Aid* Ineffective and/or excessively small amounts of subsidies shall
be abolished or consolidated.

For certain types of subsidy programs a time limit shall be set for
their expiration.

*(2) Simplification of Procedures related to Subsidy and Grant-in-
Aid Programs* Procedures related to subsidy and grant-in-aid pro-

grams shall be reviewed to make them more simplified, less burdensome and less time-consuming.

6. Administrative Affairs

(1) Regulatory Reform Unnecessary regulations shall be abolished and excessive regulations shall be relaxed.

Unless serious difficulties would be thereby created regulatory authority shall be delegated to local branch offices of the national government or to local governments either of which are closer to the regulated. Licensing and authorization procedures shall be simplified.

One thousand twenty four items are specifically listed for reforms to be taken by the end of fiscal 1978.

(2) Rationalization of Certain Inspection, Verification and Certification Programs Certain inspection, verification, and certification programs directly carried out at present by government agencies shall be abolished or left to private organizations with sufficient facilities and qualified personnel.

(3) Rationalization of General Administration Services General administrative services at government offices such as the operation of passenger cars and telephone switchboards shall be rationalized.

Other general administrative services, such as the maintenance of government buildings, which have already been partially rationalized shall be rationalized further.

8 Creative Conservatism: Public Policy In Japan

Public policy is an excellent window through which to view Japanese politics and the politics of other industrialized countries. It is particularly suggestive of the relationship between the timing of a country's industrialization and its internal distribution of power. The study of public policy also helps one to unravel the complex problem of how a country deals with specific issues at different points in time. To what extent is there a similar pattern in Japanese policy actions? To what extent do these change with time and with the character of the issue at hand? How are these patterns similar to or different from those of other industrialized countries? From a third perspective, public policy is a valuable index to the problems of democracy. To what extent do democratic principles influence policy making processes and public choices? Do the politics of public policy reinforce or undermine these principles? How democratic is Japan compared to other countries? The answer to these questions is rooted in the creative conservatism that characterizes contemporary Japanese public policy.

Industrialization and Power

Most industrialized democracies are currently well on the road to becoming welfare states. Government is the main vehicle, carrying a vast array of services to the citizen. It is the prime regulator of important social transactions from birth and marriage through burial and inheritance, and of many others such as use of public parks, air travel, and immigration. The economy feels the steady presence of the state in individual and collective commercial transactions, in banking, and in taxation and government spending. The norms and cultural aspirations of citizens are shaped by the pronouncements of political leaders. Government is bigger, more costly, and intrusive than ever before in history. What is most striking about Japan is that if it is moving along this road it is far behind the other industrialized democracies; if the path to the modern welfare state must inevitably be travelled by all, Japan is a reluctant voyager in no apparent hurry to arrive.

How and why is Japan so different? An important part of the answer lies in the character and the timing of its industrialization. Most early industrializers were divided along religious, economic, geographic, ethnic or cultural lines. Many were seeking guarantees against the negative consequences of authoritarian rule. Decentralized state institutions and guarantees of civil rights and liberties were the only way to reconcile existing social cleavages with democratic values. No single social group could be assured of getting all that it wished, but the most powerful were able to exact assurances that state power would not be directed against them. Social diversity demanded a pluralist state.

The extent to which this holds true differs from one country to the next. Britain and the United States were less centralized than France and Germany. But by the end of the nineteenth century, for political reasons all were forced to circumscribe state power considerably. This weakening made it comparatively easy for newer social sectors to gain a share of governmental power.

For purposes of comparison to Japan, the most striking consequences in Western countries were those of organized labor. When labor sought to organize collectively during the mid-to late-nineteenth century, it faced relatively decentralized institutions of power in Europe and North America. International ideologies of class conflict and the news of individual labor victories quickly transcended national boundaries. As a result, labor found it possible, although by no means easy, to organize into unions, to gain a modicum of power in the workplace, and ultimately to parlay electoral rights into regularized influence over the government. These gains shaped the character of public policy in these countries in fundamental ways. It became expedient, desirable, or necessary to expand the scope of state activities. By increasing benefits to

individual citizens, by regulating powerful social groups and institutions, by controlling private use of public benefits, public policy
transformed these countries into welfare states.

Among the world's highly industrialized countries, Japan stands
out as the most noteworthy exception to this pattern. Its industrialization began later and in greater geographic, cultural, and
intellectual isolation than its European and North American counterparts. The country was socially more homogenous than any early
industrializer, and the coalition that dominated Japan after the
Meiji Restoration rapidly gained cohensiveness. Neither social
heterogeneity nor vigorous democratic inclinations pressed for
limits on state power. International vulnerability, in fact, demanded the opposite. Japan therefore developed a state-centric
constitution, a relatively weak parliament, and a severely circumscribed electoral system. Economic power was similarly concentrated in a small number of conglomerates and a centralized banking system. There was a national ideology favoring hierarchy and
collectivity, fostered by a centralized educational system, cultural
isolation, and elite manipulation.

When the socioeconomic conditions that had given rise to unions
in all other industrialized countries began to develop in Japan, the
public and private barriers to union development were far stronger
than they had been elsewhere. Electoral and party links to state
power were difficult for labor to utilize effectively. Lateness in
industrialization had given Japan's political and economic elites the
capacity to learn from the experiences of earlier industrializers.
They were able to anticipate many of labor's claims, responding to
some while stifling others. State power, ideological manipulation,
industrial paternalism, and structures such as the enterprise union
were but a few of the creatively applied weapons in the conservative
arsenal.

Although Japanese labor unions greatly increased their powers in
the period following World War II, they never fully overcame the
historical inheritance of the prewar period. The conservative coalition was shaken, but remained largely intact. The powers of the
state were far more sharply circumscribed than they had been under
the Meiji Constitution, but the tradition of strong centralized authority remained deeply embedded in the national consciousness
and was matched in the practical allocation of power and authority.

Although the unions were capable of organizing large segments of the working population, the historical conditions that had given rise to widespread unionism in most other industrialized countries were vastly different by the 1940s and 1950s. Furthermore, when Japanese unions organized, they retained the prevailing pattern of enterprise unionism. Although the labor movement was numerically comparable to movements in many other industrialized countries, Japanese unions remained incapable of gaining a major role in national policy formation. In this regard, Japan was unique among the advanced industrialized states of the world.

Moreover, by the time that Japanese unions had become somewhat strong, politics in all industrialized democracies had become increasingly technical and bureaucratic, while parliamentary institutions were losing political power. Even in Britain and the United States, where history gave the parliaments a strong position, their effectiveness was diminished. Simultaneously, the economic and social conditions that had given rise to strong trade union movements in other countries were being eroded in Japan, as elsewhere. Few Japanese had been socialized into working-class ideologies by the 1950s. And as Japan moved toward ever more complex manufacturing processes and toward the creation of a service-based economy, many of the industrial and economic conditions that had stimulated strong union movements in other countries were being eliminated.

The historical grip on power that unions had gained elsewhere was often shaken but rarely broken by such changes. In Japan, however, labor never had the initial strength that made it possible for unions to hold on to power in other countries. Therefore, largely because of the way in which labor evolved, the major impetus toward the creation of a welfare state that had occurred in other industrialized democracies never took the same form or gained the same power in Japan.

Lacking the political stimulus toward the creation of big government, Japan's business and political leadership was free to follow its traditionally conservative instincts. Government could intervene in public policy in only limited ways. When critical conservative interests were threatened, either domestically or from abroad, the government had strong and effective instruments with which to repond. But the government took few entrepreneurial roles in seeking out new areas to regulate, new services to provide, new power-dragons to slay.

These historical developments have had a persistent influence on the character of Japanese public policy. Economic growth could be pursued in the interests of major financial and manufacturing establishments while state expenditures, particularly for pensions, higher education, unemployment compensation, child allowances, and health care remained lower than in any other industrialized country. Environmental pollution was allowed to reach levels unimagined elsewhere: Labor-managment negotiations could be confined to the level of the individual enterprise, reducing the potential for a class-based labor movement that might reshape national politics. Higher education could be kept heavily privatized and of greatly unequal quality even as the system absorbed ever larger portions of the nation's high school graduates. The Japanese national bureaucracy could be kept comparatively small because demands for new programs and actions by the state were so severely circumscribed. The Japanese state took on only a limited number of programs, most of them designed to be of clear benefit to the conservative coalition. Most other actions could, with political impunity, be left to the private sector or to lower levels of government.

At the same time, when the government either chose, or was politically forced to act on all these matters, it set goals and accomplished specific improvements with impressive speed, clarity, and effectiveness. The secondary consequences of many of these actions may be open to criticism, particularly in terms of the value choices they represent. But the general efficiency of Japanese public policies in terms of meeting stated government objectives is undeniable. In this regard, Japan stands in marked contrast to many other countries, especially Britain, France, and the United States, where the opposite result has occurred.

Variations Among the Cases

How do these broad generalizations hold up in light of the detailed information that has been provided on the six cases of Japanese policymaking? To what extent to they capture the diversity of issues and the changes made over time?

The diverse contexts, agendas, processes, and consequences certainly suggest that the character of an issue matters greatly in the politics of Japanese policy. When one compares one of the six policy cases to another—economic policy to social welfare, higher education to environment, labor management to administrative reform—the variations among them are striking. Each involved different problems; goals of one policy were competitive with those of others; different political instruments were utilized for the resolution of each. Through most of the 1960s, for example, overall priority was given to economic growth. This deflected governmental attention from environmental protection, improving quality in higher education, or the expansion of social benefits. A decade later priorities had shifted greatly. The national bureaucracy shaped policies related to administrative reform and economics, whereas the judiciary and the parliament devised solutions to environmental problems. The individual factory was the central locus of most dealings between labor and management while street and campus were the scene of protests that catalyzed higher educational reforms.

It would take a separate study to do justice to the full implications of the individual cases but several observations can be made. First, simple functional categorization of issues does not promote much insight. There are at least two problems here. As the Japanese cases make clear, most policy problems involve several overlapping functional categories. Thus, the problem of retirement age involves labor-management, social welfare, and even economic policies. When the retirement of public officials is included the issue bears on administrative reform as well. The economics of taxation, social insurance schemes, and the labor shortage all push logically for an increase in the retirement age. At the same time, intra-organizational efficiency, improved social welfare, and concern for the individual push in the opposite direction. Hence the seemingly clear-cut problem of setting a retirement age cannot be easily assigned to any single functional category, nor do the problems inherent in the issue all suggest one coherent solution.

Cross-nationally, there is an additional problem with functional categorization. As has been noted throughout the book, various functional labels do not carry the same meanings in all countries. In

Japan, "economic policy" did not involve the same goals or the same means to achieve these goals as in Britain, Germany, or Sweden. The same can be said of higher educational reform, pension policies, or administrative reform. One of the most basic political aspects of public policy in any country is the definition of the crucial elements of a policy problem. To understand the politics of public policy cross-nationally, it is necessary to go beyond simple functional comparisons and to identify functional equivalents cross-nationally. Hence, the politics of Japanese environmental policy is much more meaningfully comparable to, say, that of German abortion policy or French educational policy than to the environmental politics of either of these countries. Similarly, Japanese labor-management relations are more fruitfully compared to relations between central and local governments in Sweden or to British housing policy rather than to labor-management relations in either of these countries.

A second conclusion that emerges from the comparison of the six cases is the importance particular issues have to the dominant coalition. The Japanese state and the conservative coalition have shown a high degree of autonomy in choosing the issues to which they devote attention and resources. For the bulk of the postwar period they succeeded in keeping many socially significant issues off the official agenda, pushing them down to the private sector or to local governments. Thus, Japan was able to concentrate most of its official resources on the item of chief concern: economic growth. Public opinion, protest, and initiatives directed against growth were rarely important considerations to the government.

At other times, the government was effectively forced to defend itself and the interests of the conservative coalition on issues that had hitherto been ignored. Higher educational reform and environmental protection policies in the 1970s both clearly were started to cope with protests whose collective impact posed an undeniable threat to the legitimacy of continued conservative rule as well as to economic goals. But once the government did act, it did so vigorously and decisively, not only quashing the political threat posed, but also dealing quite effectively with the problem or problems behind the threat.

A third point concerns the arena in which an issue arises or is resolved. The cases examined demonstrate that no single institutional process is followed when public policies are made in Japan. Interestingly there appears to be a strong relationship between the degree of public visibility of an issue and the extent to which actors outside the dominant coalition exert influence over its resolution. Problems involving higher education and the environment, for example, as well as wage- and work-condition bargaining, arose largely outside the parliament and the national bureaucracy. As such, they were subject to substantial influence by those outside the government and the conservation coalition. In contrast, economic planning and administrative reform took place largely within the central bureaucracy and were isolated from most public, pressure group, and opposition influences. In between these two extremes were issues which were resolved legislatively, most notably pension and health-care programs, the enactment of environmental legislation in 1970, the University Control Bill, and the like. Influence, although by no means equally balanced, by both government and opposition, could be seen on such issues.

Such observations make it important to reaffirm the political truism that institutions do matter. Whether an issue is dealt with legislatively, bureaucratically, or in other ways and whether it is dealt with by the national government or local governments can greatly influence the political content of policy decisions that are eventually reached.

The six cases provide enormous data with which to begin examining variations on the development of public problems in Japan. Understanding that Japan has a dominant coalition and a strong state is only the first step in understanding the politics of policy; similarly, the two-party system in Britain and the United States, and the strong administrative state in France are only the contexts within which policy is formed.

Much the same can be said of changes over time. Even in the space of a decade or two, tremendous changes took place in many of the six areas. Economic policy, for example, originally involved a relentless focus on sectoral development, maximization of growth in GNP, official support for exports, and restrictions on the import of capital and manufactured goods. By the beginning of the 1980s, policy had shifted away from growth toward control of inflation, liberalization of trade policies, and aid for overseas investment. Whereas bureaucratic control of technology, imports, raw materials, capital, and foreign exchange were central to economic policy during the 1950s and 1960s, by the 1980s most of these concerns had been scrapped. Budgetary politics, deficit spending, a floating yen, and the autonomy of the private firm replaced them in significance.

In the mid-1950s, the Japanese government was doing very little to provide a comfortable retirement for most of its citizens. Approximately 10 percent of the country's college-age population were attending higher educational institutions, the bulk in private institutions which received virtually no financial assistance from the government. Its national bureaucracy was showing signs of prodigious multiplication. Its environment was beginning to reveal deformities and would in a decade become hideously diseased.

At the beginning of the 1980s, in contrast, the country was being referred to by some in the popular press as a "welfare superpower" (Nakagawa, 1979); government spending for pensions, health care, and higher education was up sharply; the national bureaucracy was substantially smaller than it had been fifteen years earlier; regulations for the protection of the environment were among the strictest in the world.

Behind these many changes in individual issues, two broad longitudinal trends deserve particular mention. The first of these is that the government in most policy areas has displayed an increased sensitivity toward social welfare and the improvement of living conditions for the individual citizen. An ever-improving economy lies at the heart of such a shift. Increased government spending in such areas became much easier with a national economy seven times larger in 1977 than it had been in 1952. Simply put, more money was available than shortly after World War II.

At the same time, the government continued to rely more heavily on the private sector in coping with many social problems than did the governments of other industrialized countries. This was true in particular for labor-management relations and higher education. But economic, environmental, and social welfare policies also continued to involve strong private, rather than government, responsibility. Reliance on the private sector was reflected in an administrative reform policy designed to curtail, rather than to expand, the size of government and the scope of its activities. In contrast, most other countries which have sought to improve the living conditions of their citizenry have opted for solutions which require bureaucratic expansion and proportionately increasing government spending. Japan has blended the concern for social improvement with the principles of conservative solutions.

The second major longitudinal trend involves an increased sensitivity to international pressures. Especially in the area of economic policy, the shift has clearly been from economic nationalism to economic internationalism. Throughout most of the 1960s, the government acted as a doorman, determining what items could enter and what items could leave Japan. Strict supervision was exercised to ensure economic development congruent with national priorities. By 1980, the government's role as doorman had been virtually eliminated. Capital and goods moved freely across Japan's borders; the yen fluctuated in accord with shifts on the international money market; industry was far freer to pursue differential opportunities.

This shift to greater internationalism occurred in other areas as well. Japan's relatively low international ranking in expenditures for higher education, social welfare, and social overhead were consistently pointed out by critics of government policies in order to press for policy changes. Government policies in these areas from the late 1960s onward showed an increased responsiveness to international standards. Even international criticism of environmental destruction was a stimulant to change.

The government's increased receptiveness to such pressures is paradoxically an outgrowth of Japan's increased international strength and stature. Consigned to international oblivion immediately after World War II, Japan's leaders adopted highly nationalistic policies. The argument that the country could not afford, economically or politically, to do otherwise, won a measure of international credibility. By the 1980s, Japan's international strength was unmistakable, and with such strengths came pressures to behave as a successful nation should, that is, to adopt policies in economics, social welfare, environment, and the like that were compatible with other advanced economies.

However, on two major issues, labor-management relations and administrative reform, the Japanese government resisted international trends. In both instances, the government followed policies that were uniquely characteristic of Japan and that were not followed in other advanced industrialized states. Reluctance to observe international standards regarding public sector unionism, despite pressures from the International Labor Organization, was matched by restraint in expanding its national bureaucracy. Furthermore, Japan's reliance on the private sector to resolve many national problems is much stronger than in most other advanced industrialized countries.

It would be a mistake to play down such differences between issues or to understate the changes that took place in many areas of Japanese public policy over a relatively short period of time. The Japan of the 1980s is a vastly different place from the Japan of the 1950s or 1960s. Many of these differences were the results of changing policies in the areas investigated in the case studies. At the same time, these variations, diversities, and changes can be viewed as less striking than the complementarity, consistency, and "Japanese-ness" that infuse them all.

When viewed cross-nationally, the common factors linking Japanese policies are striking. For example, Japan emerges as having far greater consistency and continuity in its policies than other countries. Although the primary goals of one policy have occasionally conflicted with those of another, the Japanese experience rarely reveals the bureaucratic infighting and consequent policy disjunctures of France or Britain where, for example, national economic policy and regional industrial policy seem to be totally contradictory. Over a period of time, moreover, even though policy changes occurred in Japan, they very rarely had the stop-and-go quality that public policies had in countries with frequently changing governments, such as the United States, Britain, or West Germany. What explains this consistency? Undoubtedly, the most important element is the fact that a conservative coalition and a powerful state apparatus have dominated policymaking since the Occupation. The Liberal Democratic Party and its predecessors have held majorities in both houses of parliament and assigned all cabinet posts for over thirty years. Of all the major industrialized countries of the world, only Sweden and Israel showed comparable political dominance for such long periods. And in both of these cases the dominance was by a leftist coalition, rather than a conservative one. Furthermore, in both countries the dominance was broken in the late 1970s, as opposition parties representing drastically different policy orientations came to power, whereas in Japan the conservative coalition and the strong state continued to be vigorous especially after the 1980 elections. These features—long reign by a cohesive conservative coalition and a powerful state— overarch differences in policy problems and the variations in policy over a period of time. Their influence has so pervasively penetrated public policy that variations from issue to issue and over time pale in significance by comparison.

Democracy and Public Policy

The long-continuing conservative dominance and the strong state in Japan prompt a few general remarks on the problem of democracy and public policy in industrialized societies. The Japanese state and the conservative coalition that has provided its social underpinning have dominated the definition of issues, the process whereby these issues have been resolved, and ultimately the shape of official policies. This should occasion no surprises. Most governments have great power to dominate the media, control public information, gerrymander electoral districts, choose the most auspicious time for elections, utilize the state bureaucracy and judiciary to their own ends, and manipulate short-term political conditions to their own advantage. Like all governments the ruling coalition in Japan has taken advantage of these and many other tactics. Important as these powers have been, however, it would be an insult to the intelligence and political consciousness of the Japanese people to assume that sheer manipulation and dominance were primary factors in the continuation of conservative rule. The conservative coalition has remained in power as a result of having been returned to office through democratically conducted elections. Since the end of World War II, opposition parties have had ample opportunity to organize, to develop alternative policy positions, and to compete for popular support. But many of the policies followed by the conservatives have been creatively astute and at least tolerably popular, while many of the policy alternatives posed by the opposition parties have been unimaginative at best and on occasion almost totally devoid of insight and popular support.

This realization is an important starting point in the assessment of postwar Japanese politics and policy, particularly for those who are the most critical of conservative rule. It is also important to recognize the historical advantages enjoyed by the conservative coalition, advantages which have given to contemporary politics much of its shape and texture. To take but a simple example, late industrialization in Japan meant that the ruling elite, including big commerce, finance, and industry, could anticipate many of the same problems involving organized labor that had already occurred in earlier industrializers such as Britain, Sweden, Germany, and the United States. There is clear evidence that enterprise unions emerged in Japan at the instigation of government and business, an effort to ward off the tumultuous pattern of labor-management relations found in these other countries. Local governing, the police, and the coercive powers of the state were all used to suppress labor. The very success of unionization in the early years of the Occupation reveals how effective such suppressive powers of the state had been during the prewar period. Similarly, the sharp curtailment of unionization during the later years of the Occupation, the government's tightening of the laws government union organization, and the assumption of control over public sector strikes show the clear link between government action and labor's weakness.

Such historical residues benefit the conservatives. In every country, the powers of the incumbent can be parlayed into future power. For example, the choice of arenas of resolution are frequently the choices of the dominant coalition rather than of opposition forces. Thus, Japanese governmental actions were consistently important in privatizing higher educational expansion, in pressing wages and benefit negotiations down to the level of the plant, or in restricting administrative reforms to changes pressed by the Administrative Management Agency. These policies, in turn, shaped social powers in ways that consistently benefitted the dominant coalition.

Much has been said about the importance of how differently different countries define issues. But again, it is important to recognize the residue of history and the power of a dominant coalition, at some prior time, to define at least certain elements of an issue. Administrative reform could have been defined differently as, for example, it was in Britain, in order to change the class composition of the nation's top civil servants, or as it was in the Scandinavian countries, in order to make the civil service more popularly responsive. Labor-management relations in Japan would be very different if twenty-five years ago the government had recognized the right of public sector unions to strike or if it had then committed itself (or been forced to commit itself) to a nationally standardized minimum wage.

For the most part, therefore, established powers of the state and the conservative coalition dominate political definition, shape institutions, and channel different problems through them in different ways. These choices influence subsequent political outcomes and conflicts. Dominance is clearly more than the result of competing political party programs, demands and preferences aired in periodic elections. In most instances in Europe, and North America, the mechanisms linking citizen preferences to public policies are weak or obscure. There is surely no prima facie reason to presume that Japan is any different.

Rigid and powerful as the dominant coalition in Japan appears to have been historically, Japan is by no means a bastion of unmitigated conservatism. Certainly, the conservative coalition, over a period of time, has not proved itself ruthless. The state's powers have not been applied without restraint and many benefits have accrued to its citizens. As Japan's industrial development proceeded throughout the postwar period, its agricultural sector continually diminished in size and influence. Whereas at the end of the war approximately half of Japan's population was agricultural by the 1980s this figure was 12 percent, of which a large portion were only part-time farmers. As the economic and educational levels of the population shot up, the supposed virtues of social conservatism, nationalism, and economic growth for its own sake lost much of their traditional appeal. There was a steady erosion of conservative control over the instruments of state power.

The electoral process and parliamentary government provided an important element in this erosion and, in turn, forced drastic shifts in some policies of the national government. Though a dominant party, the LDP responded to certain popular pressures. From the late 1960s through the 1970s, the electoral fortunes of the LDP declined. From 60 percent of the seats in the lower house before the 1967 election, the number of LDP seats fell to below 50 percent in the 1979 election, the party retaining power only by enrolling several conservative independents after the election. At the local level, it fared even worse, with left-of-center candidates gaining control of many important cities. By mid-1974, over 40 percent of the Japanese population lived in prefectures or cities having executives from one more of the opposition parties (MacDougall, 1976, p. 42).

It can be seen that the electoral weapon proved to be highly effective for opponents of the conservative coalition. And as the fortunes of the conservatives diminished, the Japanese government began shifting many of its policy priorities. By the end of the 1970s, the government had taken many steps to control the environmental destruction that had been proceeding virtually unchecked for fifteen years. Higher education and social welfare rapidly gained in priority in national government circles. Control of inflation, increased leisure time for workers, and access to consumer goods, even those from abroad, were held to be of far greater importance than they had been in the high-growth period of the 1950s and 1960s.

The importance of elections and parliament on public policy in Japan should not be denied. There are limits on the extent to which elections influence governmental actions on any single policy issue in Japan or elsewhere. Furthermore, party solidarity in the parliament meant that, until the late 1970s when the government majority could no longer control all parliamentary committees, the institutional influence of parliament over most items of public policy was severely restrained. Nevertheless, many of the policy shifts that took place must be attributed at least partially to the fact that the electoral margin of the LDP was constantly shrinking. If in no other way than in stimulating actions designed to anticipate public or opposition demands, parliamentary democracy in Japan influenced public policies in a most meaningful way.

In the same vein it is worth noting that, causally related or not, the electoral decline of the LDP was reversed following the changes in policies during the 1970s. Several major cities, including Tokyo and Kyoto, were returned to LDP control, and in the 1980 elections for the upper and lower houses the LDP regained its strong majorities. The intriguing and, at present, unanswerable question this poses is whether the major public policy shifts that occurred during the 1970s, in apparent anticipation of the electoral crisis faced by the conservative coalition, will be reversed following this newfound strength. Alternatively, have the changes that took place acquired a momentum of their own, moving Japan closer to the creation of a welfare state without a socialist government?

Whatever occurs, one must recognize that in Japan as in other functioning parliamentary democracies, elections, political parties, and parliaments are extremely important instruments for setting limits on governmental actions and for providing potential alternatives to the ongoing activities of the government. European and American assumptions are that their influence is weighty when the government's margin of control is threatened, or can be seen as threatened, by a potentially victorious alternative coalition. Adapting a phrase from big-city politics in the United States: "You can't threaten somebody with nobody." If an electoral of parliamentary shift of, say, 5 percent could topple the government or severely threaten its power, that government would almost automatically become highly susceptible to the changing mood of numerous different public groups and sectors on a variety of issues. If a 10 percent or 15 percent shift would still leave the government in power, there is far less incentive to worry about mild fluctuations in opinion. Thus as far as public policy is concerned, the relatively rigid balance of the social coalitions competing for electoral or parliamentary power seems far more significant than the simple presence or absence of an open parliament. This balance is possibly more significant than the particular structures and procedures that control the electoral or parliamentary processes. In Japan, the power of the conservative coalition, when preponderant, overrode such institutions; only as the margin of control was reduced did the institutions grow again in significance. The overwhelming electoral success of the conservatives in the 1980 elections may, ironically, serve to reduce the influence of such institutions over public policy.

There is no implication here that because Japan differed substantially from earlier industrializers in Europe and North America, it *should* have followed in their footsteps. The comparative evidence does not suggest that there is something normatively preferable or morally inevitable about the course of political developments followed by the early industrializers. Recent reflections in these countries concerning the loss of personal individuality, the rise of bureaucracy, the complexity of government, the breakdown of community, and other problems suggest that there is ample room for reevaluating their alleged successes and failures. One can legitimately question whether their achievements have been as consistent or universally applicable as might have once been thought.

With its high levels of economic growth, literacy, culture, and life expectancy, and its low levels of unemployment, crime, disease and poverty, Japan represents its own success story. All these have been achieved along with the preservation of cohesion, group loyalty, and individual motivation. No wonder increasing numbers of Westerners are becoming fascinated with the country!

Yet, the chorus singing the paeans to Japanese success often sounds out of tune. Without belittling Japan's many genuine successes, it is important to keep in mind the costs of these successes, and the fact that these costs were by no means borne evenly by all of Japanese society. The fact that, for all intents and purposes, labor has no voice in the organs of Japanese government has profound implications. In every country there are costs to most successes and costs are usually disproportionately allocated. What is peculiar to Japan is that, more than any other single factor, organized labor's virtually total exclusion accounts for the consistently conservative coloring of policies. This conservative hue may be indelibly ingrained in the fabric of Japanese politics and may therefore last long into the future, regardless of how the conservative coalition changes or how power is restructured.

This point leads to one final observation on the relationship between politics, public policy, and democracy. One of the curious ironies of politics in modern industrialized societies is the fact that the issues that lie on the ideological fault lines along which parties organize and elections are fought are often of comparatively less significance in the long run than many issues which are not. Issues in the areas of administration, economics, higher education, environmental protection, and pensions, to take some examples, are highly complex. They cannot be encompassed by the pithy slogans used by political parties to mobilize support or opposition. For this reason, in many areas where public policy choices have the potential for long-range impact on society, social mobilization is low, public and group involvement is narrow, and government choices are autonomously arrived at. No one committed to belief in the necessity of public influence over governmental choice is likely to favor the elimination of elections, parties, and parliaments, but the limits of their ability to ensure the classical goals of democracy in highly technological countries with refined welfare systems are only beginning to be understood. Increased attention to public policies including policies that are not typically the focal point of electoral politics, may well allow for a more meaningful investigation of the relationship between politics and democracy.

References

Akita, George. 1967. *Foundations of Constitutional Government in Japan, 1868–1900.* Cambridge, Mass.: Harvard University Press.

Asahi Shimbun. Daily.

Bayley, David H. 1976. *Forces of Order.* Berkeley: University of California Press.

Campbell, John C. 1977. *Contemporary Japanese Budget Politics.* Berkeley: University of California Press.

———. 1979. "The 'Old People Boom' and Japanese Policy Making." *Journal of Japanese Studies* 5:321–57.

Chubachi, Masayoshi, and Koji Taira. 1976. "Poverty in Modern Japan: Perceptions and Realities," in Hugh Patrick, ed., *Japanese Industrialization and Its Social Consequences*, pp. 391–437. Berkeley: University of California Press.

Chūgoku Shimbun. Daily.

Cole, Robert E. 1971. *Japanese Blue Collar.* Berkeley: University of California Press.

———. 1979. *Work, Mobility, and Participation.* Berkeley: University of California Press.

Destler, I. M., et al. 1979. *The Textile Wrangle.* Ithaca, N.Y.: Cornell University Press.

Donnelly, Michael W. 1976. "Setting the Price of Rice." In T. J. Pempel, ed., *Policymaking in Contemporary Japan*, pp. 102–200. Ithaca, N.Y.: Cornell University Press.

Doi, Takeo. 1973. *The Anatomy of Dependence.* Tokyo: Kodansha International.

Dore, Ronald. 1958. *City Life in Japan.* Berkeley: University of California Press.

———. 1973. *British Factory—Japanese Factory.* Berkeley: University of California Press.

Fisher, Paul. 1973. "Major Social Security Issues: Japan." *Social Security Bulletin* 36, no. 3: 26–38.

Focus Japan.   Monthly. Tokyo.

Fukui, Haruhiro.   1972.   "Economic Planning in Postwar Japan." *Asian Survey* 12:327–48.

Fukutake, Tadashi.   1967.   *Japanese Rural Society*.   Ithaca, N.Y.: Cornell University Press.

Gerschenkron, Alexander.   1962.   *Economic Backwardness in Historical Perspective*.   Cambridge, Mass.: Harvard University Press.

Gibney, Frank.   1975.   *Japan: The Fragile Superpower*.   Rutland, Vt.: Charles E. Tuttle.

Hanami, Tadashi.   1979.   *Labor Relations in Japan Today*.   Tokyo: Kodansha International.

Harari, Ehud.   1973.   *The Politics of Labor Legislation in Japan*.   Berkeley: University of California Press.

Hashimoto, Akikazu.   1975.   *Shiji Seitō Nashi*.   Tokyo: Nikei Shinsho.

Helco, Hugh.   1974.   *Modern Social Politics in Britain and Sweden*.   New Haven, Conn.: Yale University Press.

Honda, Yasuharu. 1974.   *Nihon Neokanryōron*.   Tokyo: Kodansha International.

International Labor Organization.   Monthly. *Official Bulletin*. Geneva.

Itō, Daiichi.   1968.   "The Bureaucracy: Its Attitudes and Behavior." *The Developing Economics* 6: 446–67.

Itoh, Hiroshi, and Lawrence Ward Beer.   1978.   *The Constitutional Case Law of Japan*.   Seattle: University of Washington Press.

Japan, Economic Planning Agency.   1979.   *New Economic and Social Seven-Year Plan*. Tokyo: Economic Planning Agency.

Japan, Environment Agency.   Annual. *Quality of the Environment in Japan*. Tokyo: Environment Agency.

———.   1974.   *White Paper on the Envoronment*.   Tokyo: Environment Agency.

Japan, Gyōsei Kanri Iinkai.   1967, 1968, 1969.   *Gyōsei Kaikaku no genjō to Kadai*.   Tokyo: Gyō Kanri Iinkai.

Japan, Ministry of International Trade and Industry.   1977.   *Japan's Industrial Structure: A Long-Range Vision*.   Tokyo: MITI.

Japan, Social Insurance Agency.   1977.   *Outline of Social Insurance—Japan*.   Tokyo: Social Insurance Agency.

Japan Echo.   Monthly. Tokyo.

Japan Labor Bulletin.   Monthly. Tokyo.

Japan Report.   Bimonthly. New York.

Japan Socialist Review.   Monthly. Tokyo.

Japan Times.   Daily. Tokyo.

Japan Times Weekly.   Weekly. Tokyo.

Johnson, Chalmers.   1974.   "The Reemployment of Retired Government Bureaucrats in Japanese Big Business." *Asian Survey* 14: 953–65.

————. 1975. "Japan: Who Governs? An Essay on Official Bureaucracy." *Journal of Japanese Studies* 2:1–28.

————. 1977. "MITI and Japanese International Economic Policy." In Robert A. Scalapino, ed., *The Foreign Policy of Modern Japan*, pp. 227–80. Berkeley: University of California Press.

————. 1978. *Japan's Public Policy Companies*. Washington, D.C.: American Enterprise Institute.

Kajinshi, Mitsuhaya. 1971–74. *Nihon ni okeru Shihonshugi no Hatatsu*. Tokyo: Tokyo Daigaku Shuppan.

Kajinishi, M., et al., eds. 1974. *Nihon Shihonshugi no Botsuraku*. Tokyo: Tokyo Daigaku Shuppan.

Kaplan, Eugene J. 1972. *Japan: The Government-Business Relationship*. Washington, D.C.: Department of Commerce.

Katzenstein, Peter, ed. 1977. *Between Power and Plenty*. Madison: University of Wisconsin Press.

Kitamura, Kazuyuki, and William K. Cummings. 1972. "The 'Big Bang' Theory and Japanese University Reform." *Comparative Education Review* 16: 303–24.

Krauss, Ellis S. 1981. "Toward the Institutionalization of Conflict Management in Japan's Parliament." In Thomas Rohlen et al., eds. "Conflict in Japan." Unpublished manuscript.

Kubota, Akira. 1969. *Higher Civil Servants in Postwar Japan*. Princeton: Princeton University Press.

Kuriki, Yasunobu. 1977. "Keizai Kiki to Rōdō Undō." In *Iwanami Kōza: Nihon Rekishi* 22: 221–64. Tokyo: Iwanami.

Liberal Democratic Party. 1970. *Kurashi to Seiji*. Tokyo: LDP.

Lynch, John. 1968. *Toward an Orderly Market*. Tokyo: Sophia University Press.

MacDougall, Terry. 1976. "Japanese Urban Local Politics: Towards a Viable Progressive Political Opposition." In Lewis Austin, ed., *Japan: The Paradox of Progress*, pp. 31–56. New Haven, Conn.: Yale University Press.

Marshall, Byron K. 1967. *Capitalism and Nationalism in Prewar Japan*. Stanford, Calif.: Stanford University Press.

McKean, Margaret A. 1976. "Pollution and Policymaking." In T. J. Pempel, ed., *Policymaking in Contemporary Japan*, pp. 201–38. Ithaca, N.Y.: Cornell University Press.

Moore, Barrington. 1967. *Social Origins of Dictatorship and Democracy*. Boston: Beacon Press.

Nagai, Michio. 1971. *Higher Education in Japan*. Tokyo: University of Tokyo Press.

Nakagawa, Yatsuhiro. 1979. "Japan, the Welfare Super-Power." *Journal of Japanese Studies* 5: 5–51.

Nakane, Chie. 1970. *Japanese Society*. Berkeley: University of California Press.

Nihon Kokusei Zue. Annual. Tokyo: Kobuseisha.

Nikkeiren News. Monthly. Tokyo.

Nishihira, Shigeki. 1972. *Nihon no Senkyō*. Tokyo: Shiseido.

Nutter, G. Warren. 1978. *Growth of Government in the West*. Washington, D.C.: American Enterprise Institute.

Okamoto, Hideaki. 1972. "Industrialization: Environment and Anti-Pollution Movements: A Case." *Japan Labor Bulletin*. 11, no. 11:4–12.

Okochi, Kazuo, et al. 1973. *Workers and Employers in Japan*. Tokyo: University of Tokyo Press.

Organization for Economic Cooperation and Development. 1977. *Towards an Integrated Social Policy in Japan*. Paris: OECD.

———. 1977. *Environmental Policies in Japan*. Paris: OECD.

Patrick, Hugh, and Henry Rosovsky, eds. 1976. *Asia's New Giant*. Washington, D.C.: The Brookings Institution.

Pempel, T. J. 1975. "The Dilemma of Parliamentary Opposition in Japan." *Polity* 8:63–79.

———, ed. 1976. *Policymaking in Contemporary Japan*. Ithaca, N.Y.: Cornell University Press.

———. 1977. "Japanese Foreign Economic Policy: The Domestic Basis for International Behavior." In Peter J. Katzenstein, ed., *Between Power and Plenty*, pp. 139–90. Madison: University of Wisconsin Press.

———. 1978a. *Patterns of Japanese Policymaking*. Boulder, Col.: Westview Press.

———. 1978b. "Political Parties and Social Change: The Japanese Experience." In Louis Maizel and Joseph Cooper, eds., *Political Parties: Development and Decay*, pp. 309–41. Beverly Hills, Calif.: Sage Publications.

Rohlen, Thomas P. 1974. *For Harmony and Strength*. Berkeley: University of California Press.

Sato, Tatsuo. 1970. *Kokka Komuin Seidō*. Tokyo: Gakuyuo.

Scalapino, Robert A. 1968. "Elections and Political Modernization in Pre-War Japan." In Robert Ward, ed., *Political Development in Modern Japan*, pp. 249–91. Princeton, N.J.: Princeton University Press.

———. 1977. *The Foreign Policy of Modern Japan*. Berkeley: University of California Press.

Shimada, Haruo. 1980. *The Japanese Employment System*. *(Japanese Industrial Relations Series.)* Tokyo: The Japan Institute of Labor.

Stockwin, J. A. A. 1975. *Japan: Divided Politics in a Growth Economy*. New York: W. W. Norton.

Takemae, Eiji, and Amakawa, Akira. 1977. *Nihon Senryō Hisshi.* Tokyo: Asahi Shimbunsha.

Thayer, Nathaniel B. 1969 *How the Conservatives Rule Japan.* Princeton, N.J.: Princeton University Press.

Thurston, Donald. 1973. *Teachers and Politics in Japan.* Princeton, N.J.: Princeton University Press.

———. 1974. "Aftermath in Minamata." *The Japan Interpreter* 9, no. 1:25–42.

Tokyo Municipal News. Biannual. Tokyo.

Tratner, Walter. 1979. *From Poor Law to Welfare State.* 2nd ed. New York: Free Press.

Vogel, Ezra F. 1963. *Japan's New Middle Class.* Berkeley: University of California Press.

———. 1979. *Japan as Number One.* Cambridge, Mass.: Harvard University Press.

Wilensky, Harold L. 1975. *The Welfare State and Equality.* Berkeley: University of California Press.

Yokoyama, Kazuhiko. 1979. *Shakai Hōshoseido no Shikumi to Mondaiten.* Tokyo: Kyōikusha.

Yomiuri Shimbun. Daily. Tokyo.

Zusetsu Rōjin Hakusho. [1980.] Tokyo: Sekibunsha.

Index

Administrative Management Agency, 257, 261, 262, 264, 265, 267, 275, 276–77, 280, 285, 291, 308; Administrative Management and Inspection Committee, 276–77, 285

Administrative reform, 8, 9, 20–21, 43, 44, 255–95, 300, 305–6, 308–9, 312; absence during U.S. Occupation, 15–16. *See also* Bureaucracy; Civil service; State, Japanese, size

Advisory councils, 17–18, 101–2, 294

Agriculture, 25, 26, 29, 30–31, 32, 35, 43, 92, 309

Air Pollution Control Law, 232

Akita, George, 12, 13

Amaike, Seiji, 104

Amakawa, Akira, 94

Amami Island group, 17

Antimonopoly Law, 59

Ashford, Douglas, xviii

Association for Harmony and Conciliation, 95

Australia, government spending, 271

Austria, 136; late industrializer, 136; welfare, 134

Automobile industry, 59–61

Automobile Industry Association, 60

Bank of Japan, 8, 59, 61, 67

Basic Law for Environmental Pollution Control, 231

Bayley, David H., 3

Beer, Lawrence Ward, 19

Belgium, industrial competition, 49

Britain, xiii, 13, 109, 299, 300, 306; bureaucracy, 8, 21, 256, 260, 264, 267, 269, 270, 306, 308; "Butskellism," 6; centralization, 297; conflict in, 97; consensus, 6; constitution, 15; early industrialization, 48, 208; economic policy, 7, 9, 58; elderly, 146; exports to, 64; GDP, 221; geography, 21; higher education, 171, 189, 193; immigration, 237; industry, 49; labor, 31, 32, 92, 93, 94, 96, 97, 109, 150; labor policy, 99, 100; media, 25; parties and elections, 38, 40; pensions, 144, 148, 151; policy inconsistency, 43; pound, 8; strikes, 6, 90; taxation, 271; unemployment, 90; wages, 91; welfare, 56, 134, 151, 152, 260

Buddhism, 24

Bureaucracy, 4, 13, 16, 21, 23–24, 27, 36, 41, 43, 50, 133, 140, 146, 184, 255–95, 300, 301, 304, 306; administrative rationality, 257, 260; administrative reform, 9, 255, 257–58, 259–60, 261–62, 267–68, 270, 271, 275–76; 305, 308, 312; bureaucratic protectionism, 259, 261; efficiency, 255, 256, 257, 258, 260, 261; efforts to limit size, 255, 259–60, 261–62, 264–67, 267–68, 270; elite access to, 269; flexibility, 260, 264; patronage, 256–57; separation of politics and admin-